CAMBRIDGE LIBRARY COLLECTION

Books of enduring scholarly value

Religion

For centuries, scripture and theology were the focus of prodigious amounts
of scholarship and publishing, dominated in the English-speaking world
by the work of Protestant Christians. Enlightenment philosophy and
science, anthropology, ethnology and the colonial experience all brought
new perspectives, lively debates and heated controversies to the study of
religion and its role in the world, many of which continue to this day. This
series explores the editing and interpretation of religious texts, the history of
religious ideas and institutions, and not least the encounter between religion
and science.

The Epistle of St. James

Fenton John Antony Hort (1828–1892) was Professor of Divinity at
Cambridge and the editor, with B.F. Westcott, of an influential edition of
the Greek New Testament. His detailed commentary on the Greek text of
the Epistle (Letter) of St James was left incomplete at his death. When it was
published in 1909, the editor wrote 'Each word and phrase and sentence has
been examined in the light of the whole available evidence with characteristic
freshness, and with a singularly delicate sense both of the meaning of words,
and of subtle variations of grammatical structure.' The Introduction situates
the Epistle in its New Testament context, and reflects on issues of authorship,
reception and content. Hort's scholarly insights remain of interest to modern
theologians. His work also bears witness to the strenuous efforts made by
late Victorian theologians to create a textual bulwark against the growth of
religious scepticism.

T0371566

The Epistle of St. James

*The Greek Text with Introduction,
Commentary as Far as Chapter IV, Verse 7,
and Additional Notes*

EDITED BY FENTON JOHN ANTHONY HORT

CAMBRIDGE
UNIVERSITY PRESS

CAMBRIDGE UNIVERSITY PRESS

Cambridge, New York, Melbourne, Madrid, Cape Town, Singapore,
São Paolo, Delhi, Dubai, Tokyo

Published in the United States of America by Cambridge University Press, New York

www.cambridge.org
Information on this title: www.cambridge.org/9781108007535

© in this compilation Cambridge University Press 2009

This edition first published 1909
This digitally printed version 2009

ISBN 978-1-108-00753-5 Paperback

THE EPISTLE OF ST JAMES

MACMILLAN AND CO., LIMITED
LONDON · BOMBAY · CALCUTTA
MELBOURNE

THE MACMILLAN COMPANY
NEW YORK · BOSTON · CHICAGO
ATLANTA · SAN FRANCISCO

THE MACMILLAN CO. OF CANADA, LTD
TORONTO

THE EPISTLE OF ST JAMES

THE GREEK TEXT

WITH INTRODUCTION, COMMENTARY AS FAR AS
CHAPTER IV, VERSE 7, AND ADDITIONAL NOTES

BY THE LATE

F. J. A. HORT, D.D., D.C.L., LL.D.

SOMETIME HULSEAN PROFESSOR AND LADY MARGARET'S READER IN DIVINITY
IN THE UNIVERSITY OF CAMBRIDGE

MACMILLAN AND CO., LIMITED
ST MARTIN'S STREET, LONDON

1909

CONTENTS

PREFACE

THE circumstances connected with the origin of this book have already been related by Dr Westcott in the preface to the companion edition of Dr Hort's Commentary on 1 St Peter i.—ii. 17, published in 1898. It was designed to take its place in a Commentary on the whole N.T. planned by the three friends, Westcott, Lightfoot, and Hort in 1860.

Dr Hort's share included the Synoptic Gospels, the Acts, and the Epistles of St James, St Peter, and St Jude. After a brief period of work on the Gospels, of which only a few unimportant fragments remain, Dr Hort set to work on St James. If we may judge from the condition of the MS. the Commentary on Chapter I was complete when he came back to Cambridge, as a Fellow of Emmanuel College, in 1871. His notes were, however, worked over and written out afresh when he chose St James as the subject for his first three courses of Lectures as Hulsean Professor in 1880, 1881. It is idle now to regret that his attention was called away to lecture in 1882 on Tatian's Apology, leaving the Commentary incomplete, but within sight of the end. When at length he returned to the Epistle in the Summer Term of 1889, he dealt mainly with questions of Introduction. The introductory matter printed in this volume was prepared for that course of Lectures. It was supplemented by condensed notes on select passages from the earlier chapters of the Epistle. No further progress was made with the Commentary on the Text.

The Introduction and Commentary have been printed substantially as they stand in the MS., except that for the sake of uniformity English renderings have in some cases been supplied at the head of the notes. This however has only been done in cases where the note itself gave clear indication of the rendering which Dr Hort would himself have proposed.

No one who reads this book with the attention that it requires and deserves will feel that any apology is needed for its publication, in spite of its incompleteness. In the Introduction no doubt the scholarship appears to a certain extent in what Dr Sanday, in the Preface to Dr Hort's notes on Apoc. i.—iii. published last year, aptly describes as 'undress.' And some points would naturally have received fuller treatment, if the author himself had been spared to prepare his own work for publication. But there is no reason to suppose that his conclusions would have been seriously modified by anything that has been written on the Epistle since his death. His Introduction has, it will not be superfluous to point out, an advantage from the appended Commentary, inevitably but none the less unfortunately lacking in the still more compendious introduction provided, *e.g.* in such a recognized Text-book as Jülicher's. For after all the ultimate appeal on most of the vexed questions of Introduction lies to the Text itself. And on one point at least Dr Hort's patient and minute examination of the Text supplies a conclusive answer to the charge of incoherence[1] not uncommonly brought against the Epistle on the ground of the obvious abruptness of

---

[1] On this point it is well worth while to compare *A Discussion of the General Epistle of St James* by R. St John Parry, published by the Cambridge University Press in 1903.

its style. No one can study these notes consecutively without
becoming conscious of a subtle harmony underlying the whole
Epistle, due partly to the consistent application of a few fundamental principles characteristic of the author[1], and partly to
the recurrence in different forms of the same fundamental
failing in the people to whom his warnings are addressed[2].

In regard to the evidence to be derived from the language
in which the Epistle is written it is clear that Dr Hort worked
habitually on an hypothesis, the possibility of which many
modern critics either ignore or deny. Everything here turns
on the extent to which a knowledge of Greek may be pre-
supposed among the Jewish inhabitants of Palestine in the First
Century A.D. Jülicher, for example, regards the excellence of
the Greek of the Epistle as in itself conclusive against the
traditional attribution. This seems arbitrary in the case of a
man whose father according to an early tradition (St Matth. ii.)
spent some time in Egypt. Dr Hort on the other hand regarded a knowledge of Greek as anything but exceptional in
Palestine. He thinks it possible to identify dialectic peculiarities
of Palestinian Greek[3]. He is prepared to believe in the currency[4]
of 'Greek paraphrases of the O.T. resembling the Hebrew
Targums.' The influence that he everywhere ascribes to the
LXX in moulding N.T. vocabulary presupposes a considerable
familiarity with the Greek Version of the O.T. in Apostolic
circles[5]. And he finds the Epistle of St James full of implied
references to the words of the Lord *in their Greek form*[6]. This
point is one of far-reaching importance, and if there are good
reasons for supposing that a man in St James' position could

---

[1] See notes on i. 18, 21, iii. 9 for St James' doctrine of Creation : on the
true Law i. 25, ii. 12: on his conception of the World i. 27, iii. 6, iv. 4.
[2] *E.g.* formalism i. 22, 26, 27, ii. 19 : censoriousness i. 19, iii. 1, 9, 12.
[3] See p. 46 b, 84 a.
[4] See p. 94 b.   [5] See esp. p. 97 b.
[6] See p. 91 a, p. xxxiii. etc.

not have had a thorough knowledge of Greek, it would be well
that they should be produced.

The Commentary itself, as far as it goes, is finished work in
every line. Each word and phrase and sentence has been
examined in the light of the whole available evidence with
characteristic freshness, and with a singularly delicate sense
both of the meaning of words, and of subtle variations of
grammatical structure. At times, no doubt, in Dr Hort's
work as in Dr Westcott's, the investigation of a particular word
or form of thought seems to be carried beyond the limits strictly
necessary for the interpretation of the passage immediately
under discussion. It is however only fair to recal the fact that
each separate Commentary was meant to form part of an
inclusive scheme. Both scholars combined a keen sense of
the variety of the several parts of the N.T. with a deep conviction of the fundamental unity of the whole. Their field
of view was never limited by the particular passage on which
they might happen to be commenting. No single fragment,
they felt, could be fully understood out of relation to the whole
Revelation of which it formed a part. Conciseness and, as
regards the rapid apprehension of the salient points in individual
books, something of sharpness of focus were sacrificed in consequence. But for students of the N.T. as a whole, the result is
pure gain. The labour entailed in following out the suggested
lines of thought is amply repaid by a growing sense of depth
beyond depth of Wisdom hidden under familiar and seemingly
commonplace forms of expression. And even the several books
stand out in the end in more clearly defined individuality.

This characteristic of Dr Hort's method minimizes the dis-
advantages arising from the fragmentariness of the finished
work. The discussion of representative sections of different
writers has given him wider scope for the treatment of the
various departments of N.T. Theology than would have been

afforded by a Commentary formally complete on a single Epistle. The First Epistle of St Peter occupies no doubt a peculiarly central position in N.T. The relation in which it stands to the Epistles to the Romans and to the 'Ephesians' led Dr Hort to treat many of the characteristic problems of the Pauline Gospel, and its relation to the Epistle of St James is remarkably illustrated by the fact that in commenting on St Peter Dr Hort not infrequently summarizes the results of investigations recorded in full in this volume. Yet even I St Peter would not have given him the scope afforded by these chapters of St James for treating of the fundamental problems of individual (as distinct from social) Ethics, and of Psychology.

In spite therefore of its apparent fragmentariness Dr Hort's work is marked by a real unity, and possesses a permanent value for all serious students of N.T. In details no doubt both of vocabulary and syntax his results will need to be carefully checked in the fresh light which is coming from the Papyri. But in work so broadly based, fresh evidence we may well believe will confirm far more than it will upset.

But, some one may say, granted all this, what is meant by the permanent value of a Commentary ? Are not Commentaries like all scientific text-books, only written to be superseded ? In every other department of study, however gifted a scholar may be, he must be content that his particular contribution to the advancement of knowledge shall be merged and lost in the general sum. Is there any reason to think that the case is different in Theology ? Strangely enough there is.

The subject-matter of the science of Theology is provided by the Bible. 'That standard interpretation[1]' of the primary Gospel 'was ordained to be for the guidance of the Church in all after ages, in combination with the living guidance of the

[1] p. ix.

Spirit.' Each age must go back for itself to the fountain head. Yet for the thinkers in each age there are abiding lessons to be learnt from the labours of their predecessors. It is not surprising, therefore, that all the outstanding leaders in Theological thought, the men of creative insight, who have moulded the minds of their fellows throughout the Christian centuries, *e.g.* Origen, Theodore, and Augustine, have been great primarily as interpreters of Scripture, content to sacrifice any glory of 'originality,' all licence of unfettered speculations, that they might be the servants of a Text. And the work to which they gave their lives is living work to-day. Their Theologies have still a message for us, in spite of antiquated method and defective intellectual equipment: full of light which we can ill afford to neglect. Though 'they must remain a dead letter to us, till they are interpreted by the thoughts and aspirations of our own time, as shone upon by the light of the Spirit who is the teacher of Christ's disciples in every age[1].'

The fact is that just as in the original communication of the Divine Revelation the personality of the writer is an integral part of the message which he was chosen to convey, so the personality of each interpreter of these 'living oracles' is a vital element in all the fresh light that he is able to perceive in them. Any contribution that he makes to their fuller understanding remains to the end of time recognisably his, for those who have eyes to see. Here, as in the case of all other builders on the one foundation, the fire tries, and the day will declare each man's work of what sort it is: though it is only the few here and there who are called out by, and exercise a dominant influence in, the successive crises in the development of Christian thought, whose names survive upon the mouths of men, and whose work is studied for its own sake in later generations.

[1] Hort on *The Ante-Nicene Fathers*, p. 138.

Now Lightfoot, Westcott and Hort have not left behind
them a body of systematic Theology. The treatise on Christian
Doctrine which was to have been the crown of Dr Westcott's
work was never completed. They founded no school marked
by common adherence to any characteristic tenets. Their
message to their age lay rather in the attitude and method
than in any specific results of their work. The crisis in
Christian thought which they were called to face affected
primarily the Authority, the Inspiration, and the Interpretation
of the Bible. And it is impossible to over-estimate the debt
which English Christianity has owed in this perilous period of
transition to the steadying influence exerted over the minds
of their contemporaries by the simple fact of their lifelong
devotion to the study of the sacred text, their fearless faith
in Truth, their 'guileless workmanship,' and their reverent
humility. At the same time it is hard not to believe that the
actual results of work done in such a spirit will be found to
possess a value in the eyes of other generations besides that
which witnessed its production.

It only remains for me to express my heartiest thanks to
my colleague, the Rev. P. H. L. Brereton, Fellow of St Augustine's
College, without whose scholarly and ungrudging assistance I
should have found it impossible in the pressure of multifarious
distractions to see this book through the press and verify the
references: to Professor Burkitt for his kind help in the note
on the Latin renderings of ἐριθία: and to the printers and
proof-readers of the University Press for their patience and
thoroughness.

J. O. F. MURRAY.

St Augustine's College,
Canterbury.
St Peter's Day, 1909.

INTRODUCTION.

THE Epistle of St James is among the less read and less studied books of the N.T.; and this for obvious reasons. With one partial exception it has not supplied material for great theological controversies. But moreover it is a book that very few Christians on consideration would place among the *most* important books. No one wishing to refer to the written records which best set forth what Christian belief and even Christian practice is would turn to it as they would turn to the Gospels or to some, at least, of St Paul's Epistles. Nay, as we all know, even distinctively Christian language in one sense of the phrase, i.e. such language as no one but a Christian could use, is used in it very sparingly. Thus no wonder that it has been comparatively little valued by Christian readers, and comparatively little examined and illustrated by Christian commentators.

Yet on the other hand it has an important place and office of its own in the Scriptures of the N.T. Its very unlikeness to other books is of the greatest value to us, as shewing through Apostolic example the manysidedness of Christian truth. Our faith rests first on the Gospel itself, the revelation of God and His redemption in His Only begotten Son, and secondly on the interpretation of that primary Gospel by the Apostles and Apostolic men to whom was Divinely committed the task of applying the revelation of Christ to the thoughts and deeds of their own time. That standard interpretation of theirs was ordained to be for the guidance of the Church in all after ages, in combination with the living guidance of the Spirit. But it could not have discharged this office if it had been of one type only, moulded by the mental characteristics of a single man, though he were an inspired Apostle. It was needed that various modes of apprehending the one Truth should be sanctioned for ever as contributing to the completeness of the faith. And that mode of apprehending it which we find in St James stamped the comprehensiveness of Apostolic Christianity in a marked manner, being the furthest removed from that of the Apostle of largest influence, St Paul.

That special type of Christianity which is represented by St James had a high intrinsic value apart from its testimony to the various because partial character of Divine truth as apprehended by men. One of the most serious dangers to Christian faith in the early ages, perhaps we may say, in *all* ages, was the temptation to think of Christ as the founder of a *new* religion, to invert His words "I came not to destroy, but to fulfil." St Paul himself was entirely free from such a view of Christianity: but the part which he had to take in vindicating Gentile freedom against Jewish encroachments made him easily appear to be the herald of a new religion. The Divine judgement of the fall of Jerusalem and the Jewish State, and also the bitter hatred with which the Jews long pursued Christians, would all tend to produce the same impression. Thus many influences prepared the way for the influence of Marcion in the second century and long afterwards, and made him seem a true champion of the purity of the Gospel. When he cast off the worship of the Creator, of Jehovah the Lord of Israel, the merely just God of the O.T., as he said, and set up the God of the N.T. as a new God, alone in the strict sense good, alone to be worshipped by Christians, he could not but seem to many to be delivering the faith from an antiquated bondage. And so again and again the wild dream of a "Christianity without Judaism" has risen up with attractive power. But the Epistle of St James marks in the most decisive way the continuity of the two Testaments. In some obvious aspects it is like a piece of the O.T. appearing in the midst of the N.T.; and yet not out of place, or out of date, for it is most truly of the N.T. too. It as it were carries on the line of intermediate testimony which starts from John the Baptist, and is taken up by the hymns in Lk. i., ii. (Magnificat, Benedictus, Nunc Dimittis). As they reach forward towards the Gospel, so the Epistle of St James looks upon the elder dispensation as having been in a manner itself brought to perfection by the Gospel.

This distinctive value of St James' Epistle is closely related to the distinctive value of the first three Gospels. The relation is not merely of affinity, but almost of direct descent. The Epistle is saturated with the matter of those Gospels (or narratives akin to them). No other book so uses them. And though the completeness of Christianity would be maimed if the teaching of the Gospel of St John were away, yet the three Gospels give in their own way a true picture. Many perversions of Christianity could not have arisen if *they* had in practice as well as theory been taken with the Gospel of St John; and so the combination of St James with St Paul is a safeguard against much error.

Besides this general value of the Epistle as a whole, its details are full of matter of high interest and importance, often by no means lying on the surface. It is also far from being an easy Epistle. Many verses of it are easy, but many are difficult enough, and even in the easier parts the train of thought is often difficult to catch. Much, though not all, of the difficulty comes from the energetic abruptness of style, reminding us of the older prophets. Thus for various reasons the Epistle is one that will repay close examination and illustration.

Authorship.

Two questions arise : (1) What James is intended by Ἰάκωβος in i. 1. (2) Whether the James so intended did really write the Epistle: is it authentic or supposititious ?

There is no need to spend much time on this second question, which is almost entirely distinct from the general question of the date of important N.T. books. Some critics of ability still uphold a late date, but on very slight and intangible grounds. One has urged similarity to *Hom. Clem.*, a late book : but such little simi-

larity as there is proceeds from the fact that both are by Jewish
Christians, though in quite different generations. Others refer to
the judicial persecutions, or to the presbyters. Others, with less
reference to date, say that though Jewish it is not Jewish enough
for the James whom they rightly suppose to be intended: but then
this image of James they have constructed out of problematical
materials. Again it is said that it contains Orphic language,
strange in a Palestinian Jew (τὸν τροχὸν τῆς γενέσεως in iii. 6):
but this interpretation of the words cannot stand.

A somewhat more tangible ground is the supposed reference to
Hebrews and Apocalypse, books apparently (Apoc. certainly) written
after St James' death. In ii. 25 there is a reference to ʿΡαὰβ ἡ πόρνη
as with Abraham an example of justification by works. It is urged
that as Abraham is taken from St Paul, so Rahab is taken from the
Pauline Hebrews xi. 31 (cf. Bleek Heb. I. 89 f.). It is quite possible
that Rahab may have been cited by St Paul or disciples of his as an
example of faith: but the reference to Heb. is unlikely, for there is
no question of justification there. She is merely one of a long series
(οὐ συναπώλετο). But at all events it is enough that she was
celebrated by the Jews as a typical proselyte (Wünsche, Erläute-
rung der Evangelien, 3 f.). As Abraham was the type of Israelite
faith, so Rahab was of Gentile faith. In i. 12, τὸν στέφανον τῆς
ζωῆς is referred to Rev. ii. 10; and ii. 5, κληρονόμους τῆς βασιλείας
to Rev. i. 6, 9; v. 10. "Crown of life" is a striking phrase, not
likely to arise independently in two places: but probably of Jewish
origin, founded on O.T. (see further, in loc.). Κληρον. τ. βασιλ.
comes straight from our Lord's words Mt. v. 3, 10; Lk. xii. 32, etc.
as regards βασιλεία (the poor, as here) and both words Mt. xxv.
34; 1 Cor. vi. 9, etc. These supposed indications, practically all
isolated, crumble into nothing.

A striking fact is that Kern, who initiated the more vigorous
criticism of the Epistle in modern times by his essay of 1835, then
placed it late: yet himself wrote a commentary in 1838 in which
he retracted the former view, and acknowledged that he had been
over hasty.

It is not necessary at present to say more on authenticity, which will come under notice incidentally. But how as to the James intended? Practically two only come into consideration: James the son of Zebedee and James the Lord's brother. Who James the Lord's brother was is another question.

Was it the son of Zebedee? For this there is hardly any external evidence[1]. Cod. Corbeiensis, an interesting MS with an Old Latin text, has *Explicit epistola Jacobi filii Zebedaei.* The date is cent. x (Holder ap. Gebhardt *Barn.*[2] xxiv f.); but the colophon is probably much more ancient. The Epistle is not part of a N.T. or of Epistles, but is in combination with three other Latin books all ancient, the four together forming the end (true end) of a vol. of which the first three-quarters (69—93) are lost (Bonnell ap. Hilgenf. in *Zeitsch.* 1871, 263). Philaster on Heresies (soon after the middle of cent. IV); Novatian (called Tert.) *de cibis judaicis* (cent. III); and an old translation of the Ep. of Barnabas, next to which (i.e. last) it stands. Thus it is highly probable that the Corb. MS was copied from one written late in cent. IV, or not much later, i.e. at a time when the Epistle of St James was treated in the West as a venerable writing, but not as part of the N.T. This could hardly have been the case after cent. IV, owing to the authority of Jerome, Augustine and the Council of Carthage (prob. 397).

Another probable trace of this tradition in the West is in Isid. Hisp. *de ortu et obitu patrum* 71: Jacobus filius Zebedaei, frater Joannis, quartus in ordine, duodecim tribubus quae sunt in dispersione gentium scripsit atque Hispaniae et occidentalium locorum gentibus evangelium praedicavit etc. It has been suggested that "scripsit" is an interpolation. Apparently the only reason is because (in some MSS (?) not noticed by Vallarsi) Jerome *de vir. illust.*

---

[1] Syr. often cited, on account of a Syriac note common to the three Epistles:

Of the Holy Apostles
James Peter John
Spectators of the Resurrection of Jesus Christ
The several Epistles
printed in the Syriac tongue and characters.

But this is now understood to be due to Widmanstadt.

after Matthew has: J. Zebedaei filius duodecim tribubus quae sunt
in dispersione omnibus praedicavit evangelium Dni. nostri J.C. etc.
(Martianay, *Vulgata*, p. 191: cf. Sabat. III. 944). But this may just
as easily be a shortened abbreviation of Isidore. This addition in
Jerome is by Martianay referred to some Greeks (a Graecis nescio
quibus); but what Greeks are meant? The motive probably was to
make him an apostle, the identification with the son of Alphaeus
not being known to those who gave the title; also the connexion of
Peter, James and John. Practically the same motive still exists;
but it is not an argument. Plumptre (pp. 7—10) quite sufficiently
answers Mr Bassett's reasons. They all are merely points in which
words said in the Epistle are such as might easily have been said by
one who saw and heard what the son of Zebedee did, but suit
equally the other James in question. Besides Apostleship the other
motive is to obtain an early date, on which more hereafter. At
all events it is obvious that the existence of recipients such as the
Epistle presupposes would be inconsistent with all that we know of
the few years before St James' death. Indeed if he had written, it
is most strange that no better tradition should exist; most strange
also that there should be no record of such a special position and
activity as would lead to his writing in this authoritative tone.

We come therefore as a matter of course to James the Lord's
brother. About him a large literature has been written: it is
worth while here only to take the more important points. To take
first what is clear and accepted on all hands, he was *the* James of
all but the earliest years of the Apostolic age. Three times he
appears in the Acts, all memorable occasions :—(1) xii. 17. When
Peter is delivered from the imprisonment which accompanied the
death of James the son of Zebedee, he bids his friends go tell
the news to "James and the brethren," which shews that already
he was prominent, to say the least. (2) xv. 13. At the conference or council at Jerusalem, arising out of the Judaizers'
attempt to enforce circumcision at Antioch, when Peter has spoken
in favour of liberty, and Barnabas and Paul have recounted their
successful mission in Asia Minor, James likewise recognises Gentile

Christianity, but proposes restrictions which were virtually a compromise; finally he refers to the Jews and their synagogues in different cities. (3) xxi. 18. When Paul comes to Jerusalem (for the last time, as it proved) and is welcomed by the brethren, he goes in next day to James, all the elders being present: he greets them and recounts his missionary successes. They (James and the elders) glorify God for what had happened, and then mentioning the great number of Christian Jews at Jerusalem, all zealots for the law, and ill-disposed towards St Paul, suggested his performance of a Jewish rite of purification in the temple to shew that he himself had not abandoned Jewish practice though it was not to be imposed on Gentiles. Thus, again, substantially accepting Gentile freedom, but urging subordinate concession to Jewish feelings.

Now as regards St Paul's Epistles:—(1) 1 Cor. xv. 7 (to which we must return). Christ was seen by James, then by all the Apostles. (2) Gal. i. 19. Referring to the first visit to Jerusalem after the conversion, "other of the apostles saw I none, save James the Lord's brother." (3) Gal. ii. 9. The second visit to Jerusalem mentioned in Galatians, but apparently the third altogether, and probably identical with that of Acts xv. (see Lightft. *Gal.*[10] pp. 123 ff., 303 ff.). Here James, Cephas, John, οἱ δοκοῦντες στύλοι εἶναι, recognising the grace given him, give them the right hand of fellowship, that Paul and Barnabas should go to the Gentiles, they to the circumcision, with a proviso that they should remember the poor (brethren of Judaea), which, he says, for this very reason I made it a point to do. (4) Gal. ii. 12. Certain came from James (from Jerusalem to Antioch). [See *Jud. Christ.* pp. 79 ff.] Doubtless we must add Jude 1, ἀδελφὸς δὲ Ἰακώβου: but this is of less consequence. Here then we have James as the leading person at Jerusalem from the time of Peter's imprisonment to Paul's last visit. Here the N.T. leaves him. More we learn from Hegesippus (Eus. ii. 23; cf. iv. 22) about his way of life ("the Just"), his reputation among the people, and his martyrdom. His death is also mentioned by Joseph. *Ant.* xx. 9. 1, for there is no sufficient reason to suspect the passage to be interpolated.

We now come to matters of question and debate. Was he one
of the Twelve? i.e. Was he the son of Alphaeus? Why was he
called the Lord's brother? Without attempting to trace out all the
intricacies of the scriptural argument[1] a word must be said on the
cardinal points.

First Gal. i. 19: ἕτερον δὲ τῶν ἀποστόλων οὐκ εἶδον, εἰ μὴ Ἰάκωβον
τὸν ἀδελφὸν τοῦ κυρίου. Here, according to the most obvious sense,
St Paul implies that James was one of the Apostles, while he
directly calls him the brother of the Lord. Is this obvious sense
right? i.e. Can ἕτερον εἰ μή reasonably bear another meaning? On
the whole, I think not. For the very late exchange of εἰ μή and
ἀλλά in N.T. there is no probability whatever. In three other
books of the N.T. in less good Greek (Mt. xii. 4; Lk. iv. 25 f.;
Rev. ix. 4) the meaning *looks like* this, but fallaciously. Either the
εἰ μή goes with the preceding clause as a general statement, dropping
the particular reference, or (more probably) there is a colloquial
ellipse of another negative (cf. Mt. xii. 4, οὐδέ τινι εἰ μὴ τ. ἱερεῦσιν
μόνοις; Lk. iv. 26, οὐδὲ πρός τινα εἰ μὴ εἰς Σάρεπτα; Rev. ix. 4, οὐδέ
τι εἰ μὴ τ. ἀνθρώπους). The force is thus not simply "but," but
"but only." St Paul himself has some rather peculiar uses of εἰ
μή. Rom. xiii. 8, εἰ μὴ τὸ ἀλλήλους ἀγαπᾶν; 1 Cor. ii. 11, τίς γὰρ
οἶδεν...τὰ τ. ἀνθρώπου εἰ μὴ τὸ πνεῦμα κ.τ.λ.; (probably not Gal. ii.
16, οὐ δικαιοῦται...ἐὰν μή). Again with an initial ellipse 1 Cor. vii.
17, εἰ μὴ ἑκάστῳ κ.τ.λ. ("only"); Rom. xiv. 14, εἰ μὴ τῷ λογιζομένῳ;
Gal. i. 7, εἰ μή τινές εἰσιν κ.τ.λ. Thus it is not impossible that
St Paul might mean "unless you choose to count" etc. But in
a historical statement on a delicate matter he would probably with
that meaning have hinted it by a particle, as by εἰ μὴ ἄρα, εἰ
μή γε. Thus it is much more probable that he did simply accept
James as "an apostle," while yet his mentioning so important a
person (see ii. 9) only as an after thought, not with Peter, does
suggest some difference of authority or position between them.

Next what did he mean by an apostle? Was it necessarily one

[1] Excellently given in Ltft., and summarised (rather too shortly) by Plumptre
pp. 10 ff.).

of the Twelve? Here we must walk cautiously, and observe carefully the limits of usage. The range of the term in the N.T. is
very peculiar. In Mt. and Mk. it is confined to the first mission
and return of the Twelve, and is so introduced as to suggest that
the previous narratives had it not (Mt. x. 1, 2, 5; Mk. iii. 14; vi.
30). In Jn. it is only used in its general sense of envoy (xiii. 16),
οὐδὲ ἀπόστολος μείζων τ. πέμψαντος αὐτόν. In these three "the
Twelve" or "the disciples" take its place. But in Lk. it comes in
more freely, though still not so commonly as "disciples."

In Acts (from i. 2) it is the frequent and almost (contrast vi. 2)
exclusive designation of the Twelve and of them alone, with one
remarkable exception. From xi. 20 Antioch begins to be a centre
of Christian life and activity external to Jerusalem. Barnabas is
sent (xi. 22) by the Church at Jerusalem to investigate what was
going on. He approved it, fetched Paul from Tarsus, and they
worked at Antioch together; and together they carried a contribution to the brethren in Judaea (xi. 28 ff.). Then (xiii. 1-4) in a
very marked way they are described as set apart by a special command of the Holy Spirit, having hands laid on them and being
formally sent forth. This was the first Missionary Journey: on the
course of it they are twice (xiv. 4, 14) called "the apostles," but
never after. This usage in xiv. is often urged to shew the latitude
of usage. It seems to me to have quite the opposite meaning: it
shews that the apostolate of the Twelve was not the only office that
could bear the name: but the application is to one equally definite,
though temporary, a special and specially sacred commission for a
particular mission of vast importance for the history of the Church,
being the first authoritative mission work to the heathen (in
contrast to sporadic individuals), the first recorded extension of the
Gospel beyond Syria, and by its results the occasion of bringing to
a point the question of Gentile Christianity and the memorable
decision of the Council or Conference of Jerusalem.

1 Pet. i. 1; 2 Pet. i. 1: "an apostle of Jesus Christ" (as in
St Paul). 2 Pet. iii. 2; Jude 17: "the apostles" used in a way
which neither requires nor excludes limitation. Rev. xxi. 14: twelve

names of twelve apostles of the Lamb on the twelve foundations
of the wall of New Jerusalem; xviii. 20 (more indeterminately).
But ii. 2, the angel of the Church at Ephesus has "tried them that
say they are apostles, and are not, and found them false," which
seems to imply both a legitimate and illegitimate use outside the
Twelve. Heb. iii. 1, Christ Himself "apostle and high priest of
our profession," equivalent to "envoy" as in Jn.

St Paul emphasizes his own apostleship in salutations etc., and
the energy with which he asserts his own claim as connected with
a special mission from Christ Himself on the way to Damascus is
really incompatible with looseness of usage. The Twelve were con-
fessedly apostles: so was he: but this was not worth saying if the
title might be given to others not having as definite an authority.
This comes out clearly when we consider the passages in which he
acknowledges the priority of the Twelve in time (1 Cor. xv. 9;
Gal. i. 17; cf. 2 Cor. xi. 5; xii. 11). How then about the apparent
exceptions in his use? Among these we must not reckon Rom. xvi.
7 (οἵτινες ἐπίσημοι ἐν τ. ἀποστόλοις). The next clause speaks of them
(Andronicus and Junius) as having become Christians earlier than
himself, so that doubtless they had been at Jerusalem, and so would
be, as the words would quite naturally mean[1], "men of mark in the
eyes of the apostles," "favourably known to the apostles." The
only real passages are 2 Cor. viii. 23 (Titus and others), ἀπόστολοι
ἐκκλησιῶν between ἀδελφοὶ ἡμῶν and δόξα Χριστοῦ; and Phil. ii. 25
(Epaphroditus), τ. ἀδελφὸν καὶ συνεργὸν καὶ συνστρατιώτην μου, ὑμῶν
δὲ ἀπόστολον; both marked by the added words as used in the
limited sense of "envoys of churches," somewhat as in Acts xiv.
This throws no light on "other of *the* apostles," apparently absolute
and equivalent to apostles of God or of Christ.

Thus far we find St Paul's use not vague at all, but limited to
(1) the Twelve, (2) himself, (3) envoys of churches, but in this case
only with other words (defining genitives) added. Yet it does not
follow that he would refuse it to St James unless he were of the

---

[1] For this use of ἐπίσημος ἐν, and the opposite ἄσημος ἐν, there is good
classical analogy. It is analogous to 1 Cor. vi. 2, εἰ ἐν ὑμῖν κρίνεται ὁ κόσμος.

Twelve. Supposing he had some exceptional claim like his own, he might allow the name. 1 Cor. xv. 5–8 seems to shew that it really was so:

"seen of Cephas, then of the Twelve,
seen of James, then of all the apostles."

The use of *all* implies the Twelve and something more, and it is not unlikely that the relations correspond of single names and bodies.

Whether St James was the only additional apostle, we cannot tell: but probably he was. His early and peculiar authority would be accounted for if he had some exceptional Divine authorisation analogous to St Paul's. Not to speak of confused traditions about this, St Paul's mention of Christ's appearance to him (1 Cor. xv. 7) points to a probable occasion, and *the Gospel according to the Hebrews* had a story referring to this event (Jerome, *de vir. illustr.* 2). Such an event as the conversion of a brother of the Lord by a special appearance after the Resurrection might easily single him out for a special apostleship.

Thus Galatians i. 19 is compatible either with his being one of the Twelve, or an additional member of the apostolate by an exceptional title; and 1 Cor. xv. rather suggests the latter.

The details of the "brotherhood" question must be left to the books on the subject. Speaking generally there are four theories:

(1) Helvidian: brothers strictly, sons of Joseph and Mary.

(2) Palestinian or Epiphanian: brothers strictly in scriptural sense, though not the modern sense, sons of Joseph but not Mary.

(3) Chrysostom (confusedly) and Theodoret: cousins, as children of Clopas.

(4) Hieronymian: cousins, as children of Alphaeus.

The third is of no great historical importance or intrinsic interest: it is apparently founded on a putting together of Mt. xxvii. 56 ‖ Mk. xv. 40 with Jn. xix. 25 (contrast Ltft. *Gal.*[10] pp. 289 f.). But in modern times it is usually combined with the fourth by the (in itself probable) identification of Clopas with Alphaeus.

The Hieronymian, largely accepted in the Western Church, and with rare exceptions in England before Lightfoot, is probably, as

Lightfoot shews, *historically* only an ingenious scholar's theory in century iv. *Intrinsically* it gives an unnatural and for any but patriarchal times unexampled sense to "brethren"[1]. It occurs in the Gospels, Acts, and St Paul: nay (Mt. xii. 46–50 ‖ Mk. iii. 31–35 ‖ Lk. viii. 19–21) the original narrative puts it into the mouth of those who told Him that His mother and His brethren sought to speak with Him. It makes the "unbelief" of the brethren unintelligible, and involves various petty difficulties in subordinate details. I mention only one of the details, as deserving more attention than it has received, Jn. xix. 25. The cousinhood theory turns on Mary wife of Clopas being sister to the Virgin, and this on there being only three persons here, not four. Both arrangements are possible: two pairs more natural, "mother" the common word of the first, "Mary" of the second. But more striking is the antithesis of soldiers and women. As Ewald pointed out, the soldiers would be four, or a combination of fours (see Wetst. on Acts xii. 4). Thus St John would evidently have had dwelling in his mind the two contrasted groups of four, the four indifferent Roman soldiers at sport and gain, the four faithful women, two kinswomen, two disciples.

On the whole the biblical evidence, which alone is decisive, is definitely unfavourable to the cousinhood theory; and, as far as I can see, it leaves open the choice between the Helvidian and the Palestinian. Some might say that "brethren," if less inapplicable than to cousins, would still be unlikely on the Epiphanian view. But the language of Mt. and Lk. is decisive against this predisposition. Joseph was our Lord's not *genitor* but *pater*. Lk. ii. 33, ὁ πατὴρ αὐτοῦ καὶ ἡ μήτηρ; 48, ὁ πατήρ σου καὶ ἐγώ; 27, 41, 43, οἱ γονεῖς [αὐτοῦ]; and both Mt. and Lk. carry the genealogy to Joseph. Yet both assert the miraculous conception, and it is impossible on any rational criticism to separate the two modes of speech as belonging to different elements. The birth from the Virgin Mary exclusively and the (in some true sense) fatherhood of Joseph are asserted together; and if Joseph could rightly be called father, his

---

[1] See Additional Note, p. 102.

children could rightly be called "brethren." Still this leaves
neutrality only.

On the other hand the traditional authority is by no means
undecided. For the Helvidian we have only the guess of the
erratic Tertullian and obscure Latin writers of century iv. For the
Epiphanian we have in the earlier times some obscure writings
probably connected with Palestine as the *Protevangelium Jacobi*,
the Alexandrian Fathers, Clement and Origen (sic), and various
important writers of the fourth century. It was of course possible
that such a tradition should grow up, before Jerome's solution was
thought of, by those who desired to maintain the perpetual virginity
of Mary. But still the absence of any trace of the other, even
among Ebionites, is remarkable, and the tradition itself has various
and good attestation. The evidence is not such as one would like
to rest anything important upon. But there is a decided pre-
ponderance of reason for thinking the Epiphanian view to be right.

Hence the writer of the Epistle was James the Just, bishop or
head of Jerusalem, brother of the Lord as being son of Joseph by a
former wife, not one of the Twelve, a disbeliever in our Lord's
Messiahship during His lifetime, but a believer in Him shortly
afterwards, probably in connexion with a special appearance vouch-
safed to him.

Before we leave the person of James, we must speak of his
death and the time of it. According to Josephus (*Ant.* xx. 9. 1)
the high priest Ananus the younger, "a man of peculiarly bold and
audacious character" (θρασὺς τ. τρόπον καὶ τολμητὴς διαφερόντως), a
Sadducee, and accordingly, Josephus says, specially given to judicial
cruelty, took advantage of the interregnum between Festus and
Albinus to gather a συνέδριον κριτῶν, at which "James the brother
of Jesus, who is (or, was) called Christ, and some others" were
condemned to be stoned to death as transgressors of the law. He
adds that the best men of the city were indignant, some wrote to
King Agrippa, others met Albinus on the way to point out the
illegality of the act, and the result was that Ananus was deposed.
An interpolation has been supposed here; but the whole story

hangs together, and Lightfoot with good reason supports it, pointing
out that in a real interpolation the language is by no means so
neutral. The date of these events can be accurately fixed to 62,
which must therefore be the date of St James' death if the passage
about him is genuine.

Hegesippus' account is much more elaborate (see Ltft. *Gal.*[10]
366 f.). Dr Plumptre makes a good fight for some of the particulars,
on the ground that St James was apparently a Nazarite. But on
the whole Lightfoot seems right in suspecting that the picture is
drawn from an Ebionite romantic glorification of him, the Ἀναβαθμοὶ
Ἰακώβου, part of which is probably preserved in the *Clementine
Recognitions.* Hegesippus ends with the words καὶ εὐθὺς Οὐεσπασι-
ανὸς πολιορκεῖ αὐτούς, which is commonly understood to mean that
St James suffered only just before the siege, say in 68 or 69. If so,
no doubt this must be taken as an error as compared with Josephus.
But a writer of a century later might very well speak of the judgement as immediate even if eight years intervened. At all events
we must hold to 62 as the date.

The Readers.

These are distinctly described as the Twelve Tribes in the
Dispersion. Nothing is apparently clearer. Some say to the
Church at large, as referring to the true Israel. But this comes in
very strangely at the head of a letter with no indication of a
spiritual sense, and coupled with ἐν τ. διασπορᾷ; and especially so
from St James. If Gentile Christians are intended at all, then they
are considered as proselytes to Jewish Christians. This however is
not likely. Gentile Christians were very numerous, and are not
likely to be included in so artificial a way. Nor do the warnings of
the Epistle contain anything applicable to them distinctively.

On the other hand with much more plausibility the Readers
have been taken as either Jews alone, or Jews *plus* Jewish Christians.
That Jewish Christians were at least chiefly meant seems proved by
"the faith of our Lord Jesus Christ" (ii. 1), probably also by "the good

name " (ii. 7), and perhaps " the coming of the Lord " (v. 7) ; and it
is confirmed by the circumstances of those addressed   It is neither
unnatural nor wrong that St James should regard Jewish Christians
positively as the true Israel, the true heirs of Abraham.   With
Gentile Christians he was not concerned.   Jewish Christians were
to him simply the only true and faithful Jews.   His own position
as head of the Jerusalem Church gave him a special right to address
Jewish Christians, but no such special right to address others ;
though doubtless he would not refuse to speak to such as were
associated with Christian Jewish communities.

The only question therefore is whether he meant to include
unbelieving Jews.   If the story in Hegesippus is true, he was
honoured by all the people, and even Josephus' account shews that
his death might cause offence to men who were not Christians.
Still the Epistle contains no evidence that he had them in view
(neither the δώδεκα φυλαῖς, nor the slightness of definitely Christian
teaching prove anything), and it is fairly certain that he wrote to
Christian Jews and to them alone.   [Yet see on iv. 4.]

Next to what Christian Jews?   "Those in the dispersion."
Cf. 1 Pet. i. 1; Jn. vii. 35.   Certainly therefore not those of
Palestine, nor including them.   No others probably are excluded ;
but it does not follow that he sent copies of his Epistle broadcast
over the world, to wherever Christian Jews might be found.   The
distribution might have been by means of returning visitors to
feasts.   Neither method is unlikely.   Perhaps we may go further
and say that he would naturally chiefly have in view those of Syria
beyond Palestine, and possibly Babylonia.   And in Syria especially
those of Antioch.   Josephus, *B.J.* vii. 3. 3, speaks of the Jews as
sprinkled among the nations κατὰ πᾶσαν τ. οἰκουμένην, but especially
mingled with Syria on account of the neighbourhood, and peculiarly
numerous at Antioch on account of the size of the city.   The Acts
shew how important Antioch was in the early Church.   In writing
in the first instance to Antioch he would be writing to the chief
centre of Hellenistic Judaism, from which what he wrote would go
forth elsewhere.   At the same time he might have a good deal in

view the city itself and its circumstances, which he would know by the yearly visitors. This supposition (of course it is not more) agrees with the fact that the Epistle was read in the Syriac Canon at the time when 1 Pet. and 1 Jn. were the only other Catholic Epistles so received. Various explanations of this fact are possible[1], but a very natural one would be that Antioch was itself the primary recipient.

Circumstances and Date.

These must be inferred from the contents, and do not admit of certainty. The two points which have attracted most attention are the paucity of Christian language and the passage about justification.

The first seems to me to afford nothing tangible. The character and position of St James make it quite conceivable that a state of feeling and language, which with the other leaders of the Church would naturally belong only to an early stage of growth, would with him be comparatively permanent. The amplest recognition of St Paul's work and of Gentile Christianity would be consistent with a preservation of a less developed type of Christian doctrine than St Paul's. Hence the immature doctrine must be treated as affording no evidence one way or the other.

Next as to the justification passage. This has given rise to endless debate. (1) Was it written independently of St Paul? If so, probably before St Paul wrote on the subject, and therefore at a very early date. Or (2) was it written to correct St Paul? Or (3) to correct a perverse misunderstanding of St Paul? (2) and (3) of course imply a date subsequent to Galatians and Romans, i.e. after 58.

(2) may be set aside as highly improbable. Apart from the language of the Acts, the Epistle itself cannot be so understood. Laying side by side St Paul's Epistles on this matter and St James, in spite of resemblances and contrasts it is difficult to believe that one was aimed at the other. A real antagonist would have followed

---

[1] It is possible that the language of the Epistle reflects in great measure the circumstances of the Church at Jerusalem.

St Paul more closely, and come definitely into collision, which St James never does.

For (1) there is much to be said (see Plumptre). Its great difficulty is to shew how language so similar in *form* about δι- καιοῦσθαι ἐκ πίστεως could spring up independently in the two sources. It is not a question of a mere phrase, but a controversy. There is no substantial evidence as yet that it was a Jewish controversy, and St Paul's language does not look as if it was.

For (3) may be urged the facts which throw doubt on (1) and (2). There is a similarity of phrase such as makes indirect derivation of one from the other probable, and the error which St James combats was not at all unlikely to arise from a misuse and mis-application of St Paul. More will be said when we come to the passage. If (3) be true then the Epistle must belong to the con- cluding years of St James' life, and this is probable for other reasons. The Epistle implies not only a spread of Christianity among the Diaspora, but its having taken root there some time. The faults marked are those of lukewarmness, of what would arise after a time in settled communities that were losing their early freshness and vigour. The persecutions to which it refers might doubtless have occurred early without our knowing anything about them. But the tone of St James on this head reminds us of 1 Pet. and Heb. No year can be fixed with any certainty : but 60 or a little after seems not far wrong. The essential point is not the year but the period, later than the more important part of St Paul's ministry and writings.

Reception.

Two things are to be distinguished, use and canonical authority. The earliest Bible of the Christian Church was the O.T. The books of the N.T. were only added by degrees, and variously in different places ; sometimes also with various degrees of authority. The Catholic Epistles came more slowly to their position, 1 Pet. and 1 Jn. being the earliest. The first traces of St James, now recognised almost on all hands, are in 1 Clement about 95. He apparently

combines Paul and James (Westcott, *Canon N.T.* p. 25). Next in
Hermas, also Roman, probably a little before 150. In these two
there is no distinctly authoritative use; but the whole way in which
they use N.T. books leaves it uncertain how they regarded the
Epistle.

Next Irenaeus, towards the end of the second century, representing partly Asia, partly Rome. His use of James has been often
denied, and quite rightly as regards authoritative use; but I feel
sure he knew the book, though only as an ancient theological
writing. He never cites it, but uses phrases from it, which taken
singly are uncertain, but they confirm each other. Thus it is
nothing in itself that he says (iv. 13. 4) that Abraham "amicus
factus est Dei." But it is something that it occurs in a passage
contrasting the Law of Moses and the Word of Christ as an enlarge-
ment and fulfilment of the Law, speaking of "superextendi decreta
libertatis, et augeri subjectionem quae est ad regem," which looks
very like the νόμον τελεῖτε βασιλικόν of ii. 8 and νόμον τέλειον τὸν τ.
ἐλευθερίας of i. 25. And this becomes certainty when not long
afterwards (iv. 16. 2) we get the consecutive words about Abraham
"credidit Deo et reputatum est illi ad justitiam, et amicus Dei
vocatus est"; i.e. the justification from Genesis is instantly followed
by the "Friend" clause, exactly as in Jam. ii. 23. There is no
reason to suppose that the last words as well as the former were
borrowed by St James from a traditional form of text. Subsequently (iv. 34. 4) he uses the peculiar phrase "libertatis lex,"
explaining it thus: "id est, verbum Dei ab apostolis...adnuntiatum."
Again (v. 1. 1) we get within 7 lines "*factores* autem *sermonum*
ejus facti" (cf. i. 22) and "facti autem *initium facturae*" (cf. i. 18);
neither being likely to suggest the other except as being very near
in the Epistle. These instances give some force to what would
otherwise be problematical: (iii. 18. 5) "*Verbum* enim Dei...ipse
hoc *fecit* in cruce," and shortly afterwards (19. 1) "non *recipientes*
autem *verbum* incorruptionis" (cf. i. 21). As regards authoritative
use, we have a definite statement from Cosmas (in cent. vi.),
Topogr. Christ. vii. p. 292, that Irenaeus declared 1 Pet. and 1 Jn.

alone to be by the apostles; and it is highly probable that, taking apostles in the Twelve sense, he would accordingly exclude St James. The Epistle is also absent from the *Muratorian Canon*, probably a Roman document of the age of Irenaeus.

Crossing the Mediterranean to the Latin Church of North Africa, we find no trace of the Epistle in Tertullian or Cyprian. One allusion to "unde Abraham amicus Dei deputatus" (Tert., *adv. Jud.* 2) proves nothing. The early or African old Latin version omitted it.

Moving eastward to the learned Church of Alexandria, Clem. Alex. is difficult. Certainly he did not use the book as Scripture; but I feel sure that he knew it, though he does not name it. In *Strom.* vi. p. 825 (Potter): "except your righteousness multiply beyond the Scribes and Pharisees, who are justified by abstinence from evil, together with your being able along with perfection in these things to love and benefit your neighbour, οὐκ ἔσεσθε βασιλικοί, for intensification (ἐπίτασις) of the righteousness according to the Law shews the Gnostic." Here βασιλικός is coupled with love to neighbour just as in ii. 8, and the tone of the passage is quite in St James' strain. In *Strom.* v. p. 650 we have the peculiar phrase τὴν πίστιν τοίνυν οὐκ ἀργὴν καὶ μόνην, agreeing with the true reading of ii. 20. There are several allusions to Abraham as the "Friend." τό ναί occurs three times as in v. 12, but perhaps from Evangelical tradition. Other passages may come from 1 Pet. Cassiodorus, late in cent. vi., says (*de instit. div. litt.* viii.) that Clement wrote notes on the Canonical (= Catholic) Epistles, i.e. 1 Pet., 1 and 2 Jn., Jam. What is certainly a form of these notes still exists in Latin, but there are none on Jam., while there are on Jude. So that evidently there is a slip of author or scribes, and practically this is additional evidence against Clement using Jam. as Scripture.

It is somewhat otherwise with his disciple Origen, who very rarely, but still occasionally, cites Jam., speaking of it as "the current Epistle of St James," and again referring to it as if some of his readers might demur to its authority. In the Latin works there are more copious references, but these are uncertain. On the whole a vacillating and intermediate position. Origen's disciple Dionysius

Alex. once cites i. 13 apparently as Scripture. Another disciple, Gregory of Neocaesarea, if the fragment on Jeremiah (Ghislerius i. p. 831) be genuine, refers though hardly by way of authority to i. 17.

These are all the strictly Antenicene references. But there is one weighty fact beside them : Jam. is present in the Syriac Version which excluded some others. The present state of this version comes from the end of cent. III or early IV, and *Jam.* may have been added then: but it is more likely that it had been in the Syriac from the first, i.e. in the Old Syriac. The early history of the Egyptian versions is too uncertain to shew anything.

Eusebius places it among the *Antilegomena*, practically accepted in some churches, not in others. In speaking of Jam. (ii. 23. 25), he says that "the first of what are named the Catholic Epistles is his. Now it should be known that it is treated [by some] as spurious (νοθεύεται μέν); and indeed not many of the old writers mentioned it, as neither did they what is called that of Jude, which itself also is one of what are called the seven Catholic Epistles ; yet we know that these two with the rest have been in public use (δεδημοσιευμένας) in very many churches." Thus Eusebius, cautious as always in letting nothing drop that had authority, is yet careful not to commit himself.

From this time forward the book had a firm place in the Greek Churches. It was used very freely by Didymus and Cyril Alex. ; and the Antiochene Fathers (like Chrysostom), who kept to the Syrian Canon and did not use books omitted by it, *did* use Jam. The only exception is a peculiar one. Theodore of Mopsuestia was one of the greatest of all theologians and specially as a critic of the Bible, whence he became the chosen interpreter of the Mesopotamian Churches. He was somewhat erratic and rash in his ways, and lies under a kind of ban more easily to be explained than justified. Most of his works have perished except fragments, so that we have to depend on the report of a bitter antagonist, Leontius, nearly two centuries later. After noticing his rejection of Job, and referring to the testimony to Job in Jam., Leontius proceeds (*c. Nest. et Eut.* iii. 14): "For which reason methinks he banishes both this very epistle of the great James and the succeeding Catholic Epistles by the other writers (τῶν ἄλλων)." This loose statement occurring in a violent passage needs sifting. It was not likely that he would use any Catholic Epistles but Jam., 1 Pet., and 1 Jn., and this absence of use of 2 Pet., 2 and 3 Jn., and Jude would account for Leontius language, while leaving it exaggerated. But Jam. is specially mentioned, and doubtless rightly. The *Instituta regularia* (commonly called *De partibus divinae legis*) of an African Latin writer Junilius, long believed to be connected with the Syrian school of Nisibis, have lately been shewn to be a more or less modified translation of an *Introduction to Scripture* by Paul of Nisibis, a devoted admirer of Theodore, and it is full of Theodorian ideas. Its account of the books of the O.T. corresponds with Theodore's, and in the N.T. it excludes Jam. but not 1 Pet., 1 Jn. This was doubtless Theodore's own view. What was the motive? It might have been knowledge of the imperfect early reception of Jam. But in the case of the O.T. omissions, Job, Canticles, inscriptions of Psalms, Chronicles, Ezra and Nehemiah (and Esther), there is direct evidence that in at least some cases he acted on internal evidence (Job, Canticles, Inscr. Ps.): and it is quite likely that it was the same here too as with Luther.

Outside Theodore's own school we have no further omission of Jam. in the East. Late in cent. VI Cosmas, having had urged against him a passage of 2 Pet., speaks disparagingly of the Catholic Epistles in general, and mentions various facts as to past partial rejections (*Top. Christ.* vii. p. 292). His language is altogether vague and confused : but he limits himself to urging that "the perfect Christian ought not to be stablished on the strength of questioned books (ἀμφιβαλλόμενα)."

In the West reception was not so rapid. Towards the end of cent. IV Jam. is cited by three or four Italian Latin writers, as the Ambrosiast (= Hil. Rom.) on Gal. v. 10 (dicente Jacobo apostolo in epistola sua); perhaps from Jerome's influence. Also Chromatius of Aquileia and Gaudentius of Brixia, but without "apostolus"; Jerome himself, and abundantly Augustine, whose quotations equal all others put together; also the *Corbey* MS., which may have an even earlier original, the style being very rude. But not the earlier Latin writers of the century, as Hilary, Lucifer, Ambrose (though in one place a sentence of Jam. appears among the texts which he notices as cited by Arians).

The most striking fact is the language of Victorinus Afer, converted at Rome late in life, and seen there by Jerome and Augustine. His *Comm. in Gal.* i. 13 ff.: "From James Paul could not learn"; James "admixto Judaismo Christum evangelizabat, quod negat id faciendum." Elaborately on "Jacobum fratrem Dei": "The Symmachians make James as it were a twelfth apostle, and he is followed by those who to our Lord Jesus Christ add the observance of Judaism." "When Paul called him brother (of the Lord), he thereby denied him to be an apostle. He had to be seen with honour. Sed neque a Jacobo aliquid discere potuit, quippe cum alia sentiat; ut neque a Petro, vel quod paucis diebus cum Petro moratus est; vel quod Jacobus apostolus non est, et in haeresi sit." He goes on to account for the mention of the seeing of James. It was to shew that he did not reject the Galatian doctrine from ignorance. "Vidi ergo nominatim quid Jacobus tractet et evangelizet: et tamen quoniam cognita mihi est ista blasphemia, repudiata a me est, sicut et a vobis, o Galatae, repudianda"; and more in the same strain. Something here is probably due to the writer's late and imperfect Christian education. It is not likely, in the absence of all other evidence, that such language would have been used by ordinary well-instructed Christians *anywhere*. But neither could it have been possible if the Epistle had in Victorinus' neighbourhood been received as canonical. It attests a feeling about the book very unlike that after Jerome and Augustine.

To resume, the Epistle of St James was known and used from a very early time, at least at Rome, but without authority It was used also, but with rather indefinite authority, at Alexandria by Clement and Origen and Dionysius. It formed part of the Syriac Canon, and was probably used in Syrian Churches. There is no trace of it in North Africa. It is placed among the ἀντιλεγόμενα in Eusebius. In the West it was neglected till late in cent. IV, and then adopted through Jerome and Augustine. In the East from Eusebius onwards in all Greek writers except Theod. Mops. and his disciples, who probably rejected it on internal grounds.

Purpose and Contents.

The purpose is practical not controversial, mainly to revive a languishing religious state, a lukewarm formality, and correct the corruptions into which it had fallen. Persecution had evidently fallen, and was not being met with courage, patience and faith. This last word Faith occurs at the beginning, near the end, and throughout chap. 2, and expresses much of the purport of the whole. In various forms St James deals with the manner of life proceeding from a trustful sense of God's presence, founded on a knowledge of His character and purpose.

There are three main divisions :

I. (i.) Introduction, on Religion.

II. (ii. 1—v. 6.) Against (1) Social sins, (2) Presumption before God.

III. (v. 7—end.) Conclusion, on Religion at once personal and social.

(I.)

The Epistle begins with the greeting, which closes with the word χαίρειν.

The next paragraph, i. 2–18, may be called "Religion in feeling: experience (trial—temptation), God's character, and the Divine aspects of human life." It takes up χαρά from χαίρειν, and deals with πειρασμοί, the special trials (cf. 1 Pet. i. 6 ; iv. 12 ; also Heb. ii. 18 etc.) which serve as examples of all πειρασμοί.

First 2–4, on patience (cf. Lk. xxi. 19 = Mt. x. 22 ; xxiv. 13 ‖ Mk. xiii. 13). But in this section there are digressions, the chief being 5–11; first 5–8, on asking without doubting (Mt. xxi. 21 ‖ Mk. xi. 23), and then 9–11, on the humble and the rich (cf. Sermon

on the Mount). 12, The crown of life, the result of patience (σω-
θήσεται Mt., Mk. = κτήσεσθε τ. ψυχὰς ὑμῶν Lk.; cf. Heb. x. 34).
13, Trial not a temptation by God, but (14 f.) by a man's own
desire. 16–18, Digression on God's character, as altogether good,
and perfect, and the Author of man's high dignity. These verses
are implied in the rest of the epistle.

i. 19–27. Religion in action. The moral results of this faith
are (19–21) quickness to hear, slowness to passionate speech. 22–25,
Hearing, not however as against doing. 26 f., Freedom from defilement not ceremonial, but temperance of speech, beneficence to
others, guilelessness of self.

(II.)

ii. Insolence of wealth (towards fellow men). 1–4, The miscalled Christian faith which dishonours the poor in synagogue.
This is a violation of the principle which follows. 5–9, The poor
as blessed (cf. Sermon on the Mount), and human respect of persons.
10–13, The integrity or unity of the law as a law of liberty, and
its import mercy. What follows is the positive side of 1–13.
14–26, The miscalled faith which dispenses with works.

iii. License of tongue, springing from pride. 1, Not "many
teachers." 2–6, The great power of the tongue, though a small
member. 7 f., Its lawlessness and wildness. 9–12, Its capacities
of good and evil. 13–14 (in contrast to bitter teaching), Wisdom
to be shewn in works (cf. 17 f.) of gentleness. 15–18, The difference
of the two wisdoms exhibited in bitterness and peace.

iv. 1–12. Strife springing from love of pleasure (πόλεμοι contrast to εἰρήνη iii. 18). 1–3, Wars due to evil desire. 4–6, God
and the world as objects of love. 7–10 (digression), Subjection to
God. 11 f., Evil-speaking of others a breach of a law (cf. 1 Pet.
ii. 1. Probably "love thy neighbour as thyself").

iv. 13–v. 6. Presumption of wealth (towards God). Prophetic
warnings to the confident merchants (iv. 13–17) as to stability of
the future; to the rich (v. 1–3) as to impunity, specially (4–6)

as oppressors of the poor. This leads back to persecution as at
the beginning.

(III.)

v. 7–end. Trustful patience towards God and towards man
(one aspect of the inseparableness of the two commandments. Cf.
Mt. xxii. 37 ff.). 7–11, Patience before God (as i. 1–4, 12) *now*
with patience towards men. 12, Reverence towards God, probably
as part of patience. (Negative.) 13–20, The same, positive. The
true resource Prayer, itself to be social, i.e. intercessory, whether
(14 f.) in physical or (16) moral evil. (17 f., Digression on prayer
in general.) 19 f. resumes 16.

[St James is full of unities, e.g. the unity of the O.T. and N.T. :—

(a) The λόγος ἀληθείας (i. 18) is at once the original gift of
reason, and the voice of God in the Christian conscience enlightened
by the Gospel, doubtless with the intermediate stages of instruction
(cf. Ps. cxix.).

(b) The Law is at once the Mosaic (ii. 11), the Deuteronomic
(ii. 8, actually Leviticus, but in spirit Deuteronomic; i. 12; ii. 5),
and the Evangelic (ii. 5).

(c) The principle of mercy as against judgement (ii. 13).]

Style.

The Greek is generally good ; the style very short and epigram-
matic, using questions much. There is great suppressed energy,
taking shape in vigorous images. Much of the old prophetic spirit
(Deuteronomic and later Psalms, esp. cxix.), but uniting with it the
Greek Judaism found in the Apocryphal Sapiential Books and to a
certain extent in Philo. But the style is especially remarkable for
constant hidden allusions to our Lord's sayings, such as we find
in the first three Gospels.

ΙΑΚΩΒΟΥ

ΙΑΚΩΒΟC θεοῦ καὶ κυρίου ᾿Ιησοῦ Χριστοῦ

I. 1. ᾿Ιάκωβος] For the person intended see Introd., pp. xi ff. The name is ᾿Ιακώβ in LXX., but has been doubtless Graecised as a modern name, as so many names in Josephus. Probably it was common at this time: three are mentioned by Josephus, and curiously one the brother of a Simon (*Ant.* xx. 5, 2), another coupled with a John (*B. J.* iv. 4, 2). The third is an Idumaean (*B. J.* iv. 9, 6). [James brother of Jesus Christ is also mentioned (*Ant.* xx. 9, 1) (if the passage be genuine). See pp. xv, xxi f.]

θεοῦ καὶ κυρίου ᾿Ι. Χ. δοῦλος] The combination θεοῦ καὶ κυρίου ᾿Ι. Χ., though grammatically possible, is against Scriptural analogy, and would involve a very improbable want of balance. The absence of the article is due to abbreviation and compression of phrase. See note on 1 Peter i. 1 (p. 15 *b*). An unique phrase as a whole, it unites the O.T. θεοῦ δοῦλος (-οι) (Acts iv. 29; 1 Pet. ii. 16; Apoc. *saepe* and esp. i. 1; and, in greeting, Tit. i. 1 Παῦλος δοῦλος θεοῦ, ἀπόστολος δὲ ᾿Ι. Χ.) with St Paul's δοῦλος Χ. ᾿Ι. (᾿Ι. Χ.) (fully in Rom. i. 1; later Phil. i. 1, δοῦλοι Χ. ᾿Ι.; as also Jude 1; cf. 2 Pet. i. 1).

This coupling of God and Christ in a single phrase covered by δοῦλος is significant as to St James' belief. Without attempting to say *how much* is meant by it, we can see that it involves at least some Divineness of

nature in our Lord, something other than glorified manhood. This is peculiarly true as regards a man with Jewish feelings, unable to admit lower states of deity. It thus shews that he cannot have been an Ebionite. Even St Paul's salutations contain no such combination except in their concluding prayers for grace and peace. An analogous phrase is in Eph. v. 5, ἐν τῇ βασιλείᾳ τοῦ χριστοῦ καὶ θεοῦ.

The conception is not of two distinct and co-ordinate powers, so to speak; as though he were a servant of two lords. But the service of the one at once involves and is contained in the service of the other. Christ being what He is as the Son of the Father, to be His servant is impossible without being God's servant; and the converse is also true. κυρίου ᾿Ι. Χ. is the full phrase illustrated by the early chapters of Acts; esp. ii. 36: God had made Jesus both Lord and Christ. This true sense of χριστός is never lost in N.T.; it is never a mere proper name like ᾿Ιησοῦς, which though a significant name is still a proper name like any other. "Χριστός" has indeed, as a title, a little of the defining power of a proper name, because it represents not merely its etymology "Anointed" but מָשִׁיחַ. ᾿Ι. Χ. is not merely "Jesus the Anointed" but "Jesus, He who has been looked for under the name 'the Anointed,' having therefore the characteristics already

δοῦλος ταῖς δώδεκα φυλαῖς ταῖς ἐν τῇ διασπορᾷ
χαίρειν.

associated with the name, and more."
Accordingly, though we often find
Χ. Ἰ. where Χ. is intended to have
special prominence, we never have
κ. Χ. Ἰ. but only κ. Ἰ. Χ., as here,
Ἰ. standing between κ. and Χ. and
thereby declared to have the character
of both, but specially linked with Χ.,
κ. being prefixed to both together.

δοῦλος, *servant*] Probably in the
widest sense, answering to Κύριος,
equivalent to "doing His work in
His kingdom, in obedience to His
will" (cf. Acts iv. 29). It is misleading to call δοῦλος "slave," as many do,
for it lays the whole stress on a
subordinate point. It expresses in
the widest way the personal relation
of servant to master, not the mere
absence of wages or of right to depart.
But St John in Apoc. (x. 7) uses the
O.T. phrase "His own servants the
prophets," from Amos iii. 7 ; Dan. ix.
6, 10; Zech. i. 6, and probably has
this in mind in calling himself "the
servant of God" (i. 1). And it is not
unlikely that St James also has it in
view, not necessarily as implying himself to be a prophet, as Jn probably
does, but as standing in an analogous
relation to God and His kingdom.

ταῖς δώδεκα φυλαῖς] Equivalent to
Israel in its fulness and completeness.
It has nothing to do with the return
or non-return of the different tribes
from captivity. Josephus believed
the ten tribes to have remained in
great numbers beyond the Euphrates,
and in 4 Esdras xiii. 45 they are said
to be in *Arzareth*, which Dr Schiller-
Szinessy (*Journ. of Philology*, 1870,
pp. 113 f.) has shewn to be only the
אֶרֶץ אַחֶרֶת ("another land") of Deut.
xxix. 28, referring to *Sanhed.*, shewing that that verse was referred to
the ten tribes. They are also the
subject of later traditions. But whatever may have been thought about

the actual descendants of the twelve
tribes, and their fate, the people was
thought of as having returned as a
whole.

After the return, when Judah and
Benjamin apparently alone returned
to any very considerable extent, the
reference to tribes, as a practically
existing entity, seems to have come
to an end, except as regards the
descent of individuals through recorded genealogies, and the people
that had returned was treated as
representing the continuity of the
whole nation, Judah and Israel together. (See Ezek. xlvii. 13; Ezra
vi. 17; viii. 35.) This would have
been unnatural if the tribes had been
previously the primary thing, and
the people only an agglomeration of
tribes : but in reality the true primary
unit was the people, and the tribes
were merely the constituent parts,
the union of which expressed its
unity.

Accordingly our Lord Himself chose
twelve Apostles, and spoke of them
as to sit on twelve thrones, judging
the twelve tribes of Israel. And in
the Apocalypse 12,000 are sealed
from each of twelve tribes. Cf. xxi.
12—14.

Hence τ. δ. φ. is equivalent to τὸ
δωδεκάφυλον (ἡμῶν), Acts xxvi. 7,
which occurs like Clement i. 55 (cf.
31, τὸ δωδεκάσκηπτρον τοῦ Ἰσραήλ,
answering to *Test. xii. Patriarch.
Napht.* 5, τὰ δώδεκα σκῆπτρα τ. Ἰσραήλ
from 1 Kings xi. 31 ff.; see LXX.), and
Joseph. *Hypomnesticum* (Fabricius
Cod. Pseud. V.T. ii. p. 3) τοὺς δώδεκα
φυλάρχους ἐξ ὧν τὸ δωδεκάφυλον τοῦ
Ἰσραὴλ συνίσταται. Both forms of
speech in *Lib. Jacobi* i. (1, 3).

By keeping up this phrase St James
marked that to him the designation
of the Israel which believed in Christ
as the only true Israel was no mere

² Πᾶσαν χαρὰν ἡγήσασθε, ἀδελφοί μου, ὅταν πει-

metaphor. To him a Jew who had refused the true Messiah had ceased to have a portion in Israel.

ἐν τῇ διασπορᾷ] The term comes from Deut. xxviii. 25 (LXX.), and also sparingly from later books; also from the more frequent use of the word διασπείρω, which in this connexion is freely used, as well as διασκορπίζω, for זָרָה, to scatter, or blow abroad. The cognate זָרַע, to sow, is used in this sense only, Zech. x. 9 (LXX. καὶ σπερῶ αὐτοὺς ἐν λαοῖς). Even here the notion is merely of scattering, not of sowing seed destined to germinate, and probably this was all that the LXX. anywhere meant. The idea of the Jews among the nations being a blessing to them and spreading light is found in the prophets, but not, I think, in connexion with the image of seed. The corresponding Hebrew word is simply גּוֹלָה, exile (lit. stripping), and hence the exiles collectively.

From the original seat at Babylon, which still continued a main home of the Dispersion, it spread under Alexander and his successors westward into the Greek world, Syria, Egypt (Alexandria and Cyrene), Armenia, Asia Minor, and at last Rome. It was like a network of tracks along which the Gospel could travel and find soil ready prepared for it in the worship of the true God, and the knowledge and veneration of the ancient Scripture.

χαίρειν] See Otto in *Jahrb. f. deutsche Theol.*, 1867, pp. 678 ff. The common greeting in Greek letters. The Semitic was of course שָׁלוֹם or (Chald.) שְׁלָם. In letters in the Apocrypha χαίρειν often occurs, as also εἰρήνην or εἰρήνη (together, χ. and εἰρήνην ἀγαθήν, 2 Macc. i. 1). Hence it must have been freely used by Jews as well as heathens. In N.T. it occurs

three times : Acts xxiii. 26, Claudius Lysias to Felix (heathen); xv. 23, Jerusalem letter to Gentile Christians at Antioch, etc.; and here. It has been pointed out that the Jerusalem letter was also not improbably written by St James, but nothing can be built on a coincidence in itself so natural. Here, the Greek form is probably preferred to εἰρήνη, etc. for the sake of the next verse.

2. πᾶσαν χαράν, *all joy*] Not "every (kind of) joy," as from the variety of trials; nor yet "joy and nothing but joy" negatively, but simply "all" as expressing completeness and unreservedness. Hence it *includes* "very great," but is not quantitative, rather expressing the full abandonment of mind to this one thought. Thus Aristides i. 478 (224), τὸ δὲ μηδ' ἐξ ὧν ἑωράκαμεν ἀξιοῦν πεπαιδεῦσθαι πᾶσα ἂν εἴη συμφορά; also Epictetus (*ap.* Gebser *Ep. of James* p. 8) 3, 22 εἰρήνη πᾶσα; 2, 2 πᾶσά σοι ἀσφάλεια, πᾶσά σοι εὐμάρεια; 26 πᾶσα εὔροια; and Phil. ii. 29; 2 Cor. xii. 12; Eph. iv. 2.

χαράν] Joy, from ground of joy, by a natural figure. The χαράν catches up χαίρειν. "I bid you rejoice. And this I say in the most exact sense, though I know how much you have to bear that seems anything but matter of rejoicing. Just circumstances like these should you account occasions of unreserved joy."

On the sense, see 1 Peter i. 8 with v. 7. But virtually it comes from Lk. vi. 23, and the Beatitudes altogether.

ὅταν with aor. subj.] Although suggested by present circumstances, the exhortation does not take its form from them. It is not "now that you are encountering," but "when ye shall," and probably also, by the common frequentative force of ὅταν, "whensoever ye shall."

περιπέσητε] Not "fall into" but "fall

1—2

in with," "light upon," "come across."
First used of ordinary casual meetings,
as of persons in the street or ships at
sea; then very commonly of misfortunes of all kinds, sickness, wounds,
a storm, slavery, disgrace, etc. So
the two other N.T. places: Lk. x. 30;
Acts xxvii. 41. The idea then is that,
as they go steadily on their own way,
they must expect to be jostled, as it
were, by various trials.

πειρασμοῖς, *trials*] An important
and difficult word, entirely confined
to O.T., Apocr., N.T., and literature
founded on them; except Diosc. p. 3ᴮ,
τοὺς ἐπὶ τ. παθῶν πειρασμούς, experi-
ments, trials made, with drugs in the
case of diseases, i.e. to see what their
effect will be.

But the word goes back to πειράζω,
which is not so closely limited in range
of authors. First, "tempt" is at the
utmost an accessory and subordinate
sense, on which see on *v.* 13. It is
simply to "try," "make trial of," and
πειρασμός "trial."

Nor on the other hand does it,
except by the circumstances of context, mean "trial" in the vague modern
religious and hence popular sense, as
when we say that a person has had
great trials, meaning misfortunes or
anxieties. Nothing in Greek is said
πειράζειν or called a πειρασμός except
with distinct reference to some kind
of probation.

Young birds are said πειράζειν τ.
πτέρυγας (Schol. Aristoph. *Plutus* 575).
But more to the point, Plutarch (*Cleom.*
7 p. 808 *a*) says that Cleomenes when a
dream was told him was at first troubled
and suspicious, πειράζεσθαι δοκῶν, supposing himself to be the subject of an
experiment to find out what he would
say or do. And still more to the point
Plutarch *Moralia* 15 p. 230 *a*, Namertes
being congratulated on the multitude
of his friends asked the spokesman εἰ
δοκίμιον ἔχει τίνι τρόπῳ πειράζεται ὁ
πολύφιλος; and when a desire was expressed to know he said 'Ατυχίᾳ.
The biblical use is substantially the

same. In O.T. πειράζω stands almost
always for נִסָּה (also ἐκπειράζω) and
πειρασμός for the derivative מַסָּה.
נִסָּה is used for various kinds of trying,
including that of one human being
by another, as Solomon by the Queen
of Sheba, but especially of man by
God and God by man. Of man by God
for probation, under the form of God
exploring; of God by man always in an
evil sense, "tempting" God, trying as it
were how far it is possible to go into
disobeying Him without provoking
His anger; with this last sense we
are not concerned. The trying or
"proving" (A.V.) of man by God is
sometimes, but not always, by suffering. In one chapter (Deut. viii. 2) it is
coupled with עָנָה, κακόω, "humble" or
"afflict"; but the context shews that
"proving" is meant, as it is also in
Judg. ii. 22; iii. 1, 4. The cardinal
instance is Abraham (Gen. xxii. 1).
Πειρασμός chiefly refers to temptations
of God by men, also probations of
Pharaoh (Deut. iv. 34; vii. 19; xxix.
3). There only remains Job ix. 23,
very hard and probably corrupt (LXX.
altogether different, Vulg. *poenis*),
where "probations" may possibly be
said in bitter irony, but "sufferings"
is most improbable, considering the
derivation.

In Judith, Wisdom and Ecclus.
πειράζω similarly has both uses, viz.
of God by man, and man by God; also
πειρασμός in Ecclus., not only of
Abraham (xliv. 20; as also 1 Macc. ii.
52), but more generally; but in ii. 1:
xxxvi. 1, on the one hand the context
implies affliction, on the other the
stress lies on probations. These two
are interesting passages as preparing
the way for St James. (1) xxxvi. 1, τῷ
φοβουμένῳ Κύριον οὐκ ἀπαντήσει κακόν·
ἀλλ᾽ ἐν πειρασμῷ (whatever comes will
come by way of trial), καὶ πάλιν ἐξελεῖ-
ται. Still more (2) ii. 1, Son, if thou
settest thyself to serve the Lord God,
prepare thy soul εἰς πειρασμόν etc.
Cf. ii. 5, ἐν πυρὶ δοκιμάζεται χρυσός κ.τ.λ.

ρασμοῖς περιπέσητε ποικίλοις, ³γινώσκοντες ὅτι τὸ
δοκίμιον ὑμῶν τῆς πίστεως κατεργάζεται ὑπομονήν·
⁴ἡ δὲ ὑπομονὴ ἔργον τέλειον ἐχέτω, ἵνα ἦτε τέλειοι καὶ

In the N.T. other shades of meaning appear. Besides the ordinary neutral making trial, and God's trial of man, and man's evil trial or tempting of God, we have men's evil making trial of one whom they regarded as only a man, the Scribes and Pharisees "trying" or tempting our Lord, not tempting Him to do evil, but trying to get Him to say something on which they could lay hold.

But further a peculiar sense comes in at what we call our Lord's temptation (Mk i. 13, πειραζόμενος ὑπὸ τοῦ Σατανᾶ; Mt. iv. 1, πειρασθῆναι ὑπὸ τ. διαβόλου; Lk. iv. 2, πειραζόμενος ὑ. τ. δ.). In Mt. (iv. 3) the devil is then called ὁ πειράζων.

For ποικίλοις, *divers*, see note on 1 Pet. i. 6 (p. 41).

3. γινώσκοντες, *taking knowledge, recognising*] Not necessarily a new piece of knowledge, but new apprehension of it.

δοκίμιον, *test*] In N.T. only here and, in similar connexion, 1 Pet. i. 7, a very hard verse. In LXX. only in two places, both rather peculiar. (1) Prov. xxvii. 21, representing מַצְרֵף, a "melting-pot"; but the change of order shews that "test" was meant by LXX., "there is a δοκίμιον for silver and a πύρωσις for gold." (2) Ps. xii. 7, עָלִיל, probably a "furnace," a difficult and perhaps corrupt passage. Similarly the cognate words δόκιμος, δοκιμάζω in LXX. mostly refer to silver or gold tried and found pure, to a trial by fire. [See Deissmann *Bib. Stud. sub voc.*, and *Expositor* 1908 p. 566.] The rather rare word is always the instrument of probation, never the process. Similar places are Herodian ii. 10. 6, δοκίμιον δὲ στρατιωτῶν κάματος; Iamblichus *Vita Pythag.* 30 p. 185 fin.,

ταύτην (τ. λήθην) δή μοι θεῶν τις ἐνῆκε, δοκίμιον ἐσομένην τῆς σῆς περὶ συνθήκας εὐσταθείας.

κατεργάζεται, *worketh*] A favourite word with St Paul.

ὑπομονήν, *endurance*] The word ὑπομονή (A.V. *patience*) is hardly used by classical writers (an apophthegm in Plutarch *Moralia* 208 c, and an interpolated clause in his *Crassus* 3) to describe a virtue, though frequently for the patient bearing of any particular hardships. It stands for קָוָה and its derivatives in the sense of hope or expectation (as Ps. xxxviii. 8, καὶ νῦν τίς ἡ ὑπομονή μου; οὐχὶ ὁ κύριος;), and perhaps hope itself in the LXX. and Ecclus. (Fritzsche on xvi. 13). But late Jewish and Christian writers use it freely for the virtue shewn chiefly by martyrs: thus 4 Macc. i. 11, τῇ ἀνδρείᾳ καὶ τῇ ὑπομονῇ, and often; *Psalt. Solom.* ii. 40; *Test. xii. Patriarch. Jos.* 10; in the N.T., Lk. xxi. 19 (cf. Mt. xxiv. 13); St Paul often; Hebrews; 2 Peter; and Apoc.; later Clement 1. 5; Ignatius *ad Polyc.* 6; etc. No English word is quite strong enough to express the active courage and resolution implied in ὑπομονή (cf. Ellicott on 1 Thess. i. 3). "Constancy" or "endurance" comes nearest, and the latter has the advantage of preserving the parallelism of the verb ὑπομένω. The resemblance of this verse to Rom. v. 3 f. should be noticed, though probably accidental.

4. ἔργον τέλειον ἐχέτω, *have a perfect work* or *result*] The sense, obscure in the Greek, is fixed almost certainly by the context. The phrase is suggested by, and must include the meaning of, κατεργάζεται in *v.* 3. Endurance is represented as having a work to do, a result to accomplish, which must not be suffered to cease prematurely. En-

6 THE EPISTLE OF ST JAMES [I. 4

ὁλόκληροι, ἐν μηδενὶ λειπόμενοι. ⁵Εἰ δέ τις

durance itself is the first and a necessary step; but it is not to be rested in, being chiefly a means to higher ends. Here the Stoic constancy is at once justified, and implicitly pronounced inadequate, because it endeavours to be self-sufficing and leads the way to no diviner virtue. The work of the Christian endurance is manifold (elicited by *divers* trials, *v.* 2) and continuous, not easily exhausted; it remains imperfect (so the connexion of the two clauses teaches) while we are imperfect. This use of ἔργον is illustrated by the common negative formula οὐδὲν ἔργον, generally translated "no use," as in Plutarch *Lysander* 11, ἦν δὲ οὐδὲν ἔργον αὐτοῦ τῆς σπουδῆς ἐσκεδασμένων τῶν ἀνθρώπων: *Publicola* 13, οὐδὲν ἦν ἔργον αὐτοῦ (τοῦ ἡνιόχου) κατατείνοντος οὐδὲ παρηγορούντος. The combination of τέλειον with τὸ ἔργον occurs Ignat. *Smyrn.* 11, but it is not a true parallel.

τέλειοι, *perfect*] This word in St James, as applied to man, has apparently no reference, as in St Paul, to maturity, and still less to initiation. It expresses the simplest idea of complete goodness, disconnected from the philosophical idea of a τέλος. In the LXX. it chiefly represents תָּמִים, a variously translated word, originally expressing completeness, and occurring in several leading passages as Gen. vi. 9 (τέλειος); xvii. 1 (ἄμεμπτος); Deut. xviii. 13 (τέλειος); Job i. 1 (ἄμεμπτος); Ps. cxix. 1 (ἄμωμος). The Greek τέλειος in a moral sense, rare in the LXX. and virtually wanting in the Apocrypha, recurs with additional meanings in Philo, e.g. *Legum Allegoriae* iii. 45— 49 (in contrast with ὁ προκόπτων, ὁ ἀσκητής).

It regains its full force and simplicity in Christ's own teaching, Mt. v. 48 ("Be ye therefore perfect, even as your Father which is in heaven is perfect"); xix. 21 ("If thou wilt be perfect" contrasted with "What lack I yet?").

These passages are probably the chief sources of St James' usage.

ὁλόκληροι, *entire*] The principal word τέλειος is reinforced by the almost synonymous ὁλόκληρος, the primary sense of which seems to be freedom from bodily defect either in a victim for sacrifice or in a priest; that is, it is a technical term of Greek ritual. In extant literature we do not find it before Plato, and he may well have introduced it into literature. It soon was applied in a wider manner to all freedom from defect (cf. e.g. the Stoic use in Diogenes Laert. vii. 107) being opposed to πηρός, κολοβός, χωλός. But the original sense was not forgotten, and can be traced in the usage of Josephus and Philo, though not in the LXX.

Thus τέλειος and ὁλόκληρος (which are used together somewhat vaguely at least once by Philo, *Quis rerum div. heres?* 23 p. 489) denote respectively positive and negative perfection, excellence and complete absence of defect (cf. Trench *N.T. Synon.* § 22). It is quite probable however that St James uses ὁλόκληρος with a recollection of its original force in Greek religion, and wished his readers to think of perfection and entireness not merely in the abstract but as the necessary aim of men consecrated to God.

ἐν μηδενὶ λειπόμενοι, *coming behind in nothing*] Λείπομαι with the dative means not mere deficiency but falling short whether of a standard or of other persons, the latter when expressed being in the genitive. Essentially it is to be left behind, as in a race, and it comes to be used for the defeat of an army, strictly for its ceasing to resist the enemy and throwing up the struggle. There is thus a suggestion of *acquiescence in* shortcoming as a thing to be striven against (cf. Gal. vi. 9; Heb. xii. 3; 2 Thess. iii. 13). Compare the use of ὑστερῶ and ὑστεροῦμαι in St Paul and

I. 5]   THE EPISTLE OF ST JAMES   7

ὑμῶν λείπεται σοφίας, αἰτείτω παρὰ τοῦ διδόντος θεοῦ

Hebrews (e.g. 1 Cor. i. 5, 7, ἐν παντὶ ἐπλουτίσθητε ἐν αὐτῷ, ἐν παντὶ λόγῳ καὶ πάσῃ γνώσει...ὥστε ὑμᾶς μὴ ὑστερεῖσθαι ἐν μηδενὶ χαρίσματι).

The object of comparison is usually expressed, rarely implied (as Diodorus Sic. iii. 39; Plutarch *Nicias* 3); but λείπομαι is also used quite absolutely, as here, in Plutarch *Brutus* 39 (ἐρρωμένους χρήμασιν ὅπλων δὲ καὶ σωμάτων πλήθει λειπομένους); cf. Sophocles *Oed. Col.* 495 f. Ἐν, commonly omitted, occurs Herodotus vii. 8; Sophocles *l.c.*; and Polybius xxiv. 7 (*legat.* 50); see also Herod. vii 168.

This final clause, added in apposition (cf. i. 6, 8, 14, 17, 22, 25; ii. 9; iii. 2, 8, 17), not only reaffirms negatively what has been already said positively, but suggests once more the idea of continual progress (a "race" in St Paul's language, as Phil. iii. 14; cf. "the crown of life" in *v.* 12) implied in the earlier clauses.

The spiritual force of this and similar verses cannot be reduced within the limits of "common sense." An "ideal" interpretation can be excluded only by "frittering away a pure and necessary word of Christ Himself. The perfection in all good, after which every Christian should strive simply as a Christian, is infinite in its nature, like a heavenly ladder the steps of which constantly increase the higher we climb: but woe to him who would make landings in it out of his own invention and on his own behalf" (Ewald, *Jahrbücher* iii. 259).

5. εἰ δέ τις ὑμῶν λείπεται σοφίας, *But if any of you lacketh wisdom*] *If any*, i.e. whoever. The preceding λειπόμενοι suggests λείπεται with a somewhat different sense and construction. Λείπομαι with the genitive meaning to "be wanting in" is rare, this sense being an extension of the commoner to "be bereaved of"; it occurs Sophocles *Elect.* 474 (γνώμας λειπομένα σοφᾶς); Plato *Menex.* 19,

246 E; Pseud.-Plato *Axiochus* 366 D (repeating ἄμοιρον); Libanius *Progymn.* p. 31 A (λ. τῆς τῶν ποιητῶν ἐνθέου μανίας); besides Jam. ii. 15.

σοφίας] The context fixes, without altogether restricting, the sense of *wisdom.* "True perfectness cannot be where wisdom still is wanting; and wisdom, the inward power to seize and profit by outward trials, cannot be supplied by the trials themselves: but it may be had of God for the asking; He will send it direct into the heart." It is that endowment of heart and mind which is needed for the right conduct of life. "All salutary wisdom is indeed to be asked of the Lord; for, as the wise man says (Ecclus. i. 1), 'All wisdom is from the Lord God, and hath been with Him for ever.'...But here there seems to be a special reference to that wisdom which we need for use in our trials, etc." (Bede).

This human and practical idea of wisdom is inherited from the meditative books of the O.T. and the later works written on their model. Compare "the fear of the Lord that is wisdom" (Job xxviii. 28), where wisdom is the knowledge of the most essential facts and the power to walk instinctively by their light. It is remarkable to find wisdom holding this position in the forefront of the epistle, quite in the spirit of the elder theology. See further the notes on iii. 13—18.

ἁπλῶς, *graciously*] The combination with *giveth* early led to the assumption that ἁπλῶς requires here the sense of "abundantly," but without authority (cf. Fritzsche *Rom.* iii. 62 ff.) and against the true context. On the other hand, a large body of evidence forbids us to admit only the meanings "simply" or "with singleness of heart," and establishes a nearer approach to "bounteously" than most good critics have been willing to allow (see below).

In the best Greek authors the guidance of etymology is strictly followed, and ἁπλοῦς as a moral epithet denotes only the absence of guile or duplicity. Later writers comprehend under the one word the whole magnanimous and honourable type of character in which this singleness of mind is the central feature. Kindred and associated epithets are γενναῖος (cf. Plato *Repub.* i. 361 B, ἄνδρα ἁπλοῦν καὶ γενναῖον... οὐ δοκεῖν ἀλλ᾽ εἶναι ἀγαθὸν ἐθέλοντα), ἐλευθέριος (Aeschines, p. 135, Reiske), and μεγαλόψυχος. Truthfulness, liberality, and gentleness variously appear as manifesting the same high sense of honour.

The transition may be seen in Xenophon *Cyropaed.* viii. 4, 32 ff., where Cyrus blames alike those who magnify their own fortune (so thinking to appear ἐλευθεριώτεροι) and those who depreciate it, and adds, ἁπλουστάτου δέ μοι δοκεῖ εἶναι τὸ τὴν δύναμιν φανερὰν ποιήσαντα ἐκ ταύτης ἀγωνίζεσθαι περὶ καλοκἀγαθίας. But the usage became clearer subsequently. Scipio (Polybius, xxxii. 13, 14) resolved πρὸς μὲν τοὺς ἀλλοτρίους τὴν ἐκ τῶν νόμων ἀκρίβειαν (i.e. his strict legal rights) τηρεῖν, τοῖς δὲ συγγενέσι καὶ φίλοις ἁπλῶς χρῆσθαι καὶ γενναίως κατὰ δύναμιν. One of Timon's friends (Lucian *Tim.* 56) professed that he was not one of the flatterers, greedy of gold and banquets, who paid their court πρὸς ἄνδρα οἷόν σε ἁπλοϊκὸν καὶ τῶν ὄντων κοινωνικόν. David is said by Josephus (*Ant.* vii. 13, 4) to have admired Araunah τῆς ἁπλότητος καὶ τῆς μεγαλοψυχίας, when he offered his threshing-floor and oxen. M. Antony's popularity is attributed by Plutarch (c. 43) to his εὐγένεια, λόγου δύναμις, ἁπλότης, τὸ φιλόδωρον καὶ μεγαλόδωρον, ἡ περὶ τὰς παιδιὰς καὶ τὰς ὁμιλίας εὐτραπελία. Brutus, having tempered his character by education and philosophy, seemed to Plutarch (c. 1) ἐμμελέστατα κραθῆναι πρὸς τὸ καλόν, so that after Caesar's death the friends of the latter attributed to Brutus εἴ τι γενναῖον ἡ πρᾶξις ἤνεγκε, considering Cassius

ἁπλοῦν τῷ τρόπῳ καὶ καθαρὸν οὐχ ὁμοίως (cf. *Philopoem.* 13). The Persians desired Ariaspes for their king, as being πρᾶος καὶ ἁπλοῦς καὶ φιλάνθρωπος (Plutarch *Artaxerx.* 30). Ὁ μὲν ἁπλούστερος, though opposed to ὁ πανουργότερος, is the high-minded friend who, when admitted indiscreetly to a knowledge of private affairs owing to his too complaisant manners, οὐκ οἴεται δεῖν οὐδ᾽ ἀξιοῖ σύμβουλος εἶναι πραγμάτων τηλικούτων ἀλλ᾽ ὑπουργὸς καὶ διάκονος (Plutarch *Moralia* 63 B). Wine is said to quench πολλὰ τῶν ἄλλων παθῶν (besides fear) ἀφιλότιμα καὶ ἀγεννῆ, and ἄοινος ἀεὶ μέθη καὶ σκυθρωπὴ ταῖς τῶν ἀπαιδεύτων ἐνοικεῖ ψυχαῖς, ἐπιταραττομένη ὑπὸ ὀργῆς τινος ἢ δυσμενείας ἢ φιλονεικίας ἢ ἀνελευθερίας· ὧν ὁ οἶνος ἀμβλύνων τὰ πολλὰ μᾶλλον ἢ παροξύνων οὐκ ἄφρονας οὐδὲ ἠλιθίους ἀλλ᾽ ἁπλοῦς ποιεῖ καὶ ἀπανούργους, οὐδὲ παρορατικοὺς τοῦ συμφέροντος ἀλλὰ τοῦ καλοῦ προαιρετικούς (*ib.* 716 A, B). We are reminded of this passage of St James by the following: "So I think that the gods confer their benefits in secret, it being their nature to delight in the mere practice of bounty and beneficence (αὐτῷ τῷ χαρίζεσθαι καὶ εὖ ποιεῖν). Whereas the flatterer's work οὐδὲν ἔχει δίκαιον οὐδ᾽ ἀληθινὸν οὐδ᾽ ἁπλοῦν οὐδ᾽ ἐλευθέριον" (*ib.* 63 F).

There are traces of a similar extension of meaning in Latin, as Horace *Ep.* ii. 2, 193, "quantum simplex hilarisque nepoti Discrepet, et quantum discordet parcus avaro" (cf. "the cheerful giver" of Prov. xxii. 8, LXX., and 2 Cor. ix. 7); Tacitus, *Hist.* iii. 86, "inerat tamen (Vitellio) simplicitas et liberalitas, quae, ni adsit modus, in vitium vertuntur"; and perhaps Vell. Paterc. ii. 125, 5, "vir simplicitatis generosissimae."

Himerius (*Ecl.* v. 19) affords the nearest verbal parallel to St James: εἰ δὲ ἁπλῶς διδόντος λαβεῖν οὐκ εὔλογον, πῶς οὐ πλέον, ὅτε μηδὲ προῖκα κ.τ.λ. Here however ἁπλῶς is not ethical at all, but retains its common classical

πᾶσιν ἁπλῶς καὶ μὴ ὀνειδίζοντος, καὶ δοθήσεται αὐτῷ·

meaning "absolutely," that is (in this connexion) "without a substantial equivalent." In St James the need for adopting this meaning is removed by the sufficient evidence for "graciously"; and it is excluded by the contrast with "upbraideth."

In Jewish writings ἁπλοῦς is generalised in a different direction to denote one who carries piety and openness of heart before God into all his dealings. So the LXX.: 1 Chron. xxix. 17 for יֹשֶׁר; Prov. xix. 1 (cf. x. 9; 2 Sam. xv. 11); Aq.: Gen. xxv. 27; Job iv. 6; Prov. x. 29; Sym.: Job xxvii. 5 for תֹּם, תָּם, and תֻּמָּה; Wisd. i. 1; 1 Macc. ii. 37, 60; 3 Macc. iii. 21; and the whole *Test. xii. Patriarch.*, esp. the *Test. of Issachar* (e.g. 3), not without reference to the original meanings, as in opposition to περίεργος.

In St James (as in Rom. xii. 8; 2 Cor. viii. 2; ix. 11, 13) the late Greek usage and the context certainly determine the chief shade of meaning, but with clear reference to singleness. "Liberally" (A.V.) would be the best translation, if we could preserve exclusively its proper ethical sense; but by "liberally" we now usually mean "abundantly," and that is not the particular aspect of God's bounty indicated here by the following words, whatever may be the case in the passages of St Paul. On the whole *graciously*, coupled as it is with *giveth*, seems the nearest equivalent.

καὶ μὴ ὀνειδίζοντος, *and upbraideth not*] The opposition is clearly to *graciously*, not to *giveth*: to upbraid is not to refuse, or even to vouchsafe "a stone for bread," but to accompany a gift with ungenerous words or deeds. Ὀνειδίζω often has this sense in classical writers from Aristotle (*Rhet.* ii. 6. 10; cf. Demosth. *de Coron.* § 269) onwards (see exx. in Wetstein). In Ecclus. it is a favourite word (with ὀνειδισμός), and occurs more than once

in strictly parallel passages: "My son, give not reproach with thy good deeds, neither painful words with every gift. Will not dew assuage the hot wind? So is a word better than a gift. Lo, is not a word more than a good gift? And both are with a gracious man (κεχαριτωμένῳ). A fool will upbraid ungraciously (ἀχαρίστως ὀνειδιεῖ), and a gift of the envious dissolveth the eyes" (xviii. 15—18). "The gift of a fool will profit thee not, for his eyes are many, instead of one. He will give little and upbraid much, and open his mouth as a crier: to-day he will lend, and to-morrow ask back; hated is such a man" (xx. 14, 15). "Have respect...unto thy friends concerning words of upbraiding, and upbraid not after thou hast given" (xli. 17, 22).

By this contrast of mean and ignoble benefactors, St James leads on from the naked idea of God as a giver to the more vital idea of His character and mind in giving (cf. i. 13, 17 f.; iv. 6; v. 7), answering by anticipation a superstitious thought which springs up as naturally in the decay of an established faith as in the confused hopes and fears of primitive heathenism. The subject is partly resumed in *v.* 17.

διδόντος...δοθήσεται] *Giveth* what? Wisdom doubtless in the first instance; but, as the immediate occasion of prayer becomes here the text for a universal lesson, St James' meaning is best expressed by leaving the object undefined. In like manner the "holy spirit," promised in Lk. xi. 13 to them that ask, is replaced in the parallel Mt. vii. 11 by "good things" without restriction.

This verse has much in common with some of Philo's most cherished and at the same time most purely biblical thoughts on God as a free giver and on wisdom as specially the

⁶*αἰτείτω δὲ ἐν πίστει, μηδὲν διακρινόμενος, ὁ γὰρ διακρινόμενος ἔοικεν κλύδωνι θαλάσσης ἀνεμιζομένῳ καὶ*

gift of God. But his language, beauti-
ful and genuine as it often is, suffers
much from being overlaid with a
philosophical contrast between this
wisdom (virtually "intuition") and
the knowledge and discernment which
come by processes of education. The
wisdom of St James, for all its immediate descent from heaven, excludes
no lesson of experience in thought or
life.

6. *αἰτείτω δὲ ἐν πίστει, μηδὲν διακρινόμενος, but let him ask in faith,
nothing wavering*] Taken from our
Lord's words in Mt. xxi. 21, Mk xi. 23;
cf. Jam. v. 15. Not the mere petition
avails, but the mind of the asker, the
trust in God as One who delights to
give. *Wavering* is no doubt the
right translation of *διακρινόμενος* in
this verse (as Mt. Mk, *ll. cc.*; Acts
x. 20; Rom. iv. 20; xiv. 23), though
singularly enough this sense occurs in
no Greek writing, except where the
influence of the N.T. might have led
to its use. It is supported by the
versions, the Greek commentators
on the N.T. from Chrysostom and
Hesychius, as well as by the context
of all the passages. It is probably
derived from the common meaning to
"dispute" (Jer. xv. 10; Acts xi. 2;
Jude 9; cf. Ezek. xvii. 20 *codd.*;
xx. 35 f.; Joel iii. 2), of which there
is a trace in the passages of Romans.
Compare the use of *διαλογίζομαι*, to
"dispute with oneself," in the Gospels.

*ἔοικεν κλύδωνι θαλάσσης, is like a
rough sea*] Κλύδων appears never
(not even Polyb. x. 10. 3) to mean a
"wave," but always "rough water"
("the rough sea" A.V. Wisd. xiv. 5)
or "roughness of water"; it is frequently coupled with *σάλος*.

*ἀνεμιζομένῳ καὶ ῥιπιζομένῳ, blown
and raised with the wind*] This appears to be the nearest approach to
the meaning of the Greek allowed by

the English idiom. 'Ανεμίζω occurs
nowhere else in Greek literature, and
might by its etymology express any
kind of action of the wind. The
equally rare analogous verb *πνευμα-
τίζω* is used where fanning is intended (Antigonus Caryst. ap. Wetst.).
The compound *ἐξανεμίζω* is preserved
only in the Scholia on Homer *Il.* xx.
440 (*ἦκα μάλα ψύξασα*, interpreted *τῇ
κινήσει τῆς χειρὸς ἠρέμα ἐξανεμίσασα*:
Steph. *s.v.*), where likewise it denotes
the gentle air made by a wave of the
hand. The cognate *ἀνεμοῦμαι* is to
"be breathed through (or, swelled
out) by the wind" (whence a singular
derivative use peculiar to writers on
Zoology), except in one passage; and
its compound *ἐξανεμοῦμαι* has the
same range, with the further meaning to "be dissolved into wind." An
epigram in the Anthology (*A. P.* xiii.
12) applies *ἠνεμωμένος* to the sea,
described as roaring (*βρόμος δεινός*)
and causing a shipwreck. With this
exception the evidence, such as it is,
implies a restriction of *ἀνεμίζω* to
gentler motions of the air: and in
St James the improbability of an
anticlimax forbids it being taken as
a stronger word than *ῥιπίζω*.

Still more definitely, *ῥιπίζω* means
strictly to fan either a fire or a person.
It is formed not from *ῥιπή*, a "rushing
motion" (as applied to air, a "blast"),
but from the derivative *ῥιπίς*, a fire-
fan; and consequently expresses only
the kind of blast proper to a fan.
This restriction appears to be observed
in a few passages of a rather wider
range. Thus *ῥιπίζομαι* is applied to
dead bodies allowed to sway freely (?) in
the air (Galen. x. 745 ed. Kühn); to sea
foam carried inland (Dion Cass. lxx. 4);
to spacious and airy chambers (*ὑπερῷα
ῥιπιστά*, Jerem. xxii. 14); to water
preserved by motion from the "death"
that would follow stagnation (Philo,

ῥιπιζομένῳ· ⁷μὴ γὰρ οἰέσθω ὁ ἄνθρωπος ἐκεῖνος ὅτι

de incor. mundi 24). Lastly an unknown comic poet (Meineke iv.
615) calls the people an unstable evil thing
(δῆμος ἄστατον κακόν), which altogether
like the sea is blown by the wind
(ὑπ' ἀνέμου ῥιπίζεται) and from being
calm raises its crest at a trifling breeze
(καὶ γαληνός...πνεῦμα βραχὺ κορύσσεται.
These leading words are clear, though
the line is corrupt). The compound
ἀναρριπίζω always means to "fan a
flame" literally or figuratively.
The prima facie notion of billows
lashed by a storm is therefore supported by hardly any evidence ; and
indeed the restless swaying to and
fro of the surface of the water, blown
upon by shifting breezes, is a truer
image of a waverer (cf. Dion Cass.
lxv. 16, Vitellius ἐμπλήκτως ἄνω καὶ
κάτω ἐφέρετο, ὥσπερ ἐν κλύδωνι). In
the tideless Mediterranean even a
slight rufflement would be noticed in
contrast with the usually level calm,
and the direct influences of disturbing
winds are seen free from the cross
effects of other agencies.

7, 8. We have to choose here
between three constructions, each
marked by a different way of punc-
tuating between the verses. (a) With
a colon, making two separate sentences
(A.V.); "let not that man think that
he shall receive anything from the
Lord: a man of two minds is unstable
in all his ways." (b) With a comma
making v. 7 a complete sentence, with
v. 8 added in apposition (R.V. text);
"let not that man think that he shall
receive anything from the Lord, a
man of two minds, unstable in all his
ways." (c) Without a stop, making
v. 7 incomplete without part of v. 8
(R.V. marg.); "let not that man think
that a man of two minds, unstable in
all his ways, shall receive anything
from the Lord."
In (a) and (b) it is "that man" that
is said not to receive from the Lord,
and so that is blamed. Now who is
"that man"—"he that wavereth" or

"if any of you etc."? The whole context excludes him that merely "lacketh
wisdom" from blame : blame here
attaches not to the absence of wisdom,
but to the failure to ask for it, or to
the asking without faith. Therefore
the constructions (a) and (b) require
"that man" to mean the waverer. As
an independent proof that he is meant,
it is urged that "that man" is itself a
reproachful designation. Undoubtedly
it might be so employed; but St James'
usage does not favour the supposition.
He has the same word for man (ἄνθρωπος) in six other places, but nowhere
with a trace of reproach and apparently always in emphatic opposition
to other beings. Thus the opposition
is to God's other "creatures" in i. 19;
to "the devils" in ii. 20 and probably
24 ; to "every kind of beasts etc." in
iii. 8 f. ; to beings not "of like passions"
v. 17 ; and so here to "the Lord."
Likewise there is no force in a
cumbrous reproachful description (ὁ
ἄνθρωπος ἐκεῖνος) thus closely preceding an explicit rebuke : in Mt. xii. 45 ;
xxvi. 24 the weight of the words is in
harmony with the peculiar solemnity
of the subjects. If no reproach is
implied, the phrase is still more inexplicable by Greek usage as applied
to the person last mentioned.
On the other hand, if he that
"lacketh wisdom" be intended, all
difficulty vanishes. The obvious way
of setting aside the last person and
pointing back to the person mentioned
before him would be in Greek the use
of the pronoun "that" (ἐκεῖνος); and
the insertion of "man" we have already seen to be explained by the
opposition to "the Lord."
Since then "that man" must naturally mean him that merely "lacketh
wisdom," and so cannot be identified
with the subject of rebuke, the constructions (a) and (b) (of which (b) is
certainly the more natural) are excluded, and the two verses become
one unbroken sentence. I am not

λήμψεταί τι παρὰ τοῦ κυρίου ⁸ἀνὴρ δίψυχος, ἀκατά-

7. κυρίου] κυρίου,

aware of any intrinsic advantage of the constructions (a) or (b) that would lead us to set aside this conclusion, though habit makes us assume a pause at the end of v. 7. Perhaps a feeling that the words "unstable in all his ways" must denote a punishment, not a sin, may have introduced the construction (a) into late MSS. of the Vulgate (inconstans est), and so into A.V.: in reality this instability is strictly neither sin nor punishment, but in some sense the transition from the one to the other. The position of the verb (in the Greek) at the beginning of the clause is explained by the length and elaborateness of its subject.

Although the man deficient in wisdom is not directly rebuked, the form of the sentence implies that he is concerned in the words spoken of others. Though not assumed to be a waverer, he is virtually warned that he may easily become liable to the reproach, and reminded of the nature of his relation as a "man" to "the Lord" of men.

8. ἀνήρ, man] A different word from that used in v. 7, and wholly without emphasis.

δίψυχος, of two minds] The image of δίψυχος (lit. "two-souled") represents either dissimulation (suggested to modern ears by "double-minded" in A.V.), or various kinds of distraction and doubt. Here faithless wavering is obviously meant, the description in verse 6 being made more vivid by an additional figure. Perhaps, as Calvin suggests, there is an intentional contrast with the manner of God's giving; "graciously" (ἁπλῶς) being according to the primitive meaning of the Greek "simply": Ita erit tacita antithesis inter Dei simplicitatem, cujus meminit prius, et duplicem hominis animum. Sicut enim exporrecta manu nobis Deus largitur, ita vicissim sinum

cordis nostri expansum esse decet. Incredulos ergo, qui recessus habent, dicit esse instabiles etc. There may also be an allusion to "loving God with all the soul" or "the whole soul," ἐν ὅλῃ τῇ ψυχῇ σου (Deut. vi. 5 ; Mt. xxii. 37). The idea was familiar to the Greeks (δίχα θυμὸν or νόον ἔχειν etc.) from Homer and Theognis (910 Bergk); cf. Xenoph. Cyropaed. vi. 1. 41. It appears less distinctly in 1 Kings xviii. 21, and perhaps 1 Chr. xii. 33 (Heb. "a heart and a heart," not LXX.). We are reminded of St James by Ecclus. i. 28, "Disobey not the fear of the Lord, and approach Him not with a double heart" (ἐν καρδίᾳ δισσῇ).

The word itself δίψυχος (διψυχία, διψυχέω) occurs here and iv. 8 for the first time. It is sprinkled over the early Fathers rather freely, and [is found occasionally in later times in the novelist Eustathius (viii. 7; xi. 17 f.), as well as in ecclesiastical writers. Probably all drew directly or indirectly from St James (Philo, Fragm. ii. 663 Mangey, uses διχονοῦς ἐπαμφοτερής, where St John Damascene has the heading περὶ δειλῶν καὶ διψύχων). The early references are Clem. I. 11, 23; in both cases διστάζοντες is added as if to explain an unfamiliar word: the latter passage (ταλαίπωροί εἰσιν οἱ δίψυχοι, οἱ διστάζοντες τῇ ψυχῇ κ.τ.λ.) seems quoted from an earlier writing (as it is likewise in Ps.-Clem. II. 11); the reference in this passage is conjectured by Lightfoot to be to the prophecies of Eldad and Medad referred to in Hermas, Vis. ii. 3, and therefore current early at Rome: they are said to have prophesied to the people in the wilderness, so that it is probably a Jewish, though possibly a Christian, book; Ep. Barnab. 19 (cf. δίγνωμος, δίγλωσσος ib.; διπλοκαρδία 20); Const. Ap. vii. 11 ("Be not of two minds in thy prayer (doubting)

στατος ἐν πάσαις ταῖς ὁδοῖς αὐτοῦ.   ⁹ Καυχάσθω δὲ [ὁ]

whether it shall be or not (cf. Herm. *Vis.* iii. 4. 3); for the Lord saith to me Peter upon the sea, O thou of little faith, wherefore didst thou doubt?"); Ps.- Ignat. *ad Heron.* 7; Hermas *passim*; and *Didache Ap.* iv. 4 οὐ διψυχήσεις πότερον ἔσται ἢ οὔ (whence the usage in Barnabas, Hermas, and *Const. Ap.*). The reproof to Peter literally "on the sea" (ὀλιγόπιστε, εἰς τί ἐδίστασας; Mt. xiv. 31) may have been present to St James' mind, as he had just drawn a comparison from the sea.

ἀκ. ἐν πάσαις τ. ὁδοῖς αὐτοῦ] As "a man of two minds" is a slightly varied repetition of "he that wavereth," in like manner "unstable in all his ways" answers to "like a rough sea etc." This parallelism is in itself enough to prove that the absence of the conjunction after "two minds" is expressive, and denotes not simple co-ordination but sequence: "a man of two minds *and so* unstable in all his ways."

ἀκατάστατος, *unstable*] Things properly are called ἀκατάστατα, when they do not follow an established order of any kind (καθεστηκότα: cf. Aristot. *Probl.* xxvi. 13). The word is rarely applied to persons. Polybius (cf. Demosth. *de fals. legat.* p. 383) seems to mean by it "fickle" or "easily persuaded" (vii. 4. 6); he couples the substantive with madness (μανία) a few lines further on. Other examples are Epictetus (*Diss.* ii. 1. 12: φοβήσεται, ἀκαταστατήσει, ταραχθήσεται) "in a state of trepidation"; Pollux "fickle" (vi. 121), and also "disorderly," i.e. "stirring up disorder" (vi. 129); the translators of the O.T. "staggering" or "reeling": Gen. iv. 12 (Sym.) ἀνάστατος καὶ ἀκατάστατος with varr., σαλευόμενος καὶ ἀκαταστατῶν (στένων καὶ τρέμων LXX.), Lam. iv. 14 (Sym.), ἀκατάστατοι ἐγένοντο (ἐσαλεύθησαν LXX.) τυφλοὶ ἐν ταῖς ἐξόδοις, Isa. liv. 11 (LXX.), "tossed with tempest" (A.V.), of Zion compared to a ship, and apparently

Hos. viii. 6 (Sym.) where the "Quinta Editio" has ῥεμβεύων; Plut. II. 714 E, says that wine makes τ. γνώμην ἐπισφαλῆ καὶ ἀκατάστατον; cf. Σ κοτόμαινα νύξ ἐστιν ἐν ᾗ μαίνεται καὶ ἀκαταστατεῖ τὰ οὐράνια in *Etym. Magn.* 719, 34. The verbal resemblance of Tob. i. 15 (ἐβασίλευσεν Σενναχηρὶμ ὁ υἱὸς ἀντ' αὐτοῦ, καὶ αἱ ὁδοὶ αὐτοῦ [al. αἱ ὁδ. τῆς Μηδίας] ἠκαταστάτησαν [80 B ; A κατέστησαν, א ἀπέστησαν], καὶ οὐκέτι ἠδυνάσθην πορευθῆναι εἰς τὴν Μηδίαν) is curious but hardly more : the meaning seems to be "his roads" (possibly "his ways of government") "were full of disorder and therefore unsafe."

On the whole it can scarcely be doubted that St James intended, or at all events had in view, the physical meaning of ἀκατάστατος employed by the translators of the O.T. ; so that the two leading words of the phrase make up a vigorous metaphor, "staggering in all his ways." But the English word "staggering" hardly suits the tone of the verse; and "unsteady" has other disturbing associations. "Unstable" (A.V.), though somewhat feebler than the Greek, must therefore be retained, and has the advantage of covering the alternative meaning "fickle." Compare Ecclus. ii. 12, "Woe to cowardly hearts and faint hands, and a sinner that walketh upon two paths."

ἐν πάσαις ταῖς ὁδοῖς αὐτοῦ, *in all his ways*] Ὁδοῖς retains its original force as "roads" or "journeys" more distinctly than the English equivalent. "In all his ways" is perhaps, as Bede says, in prosperity and adversity alike; whether suffering trial or not, he has no firm footing. The formula occurs Ps. xci. 11 and elsewhere.

The last two sentences may be thus paraphrased : "A prayer for wisdom, to be successful, must be full of trust and without wavering. Wisdom comes not to him that asks God for it only as a desperate chance, without firm belief in His power and cheerful willingness to give. Such a one is always tossed to and fro by vague hopes and fears; he is at the mercy of every blast and counterblast of outward things. While he allows them to hide from him the inner vision of God's works and ways, he cannot go straight forward with one aim and one mind, and therefore lacks the one condition of finding wisdom; he is a stranger to that converse with God, in which alone the mutual act of giving and receiving can be said to exist."

A passage of Philo deserves to be appended; much of the context is necessarily omitted. "Whatsoever things nature gives to the soul need a long time to gain strength; as it is with the communication of arts and the rules of arts by other men to their pupils. But when God, the fountain of wisdom, communicates various kinds of knowledge (τὰς ἐπιστήμας) to mankind, He communicates them without lapse of time (ἀχρόνως); and they, inasmuch as they have become disciples of the Only Wise, are quick at discovering the things which they sought. Now one of the first virtues thus introduced is the eager desire of imitating a perfect teacher, so far as it is possible for an imperfect being to imitate a perfect. When Moses said (to Pharaoh, Ex. viii. 9) 'Command me a time that I may pray for thee and thy servants etc.,' he being in sore need ought to have said, 'Pray thou at once.' But he delayed, saying, 'To-morrow,' that so he might maintain his godless feebleness (τὴν ἀπαλότητα τῆς ἀθεότητος) to the end. This conduct is like that of almost all waverers (ἐπαμφοτερισταῖς), even though they may not acknowledge it in express words. For, when any undesired event befalls them, inasmuch as they have had no previous firm trust in the Saviour God, they fly to such help as nature can give, to physicians, to herbs, to compound

drugs, to strict regimen, in short to every resource of perishable things. And if a man say to them, 'Flee, O ye wretched ones, to the only Physician of the maladies of the soul, and forsake the help which mutable (παθητῆς) nature can give,' they laugh and mock with cries of 'To-morrow,' as though in no case would they supplicate the Deity to remove present misfortunes" (De Sacrif. Ab. et Caini, 17-19).

9—11. A return to the original theme of v. 2, bringing in the characteristic contrast of rich and poor as a special application of the principle of rejoicing in trials. There is probably a reference to the Beatitudes such as they appear in St Luke (vi. 20, 24). An indirect opposition (marked by But and also by the brother) to the waverer of v. 8 is doubtless also intended. Poverty, riches, and the change from one to the other may be among the "ways," in all of which the waverer is found unstable.

9. The order in the Greek is important. ὁ ἀδελφός belongs equally to ὁ ταπεινός and ὁ πλούσιος, so that "let the brother boast" is common to both verses. As St James bids his "brethren" count it all joy when they fell in with trials, so he here points out the appropriate grounds of boasting to each member of the brotherhood, the body who might be expected to take a truer view of life than the outer world.

καυχάσθω, glory] In the O.T. and Ecclus. "glorying" or "boasting" drops altogether its strict sense, and signifies any proud and exulting joy: so הָתְהַלֵּל (ἐπαινοῦμαι) Ps. xxxiv. 3; lxiv. 11 etc.; and καυχῶμαι Ps. v. 11; cxlix. 5; Ecclus. xxxix. 8 etc. In the N.T. the word is confined to the Epp. and common there; but rarely loses its original force, probably out of St James only in the parallel Rom. v. 2, 3, 11 and in Heb. iii. 6; in other apparently similar cases the effect is produced merely by ob-

ἀδελφὸς ὁ ταπεινὸς ἐν τῷ ὕψει αὐτοῦ, ¹⁰ὁ δὲ πλούσιος ἐν
τῇ ταπεινώσει αὐτοῦ, ὅτι ὡς ἄνθος χόρτου παρελεύσεται.

vious paradox. Possibly the extension
had its origin in Jerem. ix. 23 f., quoted 2 Cor. x. 17. Here καυχάσθω repeats the χαράν of v. 2 with a slight
change, meaning joy accompanied with
pride.

ταπεινός, *of low estate*] Poverty is
intended, but poverty in relation to
"glorying" and contempt, a state
despised by the mass of mankind.
Ταπεινός means indifferently "poor"
and "poor in spirit" i.e. "meek," two
notions which the later Jews loved to
combine : it is often used in both
senses in Ecclus.

τῷ ὕψει αὐτοῦ, *his height*] Not any
future elevation in this or the other
world, but the present spiritual height
conferred by his outward lowness, the
blessing pronounced upon the poor,
the possession of the Kingdom of God.
Continued poverty is one of the "trials"
to be rejoiced in.

10. τῇ ταπεινώσει αὐτοῦ, *his being
brought low*] Suffering the loss not
of wealth only, but of the consideration which wealth brings. Ταπείνωσις
might mean "low estate," as in the
LXX.(and Lk. i. 48 from 1 Sam. i. 11);
but St James' language is not usually
thus incorrect, and the classical sense
is borne out by the context. The
correlation with v. 9 is not meant to
be exact. The rich brother is to glory
in his being *brought* low whenever
that may be, now or at any future day
(see v. 1). If the "trials" of the times
included persecution, the rich would
be its first victims. This is a marked
feature in the persecution of the Jews
by the mob of Alexandria under the
Emperor Gaius (Philo, *Leg. ad Gai.*
18; e.g. πένητας ἐκ πλουσίων καὶ ἀπό-
ρους ἐξ εὐπόρων γεγενῆσθαι μηδὲν ἀδι-
κοῦντας ἐξαίφνης καὶ ἀνοίκους καὶ ἀνεσ-
τίους, ἐξεωσμένους καὶ πεφυγαδευμένους
τῶν ἰδίων οἰκιῶν κ.τ.λ.).

ὅτι, *since*] This introduces not an

explanation of *being brought low*, but
one reason why the rich brother should
glory in it, or more strictly why he
should not be startled at the command
to glory in it. Perfection (v. 4) is
assumed to be his aim : our Lord
taught that riches are a hindrance in
the way of perfection (Mt. xix. 21 ff.):
and this doctrine loses no little of its
strangeness, when the separable, and
so to speak accidental, nature of riches
is remembered.

ὡς ἄνθος χόρτου, *as the bloom of
grass*] Taken from the LXX. rendering of Isa. xl. 6: πᾶσα σὰρξ χόρτος
καὶ πᾶσα δόξα ἀνθρώπου ὡς ἄνθος χόρτου.
χόρτος, properly "fodder," means in
the LXX. such grass, or rather herbage,·
as makes fodder. It stands rightly
for חָצִיר (cf. Job xl. 15), in the first
place here as in the two following
verses. But ἄνθος χόρτου is put for
צִיץ הַשָּׂדֶה, which is rightly translated
ἄνθος τοῦ ἀγροῦ, "the flower of the
field," in the parallel Ps. ciii. 15. The
LXX. nowhere else translate שָׂדֶה by
χόρτος, nor will it bear that meaning:
hence χόρτου is merely an erroneous
repetition. The unique image taken
from the flower of grass had therefore
an accidental origin, though it yields a
sufficient sense.

Grass is frequently used in the
poetical books of the O.T. to illustrate
the shortness of life, or the swift fall
of the wicked. To understand the
force of the image we must forget the
perpetual verdure of our meadows
and pastures under a cool and damp
climate, and recall only the blades of
thin herbage which rapidly spring up
and as rapidly vanish before the Palestine summer has well begun. By
"the flower of the field" the prophet
(and the LXX. translator) doubtless
meant the blaze of gorgeous blossoms
which accompanies the first shooting

¹¹ἀνέτειλεν γὰρ ὁ ἥλιος σὺν τῷ καύσωνι καὶ ἐξήρανεν τὸν

of the grass in spring, alike in the Holy Land and on the Babylonian plain (Stanley *Sin. and Pal.* 138 f.; Layard *Nineveh* i. p. 78).

παρελεύσεται, *pass away*] Παρέρχομαι and "pass" answer strictly to each other in their primary and their metaphorical senses: the Greek word here, as often in classical writers, means to "pass away," i.e. pass by and so go out of sight; it is employed in precisely similar comparison, Wisd. ii. 4; v. 9.

Which passes away, the rich man or his riches? Notwithstanding the form of the sentence, we might be tempted by the apparent connexion with *v.* 9 to say his riches (ὁ πλοῦτος included in ὁ πλούσιος). But in that case the only way to avoid unmeaning tautology is to take the comparison as justifying the mention of impoverishment rather than the exhortation to glorying in impoverishment; "let the rich man glory in his being brought low, for brought low he assuredly will be, sooner or later." This gives an intelligible sense; but no one having this in his mind would have clothed it in the language of *vv.* 10, 11. St James must therefore mean to say not that riches leave the rich man but that he leaves his riches. This is the interpretation suggested by the natural grammar of *v.* 10, and no other will suit the last clause of *v.* 11.

But a difficulty remains. St James would hardly say that the rich man is more liable to death than the poor, and the shortness of life common to both is in itself no reason why the rich should glory in being brought to poverty. Probably the answer is that St James has in view not death absolutely but death as separating riches from their possessor, and shewing them to have no essential connexion with him. "Be not thou afraid when one is made rich, when the glory of his house is increased; for when he dieth he shall carry nothing away: his glory

shall not descend after him" (Ps. xlix. 16, 17). "Whose shall those things be which thou hast provided?" (Lk. xii. 20). The perishableness was familiar to heathens of all nations: cf. Horace *Od.* ii. 14 "Linquenda tellus et domus et placens Uxor; neque harum, quas colis, arborum" etc. The argument goes no further than to lower the relative value set upon wealth, and cannot by itself sustain the exhortation of *v.* 10. But the exaggerated estimate of wealth here combated involved much more than exaggeration. It set up riches as the supreme object of trust and aspiration, and fostered the vague instinct that there was a difference of nature corresponding to the distinction of rich and poor. Thus in effect it substituted another god for Jehovah, and denied the brotherhood of men. To a rich man in this state of mind the lesson of the prophet was a necessary preparation for receiving the teaching of Christ.

11. ἀνέτειλεν, *riseth*] This is the common classical (gnomic) aorist of general statements founded on repeated experience. There is no clear instance of this use in the N.T. except here and *v.* 24. Rapid succession is perhaps also indicated by the series of aorists, though too strongly expressed in A.V. Not unlike is Ps. civ. 22, ἀνέτειλεν ὁ ἥλιος καὶ συνήχθησαν (so all MSS. except B).

σὺν τῷ καύσωνι, *with the scorching wind*] A rare word in ordinary Greek, and there chiefly used for some very inflammatory kind of fever (καύσωνος, θέρμης—Suid. where Bernhardy refers to Herod. *Epim.* p. 196); in Athen. iii. p. 73 A it denotes noontide heat. This seems also to be the meaning in Gen. xxxi. 40 (A all.; καύματι E) and Song of 3 Child. 44 (A Compl. al.³; καῦμα B all., καῦσος al.); also in Mt. xx. 12; Lk. xii. 55 (aestas latt.); and perhaps Isa. xlix. 10, where the Hebrew has nothing to do with wind.

χόρτον, καὶ τὸ ἄνθος αὐτοῦ ἐξέπεσεν καὶ ἡ εὐπρέπεια τοῦ
προσώπου αὐτοῦ ἀπώλετο· οὕτως καὶ ὁ πλούσιος ἐν

On the other hand in the O.T. καύσων is a frequent translation of קָדִים
(often also rendered νότος) the east
wind of Palestine (the Simoom) destructive alike by its violence and its dry
heat acquired in passing over the
desert. This sense alone occurs in all
the chief Greek translations of the
O.T., and again apparently in Ecclus.
and Judith. The only trace of it out of
the Bible is in the Schol. to Aristoph.
Lysist. 974, where a whirlwind is probably intended. St Jerome on Hos.
xii. 1 recognises both senses ("sequi-
que καύσωνα, hoc est *aestum*," and
further on "sequuntur καύσωνα, id est
ariditatem sive *ventum urentem*"),
describing the wind as "injurious to
the flowers and destroying every bud-
ding thing." Again on Ezek. xxvii. 26
he notices καύσων, "which we *may*
translate *burning wind*," as an appropriate rendering of קָדִים ("Auster"),
and then goes on to refer to Mt. xx. 12
with apparently only the heat in view
("totius diei calorem et aestum"). On
the whole there can be little doubt
that the O.T. sense is that intended
here ("the sun *with* the scorching
wind"). In Jonah iv. 8 the east wind
(καύσων) that beat upon Jonah rose
with the sun. For its effects on vege-
tation see Gen. xli. 6, 23, 27; Ezek.
xvii. 10; xix. 12. It is said to blow
from February to June [v. *Enc. Bib.*
pp. 5304 f.].

ἐξέπεσεν, *fadeth away*] This is one
of the words in this verse derived
from Isa. xl. 7, where (as in xxviii.
1, 4) it stands for נָבֵל, to fade or
droop away. The notion of dropping
off is not distinctly contained in the
Hebrew, as it is in Job xiv. 2; xv. 33,
where ἐκπίπτω is equally applied to
flowers. The strictest parallel is Job
xv. 30 in the LXX., but the Hebrew is
different. Possibly various metaphors

combined (cf. Fritzsche *Rom.* ii. 281)
to give ἐκπίπτω its genuine Greek
sense of ending in failure or nothing-
ness; so Ecclus. xxxi. 7; Rom. ix. 6;
and the "received" reading of 1 Cor.
xiii. 8. But the same force belongs
to the root prior to all special applications. πίπτω itself has a hardly
distinguishable sense (to "fail" as well
as to "fall"), which is associated with
παρέρχομαι (*v.* 10) in Lk. xvi. 17.
Hence ἐξέπεσεν was probably intended
to convey, and will certainly bear, the
sense of withering away rather than
falling off.

ἡ εὐπρέπεια τοῦ προσώπου αὐτοῦ, *the
glory of its pride*] Each of the principal words will bear two renderings.
Εὐπρέπεια might mean "comeliness,"
"grace," "beauty." Πρόσωπον might
be simply the 'face' of the grass or
flower, by a common metaphor for
its outward appearance or 'fashion.'
Εὐπρέπεια, however (used in O.T. for
various Hebrew words), usually includes a notion of stateliness, or
majesty. So Ps. xciii. 1, ὁ κύριος
ἐβασίλευσεν, εὐπρέπειαν ἐνεδύσατο; Ps.
civ. 1, ἐξομολόγησιν καὶ εὐπρέπειαν
ἐνεδύσω (א, B); Jerem. xxiii. 9, ἐγε-
νήθην ὡς ἀνὴρ συντετριμμένος ... ἀπὸ
προσώπου Κυρίου καὶ ἀπὸ προσώπου
εὐπρεπείας δόξης αὐτοῦ: Bar. v. 1,
ἔνδυσαι ('Ιερουσαλήμ) τὴν εὐπρέπειαν
τῆς παρὰ τοῦ θεοῦ δόξης εἰς τὸν αἰῶνα:
Wisd. v. 16, τὸ βασίλειον τῆς εὐπρεπείας: Wisd. vii. 29, ἐστὶν γὰρ αὕτη
(σοφία) εὐπρεπεστέρα ἡλίου: etc.

The varied figurative use of פָּנִים
("face") in the O.T. was closely followed in the LXX. by πρόσωπον, which
brought in with it from prior, though
late, Greek usages the secondary
notion of a person in a drama, or a
representative. In late Jewish Greek
the old Hebrew idiom to "accept the
face" (i.e. "receive with favour") ob-

ταῖς πορείαις αὐτοῦ μαρανθήσεται.   ¹²Μακάριος ἀνὴρ

tained fresh extensions, and thus in various ways the associations of the word πρόσωπον became more complex. It seems to mean a "person" ("personage"), as the possessor of dignity or honour, in Ecclus. xxxii. (xxxv.) 15 (12), μὴ ἔπεχε θυσίᾳ ἀδίκῳ, ὅτι κύριος κριτής ἐστιν καὶ οὐκ ἔστιν παρ᾽ αὐτῷ δόξα προσώπου, i.e. "the glory which distinguishes one person from another has no existence in His sight." Compare Wisd. vi. 7, οὐ γὰρ ὑποστελεῖται πρόσωπον ὁ πάντων δεσπότης, οὐδὲ ἐντραπήσεται μέγεθος. Not unlike is Ecclus. xxix. 27, ἔξελθε, πάροικε, ἀπὸ προσώπου δόξης: cf. 2 Macc. xiv. 24, καὶ εἶχεν τὸν Ἰούδαν διὰ παντὸς ἐν προσώπῳ, ψυχικῶς τῷ ἀνδρὶ προσεκέκλιτο. "Person" in this rather loose sense would accordingly seem to be the most exact translation here, but would involve too harsh a figure in English; and "pride" nearly expresses what is meant.

On the whole clause cf. Isa. xxviii. 1—5. The rendering here given has the advantage of recalling v. 9 ("glorying," "low estate," "height").

μαρανθήσεται, wither away] Μαραίνομαι denoted originally the dying out of a fire (cf. Aristot. de vita et morte, 5), but came to be used of many kinds of gradual enfeeblement or decay. In classical Greek there are but slight traces of its application to plants (Plutarch, Dion, 24; Lucian, de Domo, 9; Themistius, Or. xiii. p. 164 C, ἄνθος ἀμυδρὸν ἀρετῆς μαραίνεσθαι). But this is the exact sense in Wisd. ii. 8; and Job xxiv. 24, ἐμαράνθη ὥσπερ μολόχη (al. χλόη) ἐν καύματι ἢ ὥσπερ στάχυς ἀπὸ καλάμης αὐτόματος ἀποπεσών, which curiously resembles the text. Hence probably also the meaning "scorch" in the only remaining instance in the O.T. and Apocrypha, Wisd. xix. 20.

The idea of gradual passing away, which is characteristic of the classical use, is out of place here, where the rapid disappearance of the grass is dwelt upon. The fitness of the word comes solely from its association with the image just employed: it can mean no more than "die or vanish as the grass does."

πορείαις, goings] The known evidence for the reading πορίαις is insufficient; but in any case it is merely a variation of spelling. There is no authority for the existence of a word πορία signifying "gain" (πορισμός), which is a blunder of Erasmus founded on a false analogy of ἀπορία and εὐπορία. Πορεία means a "journey," and is very rarely used in any secondary sense, unless by a conscious metaphor indicated in the context. The only clear cases discoverable are Ps. lxviii. 24; (Isa. viii. 11;) and Hab. iii. 6 (whence the interpolation in Ecclus. i. 5). This is the more remarkable as τρίβοι and ὁδοί are abundantly so used in the LXX. Herder's ingenious suggestion that there is an allusion to travelling merchants (as undoubtedly iv. 13 f.) has great probability. At all events the common interpretation of "goings" as a mere trope for "doings" seems too weak here. The force probably lies in the idea that the rich man perishes while he is still on the move, before he has attained the state of restful enjoyment which is always expected and never arrives. Without some such hint of prematurity the parallel with the grass is lost.

The addition of the elaborate description in v. 11 to the simple comparison in v. 10 seems to shew how vividly St James' mind had been impressed by the image when himself looking at the grass : what had kindled his own imagination he uses to breathe life into the moral lesson. In the last clause of the verse he returns, as it were, from the contemplation to his proper subject, and ends with an echo of the last words of v. 8.

ὃς ὑπομένει πειρασμόν, ὅτι δόκιμος γενόμενος λήμψεται
τὸν στέφανον τῆς ζωῆς, ὃν ἐπηγγείλατο τοῖς ἀγαπῶσιν

"Let God alone be thy boast and thy greatest praise (Deut. x. 21), and pride not thyself upon riches, neither upon honour, neither etc., considering that these things...are swift to change, withering away (μαραινόμενα) as it were before they have fully bloomed." Philo, de vict. off. 10 (ii. 258).

12. The parenthesis (vv. 5—11) ended, St James returns to his first theme, trials. He has dealt with them (vv. 3, 4) as to their intended effects on human character, as instruments for training men to varied perfection. He has spoken (vv. 5—8) of the process as one carried on through a wisdom received from God in answer to trustful prayer, depending therefore on a genuine faith, which in its turn depends on a true knowledge of God's character. He has spoken (vv. 9—11) of the true estimate of poverty and riches, or rather of the contempt and honour which they confer, as characteristic of the right mind towards men, which should accompany and express the right mind towards God. Now he returns to trials, once more in relation to God, but from quite a new point of view, not as to their effects on character, but as to the thoughts which they at the time suggest to one who has no worthy faith in God.

μακάριος, happy] Not "blessed," but as we say "a happy man." Cf. its use in the Psalms (e.g. i. 1) and in the Beatitudes. St James drops the paradoxical form of the original theme in v. 2. Not now trial, but the patient endurance of trial is pronounced "happy." Thus the explanations in vv. 3, 4 are incorporated with the primary exhortation in v. 2.

ὑπομένει, endureth] Not "has to bear," but "bears with endurance," the verb recalling ὑπομονήν (v. 3). So Mt. xxiv. 13; Mk xiii. 13 compared

with Lk. xxi. 19. In 1 Pet. ii. 20 the force is very apparent. The phrase Μακάριος ὁ ὑπομένων (B : ὑπομείνας A, etc.) occurs Dan. xii. 12 (Thdn). Compare v. 11.

δόκιμος, approved] Again this word recalls the δοκίμιον of v. 3. It means one who has been tested, as gold or silver is tested (Zech. xi. 13, LXX. ; cf. Ps. lxvi. 10), and not found wanting. "Approved" is not quite a satisfactory rendering in modern English, though it is the best available here. "Proved" or "tried" in their adjectival sense would be less ambiguous, if the form of the sentence did not render them liable to be taken for pure participles, expressing not the result but the process of trial.

τὸν στέφανον τῆς ζωῆς, the crown of life] The precise force of this phrase is not easy to ascertain. One of the most ancient and widely spread of symbols is a circlet round the head ; expressing chiefly joy or honour or sanctity. There are two principal types, the garland of leaves or flowers (στέφανος) and the linen fillet (διάδημα, μίτρα). From one or other of these two, or from combinations of both, are probably derived all the various "crowns" in more durable or precious materials, sometimes enriched with additional ornaments or symbols. Each type is represented by a familiar instance. The chaplet with which the victor was crowned at the Greek games is a well-known illustration as used by St Paul. A fillet under the name of "diadem" was one of the insignia of royalty among the Persians, and was adopted by the Greek and Graeco-Asiatic kingdoms after Alexander. This ancient original of the modern kingly crown is never called στέφανος in classical Greek ; but the same Hebrew word עֲטָרָה, which is always rendered στέφανος by the LXX.,

20 THE EPISTLE OF ST JAMES [I. 12

denotes some royal headdress of gold (shape unknown) in 2 Sam. xii. 30 (the golden crown of the Ammonite king taken at Rabbah)‖ 1 Chr. xx. 2; (Ps. xxi. 3;) Esth. viii. 15; as well as the symbol of glory, pride, or beauty (cf. Lam. v. 16), στέφανος sometimes standing alone, sometimes being followed by a defining word (στέφανος δόξης, τρυφῆς, καυχήσεως, τῆς ὕβρεως, κάλλους, χαρίτων; also στ. ἀγαλλιάματος, Ecclus. vi. 31; xv. 6). This idiom clearly comes from the general popular use of chaplets, not from any appropriation to particular offices.

Which then of the various uses of crowns or chaplets has supplied St James with his image? In such a context we should naturally think first of the victor's crown in the games, of which St Paul speaks. On the other hand, the O.T. contains no instance of that use (it would be impossible to rely on the LXX. mistranslation of Zech. vi. 14, ὁ δὲ στέφανος ἔσται τοῖς ὑπομένουσιν, really the proper name *Helem*); and apparently the Apocrypha has no other instance than the description of virtue, in Wisd. iv. 2, which ἐν τῷ αἰῶνι στεφανηφοροῦσα πομπεύει, τὸν τῶν ἀμιάντων ἄθλων ἀγῶνα νικήσασα. In any case we must take St James' use with that of St John in Apoc. ii. 10, where again we have the crown *of life*. The phrase probably came from Jewish usage not now recorded. But when the two contexts are compared it is difficult to doubt that the Greek victor's crown is an element in the image. Even in Palestine Greek games were not unknown; and at all events St James writing to the Dispersion, and St John to the Churches of Proconsular Asia, could have no misgiving about such an allusion being misunderstood. There is of course no thought of a competitive contest; all alike might receive the crown. It is simply the outward token of glad recognition from the Heavenly Lord above, who sits watching the conflict,

and giving timely help in it. It expresses in symbol what is expressed in words in the greeting, "Well done, good and faithful servant!" The martyrs of Vienna and Lugdunum are said in the well-known epistle (Euseb. *H. E.* v. 1. 36) to receive "the great crown of incorruption" as "athletes." "The crown of incorruption" is also spoken of in the *Mart. Polyc.* 17, 19. (So also *Orac. Sibyll.* ii. pp. 193, 201, quoted by Schneckenburger.)

Life is itself the crown, the genitive being that of apposition. There is no earlier or contemporary instance of this genitive with στέφανος, except 1 Pet. v. 4: but the form of expression recals Ps. ciii. 4. "Life" is probably selected here in contrast to the earthly perishableness dwelt on in *vv.* 10 f. But it does not follow that perpetuity is the only characteristic in view. Fulness and vividness of life are as much implied. The life is an imparting of God's life: "enter thou into the joy of thy Lord[1]." The idea cannot be made definite without destroying it. The time when the reception of the crown of life begins is likewise not defined, except that it follows a period of trial. Its fulness comes when the trials are wholly passed.

ὃν ἐπηγγείλατο, *which He promised*] "The Lord" is a natural interpolation. The subject of the verb is to be inferred from the sense rather than fetched from *v.* 5 or 7; it is doubtless God. The analogy of ii. 5 shews that words of Christ would be to St James as promises of God; and such sayings as that in Mt. xix. 29; Lk. xviii. 29 f. may be intended here. But equally pertinent language may be found in the O.T., as Ps. xvi. 8-11, where the comprehensive idea of "life" well illustrates that of St James: see also Prov. xiv. 27; xix. 23. Zeller (Hilgenfeld, *J. B.* 1863, 93 ff.) tries to shew

[1] [For the way in which the N.T. fills out the older image of life see Hort's *Hulsean Lectures*, pp. 100 ff.]

αὐτόν.   ¹³μηδεὶς πειραζόμενος λεγέτω ὅτι 'Απὸ θεοῦ

that the reference here is to the
Apocalypse passage. Probably the
promise comes from Deut. xxx. 15,
16, 19, 20.

τοῖς ἀγαπῶσιν αὐτόν, *them that love
Him*] This phrase is common in the
O.T., usually joined with "keeping of
God's commandments"; but singularly
absent from the prophets (exc. Dan.
ix. 4), who speak much of God's love
to men. Here see Ps. xxxi. 23;
cxlv. 20; also Ecclus. xxxi. 19; Bel
and Drag. 38. As St James describes
endurance as leading to the crown
promised to those who love God, he
must have regarded it as at least one
form, or one mark, of the love of Him.
But then all the preceding verses
shew that he considered endurance
when perfected to involve trust in
Him, unwavering conviction of His
ungrudging goodness, and boasting in
that low estate which Christ had declared to be height in His Kingdom.
Probably, specially chosen, the words
sum up in the Deuteronomic phrase
adopted by Christ the Law as towards
God (Deut. vi. 5, ap. Matt. xxii. 37 ‖
Mk xii. 30 ‖ Lk. x. 27), just as we
have the second part of the Law in
ii. 8, conforming with St James'
treatment of the Law as spiritualised
in the Gospel.

'Αγαπῶσιν in 1 Cor. ii. 9 is substituted for ὑπομένουσιν ἔλεον in Isa.
lxiv. 4. Compare Jam. ii. 5 (on which
see Exod. xix. 5, 6); Rom. viii. 28
(τ. ἀγ. τὸν θεόν); 2 Tim. iv. 8 (τ. ἠγαπ.
τ. ἐπιφάνειαν αὐτοῦ); also the use of
אהב itself in Ps. xl. 17 ‖ lxx. 5 (οἱ ἀγ.
τὸ σωτήριόν σου).

13. In contrast to him who *endures*
trial, bears it with ὑπομονή, and thereby receives life, the opposite way of
meeting trial, yet accompanied with a
certain recognition of God, is to yield
and play a cowardly and selfish part,
and to excuse oneself by throwing the
blame on God as the Author of the

trial. Of course this, like most of
the ways rebuked by St James, is a
vice of men whose religion has become
corrupt, not of men who have none at
all.

As far as the first clause is concerned, the use of language is easy.
The πειραζόμενος of *v.* 13 takes up the
πειρασμόν of 12, and that the πειρασμοῖς of 2. Πειρασμός is still simply
"trial," "trying," the sense of suffering
being, as we saw, probably latent, as
in Ecclus., but quite subordinate.

ἀπὸ θεοῦ, *from God*] Not a con-
fusion of ἀπό and ὑπό, which would
be unlike St James' exactness of
language; the idea is origin not
agency: "from God comes my being
tried." The words in themselves are
ambiguous as to their spirit. They
might be used as the justification of
faithful endurance: the sense that
God was the Author of the trial and
probation would be just what would
most sustain him, as the Psalms shew.
But here the true phrase has been
corrupted into an expression of falsehood. The sense of probation, which
implies a personal faith in the Divine
Prover, has passed out of the word
πειράζομαι : just as God's giving was
thought of nakedly, without reference
to His gracious ungrudging mind in
giving, so here His proving is thought
of nakedly, without reference to His
wise and gracious purpose in proving.
Somewhat similar language occurs in
Ecclus. xv. 11, 12.

πειράζομαι, *tempted* or *tempted by
trial*] Now comes the difficulty: we
have passed unawares from the idea
of trial to that of temptation, by
giving what is apparently a neutral,
practically an evil, sense to "trial."
Trial manifestly may have either result: if it succeeds in its Divinely
appointed effect, it results in perfectness: but it may fail, and the failure
is moral evil. If we think of it only

πειράζομαι· ὁ γὰρ θεὸς ἀπείραστός ἐστιν κακῶν,

in relation to this evil when referring it to God, we mentally make Him the Author of the moral evil, in other words a tempter.

We are so accustomed to associate the idea of temptation with πειρασμός, that we forget how secondary the sense is. It is worth while to see what evidence it has from usage. We saw that the only O.T. and Apocryphal senses are : (1) trying of men by God (good); (2) trying of God by men (evil); (3) trying of men by man, which may be either neutral as in the case of the Queen of Sheba, or with evil purpose, but not properly a "temptational" purpose, as those who tried to entangle our Lord in His words. But the N.T. has another use. Three times in the Gospels the idea of tempting comes in, not as the sole sense but still perceptibly ; viz. in the Temptation, the Lord's Prayer, and "Watch and pray, that ye enter not into temptation" (Mt. xxvi. 41 and parallels). To see the exact force and connexion we must go back to the O.T. In Genesis God stands face to face with Abraham ; He alone is visible as trying him. But not so later. The Book of Job does not apply the words "try," "trial" (Heb. or Gk) to Job: but it is a record of a typical trial, recognised as such in Jam. v. 11 ; and while the result of the trial is perfectly good, the agency of Satan is interposed: the same process is carried on for his evil purpose and for God's good purpose, so that he is an unconscious tool in God's hand.

Exactly similar is the passage in Lk. xxii. 31, on Satan desiring to have the apostles to sift them as wheat: his evil purpose there stands in sub-ordination to the Divine purpose for perfecting Apostleship. Probably so also in the Temptation: Mt. iv. 1 πειρασθῆναι (πειραζόμενος Mk i. 13, Lk. iv. 2) ὑπὸ τοῦ διαβόλου (Σατανᾶ

Mk i. 13), i.e. the appointed probation of the Messiah takes place through the adversary who strives to tempt Him with the ways of false Messiah-ship. But in Mt. we have further ὁ πειράζων, and this in connexion with 1 Thess. iii. 5, μὴ ἐπείρασεν ὑμᾶς ὁ πειράζων, probably means not the Divinely ordained agent of probation, but he who tries with evil intent, i.e. the Tempter, "lest it prove that ye have been tried by the Tempter" (by him and not by God only). Cf. 1 Cor. vii. 5 (1 Cor. x. 13 ; Gal. vi. 1 are not certain); also πειρασμός 1 Tim. vi. 9 ; 2 Pet. ii. 9 ; Apoc. iii. 10.

So also in the Lord's Prayer πειρασμόν doubtless starts from trial, but trial considered as a source of danger rather than of effectual probation, as seems to be implied by the antithesis of (masc.) τοῦ πονηροῦ. The Lord's Prayer virtually rules the sense of μὴ εἰσέλθητε (Mt. xxvi. 41 and parallels). This implication of evil in the idea of trial apparently came from this idea of Satan's part in Divine trials. Thus the notion is not so much tempt in the sense of "allure," "seduce," as "try with evil intent."

It is difficult to find traces of Jewish influence going as far as the N.T. goes, but we do find "trial" with an evil sense attached, as the Evening Prayer in Berachoth 60 B, where sin, trans-gression, trial, disgrace stand in a line (cf. Taylor 141 f.).

ἀπείραστος...κακῶν, untried in evil] The meaning of ἀπείραστος has been much discussed. It appears in this shape in St James for the first time in Greek literature, though Boeckh has recognised it in the shortened ἀπείρᾰτος (as θαυμαστός, θαυμᾰτός, etc.) of Pindar, Olymp. vi. 54. The pre-ceding words at first sight suggest an active force "incapable of tempting to evil" (so Origen on Exod. xv. 25). A few cases of verbals in -τος in an active sense governing cases occur, but only in the tragedians. Ἀπροσδόκητος (Thuc.) and ἄπρακτος with two or three other doubtful instances are used actively by prose writers, but without governing a case. Considerable internal evidence would therefore be required before such a sense could be accepted here, while in fact it would reduce the next clause to an unmeaning repetition. Ἀπείραστος therefore, being from πειράζω, ought in strictness to be only a true passive, "not tried or tempted," "unattempted" (so Joseph. *B. J.* vii. 8. 1, μήτ' ἔργον ἀπείραστον παραλείποντες; Galen, *in Hip. Aph.* i. 1 [xvii. B 354 ed. Kühn] πειρᾶσθαι τῶν ἀπειράστων οὐκ ἀσφαλές), or "incapable of being tried or tempted": and ἀπ. κακῶν might well be "incapable of being tempted by evil things," i.e. virtually "to evil," though the phrase would in this sense be singular; so apparently Ps.-Ignat. *ad Philip.* 11 πῶς πειράζεις τὸν ἀπείραστον; (? Leuc.) *Act. Joh.* 190, Zahn [c. 57* Bonnet] ὁ γὰρ σὲ (John) πειράζων τὸν ἀπείραστον πειράζει; and a scholium in Oecumenius. In this way we gain a forcible antithesis to the following clause, but with the loss of causal connexion with the preceding.

The active and passive senses being then excluded by the context, the neuter remains, if only it can be sustained philologically. Now while πειράζω belongs to Epic and to late Greek, and has no middle except once in Hippoc. *de Morb.* iv. 327 T. ii. (Lob. ap. Buttm. ii. 267)[1], the Attics used πειράω and also the middle πειρῶμαι, whence they had the verbal ἀπείρᾱτος in both passive and neuter senses, which cannot always be distinguished. The phrase ἀπείρατος κακῶν, meaning "having had no experience of evils," "free from evils,"

[1] Moreover the difference in sense was broken down: πειράζω=πειρῶμαι in Acts xvi. 7; xxiv. 6; (reading) ix. 26. πειρῶμαι only in Acts xxvi. 21. In Heb. iv. 15 for πεπειρασμένον 'tempted' many MSS. have πεπειραμένον.

seems to have been almost proverbial: it occurs in Diod. Sic. i. 1; Plut. *Moral.* 119 F; Joseph. *B. J.* ii. 21, 4 (cf. iii. 4, 4): Athenag. *de resur.* 18 (where the Strasburg MS. has ἀπείραστος); Themist. vii. p. 92 B (Wetst.). It is quite possible that the two forms, having the strict passive sense in common, were at length used indiscriminately, ἀπείραστος borrowing from ἀπείρατος its wider range: and so we find in Theodoret *de Prov.* v. (iv. 560 Schulze), οὐδὲ γὰρ ἂν ἐδείσαμεν, εἰ παντελῶς ἀπείραστος αὐτῶν (sc. venomous serpents) ἡ ἡμετέρα φύσις μεμενήκει. But, even without supposing St James to have lost the distinction, we can readily understand that he may have seized the familiar ἀπείρατος κακῶν, and by a permissible license substituted the kindred ἀπείραστος in conformity with the πειράζω and πειρασμοί of his context.

Similarly his κακά are not, as usual in this phrase, misfortunes, but moral evils. In English the force is best given by the abstract singular, "untried in evil," i.e. without experience of anything that is evil. The argument doubtless is :—God's own nature is incapable of contact with evil, and therefore He cannot be thought of as tempting men, and so being to them the cause of evil. Compare M. Aurel. vi. 1 ὁ δὲ ταύτην (τὴν τῶν ὅλων οὐσίαν) διοικῶν λόγος οὐδεμίαν ἐν ἑαυτῷ αἰτίαν ἔχει τοῦ κακοποιεῖν, κακίαν γὰρ οὐκ ἔχει.

αὐτός, *Himself*] That is, He for His part (not so others). This the proper sense of αὐτός is compatible with a neuter as well as with a passive rendering of ἀπείραστος: the order is not αὐτὸς δὲ πειράζει.

πειράζει δὲ αὐτὸς οὐδένα] This statement cannot possibly be taken in the original sense of πειράζει. The whole passage rests on the assumption that πειρασμός as trial does come from God. The word has therefore in this place acquired a tinge partly from the misuse of it in the mouth of the man excusing himself, partly from the

πειράζει δὲ αὐτὸς οὐδένα.   ¹⁴ἕκαστος δὲ πειράζεται

κακῶν of the following clause; it means "tries" in the sense that the man talks of "trying," tries for evil, i.e. tempts.

At first sight it looks strange, taking this verse with the next, that St James in denying that God tempts is silent about Satan as the tempter, while yet he does in antithesis speak of a man's own desire as tempting him. The silence cannot possibly arise from any hesitation to refer to Satan or to his temptations : that supposition is historically excluded by the general language of the N.T. St James as a Jew of this time would be more, not less, ready than others to use such language; and it lies on the surface of the early Gospel records on which his belief was mainly founded.

It is striking that the Clementine Homilies, representing a form of Ebionism, i.e. the exaggeration of St James' point of view, lean so greatly on the idea of Satan as the tempter that they say absolutely, what St James here says only with a qualification, that God does not πειράζειν at all. In contrasting sayings of Christ with false teaching, it says (iii. 55) τοῖς δὲ οἰομένοις ὅτι ὁ θεὸς πειράζει, ὡς αἱ γραφαὶ λέγουσιν, ἔφη, 'Ο πονηρός ἐστιν ὁ πειράζων· ὁ καὶ αὐτὸν πειράσας, probably from an apocryphal Gospel. And so on the theory that any doctrine of the O.T. which the writer thought false must be an interpolation, he calls it a false-hood (iii. 43) to say that the Lord tried Abraham, ἵνα γνῷ εἰ ὑπομένει ; and (xvi. 13) with reference to Deut. xiii. 3 he boldly substitutes ὁ πειρά-ζων ἐπείραζεν for the LXX. πειράζει Κύριος ὁ θεός σου ὑμᾶς εἰδέναι εἰ κ.τ.λ.

This illustrates St James' caution. He was as anxious as Hom. Clem. to maintain at all hazards the absolute goodness of God, but he entirely believed and upheld the O.T. language.

Meanwhile to have spoken here of Satan would have been only substituting one excuse for another. It was as practical unbelief to say, I sin because Satan tempts me, as to say, I sin because God tempts me. In each case it was an external power. What was needed to bring forward was the third factor, that within the man himself, and subject to his own mastery. The whole subject involved two mysteries, that of God as good in relation to evil, that of God as Providence in relation to human responsibility. Explicitly and implicitly St James recognises both sides of each antinomy : he refuses to cut either knot by the sacrifice of a fundamental truth.

14. ἕκαστος δὲ πειράζεται ὑπὸ τῆς ἰδίας ἐπιθυμίας, but each man is tempted by his own desire] Here the particular temptation belonging to the πειρασμοί of persecution is expanded into temptation generally, to doing evil acts, not merely not persisting in good. It is violent to connect ὑπὸ τῆς ἰδίας ἐπιθυμίας exclusively with the following participles : ὑπό goes naturally with a passive transitive verb immediately preceding, unless the sense forbids. There is no need to take either verb or participles quite absolutely: as often happens ὑπό κ.τ.λ., standing between both, belongs to both, but especially to the verb as standing first.

ἐπιθυμίας, desire] This must be taken in its widest sense (cf. iv. 1) without special reference to sensuality: such desires as would lead to unfaithfulness under the πειρασμοί of persecution, to which the Epistle refers at the outset, are not likely to be excluded. It is not abstract desire, but a man's own desire, not merely because the responsibility is his, not God's, but also because it substitutes some private and individual end for the will of God : κατὰ τὰς ἰδίας ἐπι-

ὑπὸ τῆς ἰδίας ἐπιθυμίας ἐξελκόμενος καὶ δελεαζόμενος·

θυμίας occurs 2 Pet. iii. 3 (cf. Jude 16, 18) ; 2 Tim. iv. 3. The meaning of the Greek words needs nothing beyond themselves to explain them. But it is likely enough that St James had in mind, when he was writing, יֵצֶר הָרָע, or "the evil impulse," often spoken of in Jewish literature, starting from Gen. vi. 5 ; viii. 21 ("imagination"), properly the *set* or *frame* (πλάσμα) of the heart or of its thoughts, occasionally identified with Satan, but oftener not. Cf. Weber, *Syst. der alt-synagog. Pal. Theol.* 204 ff., 223 ff.

The representation of the desire as a personal tempter, probably implied in this verse and clearly expressed in the next, may contain the idea that, not being evil intrinsically, it becomes evil when the man concedes to it a separate voice and will instead of keeping it merged in his own personality, and thus subject to his authority. The story of Eve, with the Jewish allegories on the same subject, can hardly have been absent from St James' mind : but it does not meet his purpose sufficiently to affect his language. On the other hand he probably pictured to himself the tempter desire as a harlot. Here too a Christian distinction may be latent in the image : the desire tempts not by evil but by misused good (cf. *v.* 17).

ἐξελκόμενος καὶ δελεαζόμενος, *being enticed and allured (by it)*] Δελεάζω, to allure by a bait (δέλεαρ), is frequently used metaphorically, as here. Ἐξέλκω, a rather rare word, is not known to occur in any similar passage. The sense of Aristotle's πληγὰς λαβὼν καὶ παρὰ τῆς γυναικὸς ἐξελκυσθείς (*Pol.* v. 10, p. 1311 b 29) is too obscure to supply illustration. Several commentators cite as from Plut. *De sera num. vind.* (no ref.), τὸ γλυκὺ τῆς ἐπιθυμίας ὥσπερ δέλεαρ ἐξέλκειν : Plutarch's real words are (p. 554 F), τὸ

γλυκὺ τῆς ἀδικίας ὥσπερ δέλεαρ εὐθὺς ἐξεδήδοκε. The combination with δελεάζω has naturally suggested here the image of fish drawn out of the water by a line (οἱ δὲ ἕλκουσι· ἐπεὰν δὲ ἐξελκύσθῃ ἐς γῆν—Herod. ii. 70, of the crocodile), in spite of the obvious difficulty that the bait ought to precede the line : but the whole conception is unsuitable to the passage. The simple ἕλκω is used for the drawing or attracting operation of a love-charm (ἴυγξ : so Pind. *Nem.* iv. 56 ; Xen. *Mem.* iii. 11, 18 ; Theocrit. ii. 17 ff.; as *duco* Verg. *Ecl.* viii. 68) ; and soon came to be applied to any pleasurable attraction (Xen. *Symp.* i. 7 ; Plat. *Rep.* v. p. 458 D with πείθειν, but ἐρωτικαῖς ἀναγκαῖς; vii. 538 D, ἐπιτηδεύματα ἡδονὰς ἔχοντα, ἃ κολακεύει μὲν ἡμῶν τὴν ψυχὴν καὶ ἕλκει ἐφ' ἑαυτά, πείθει δὲ οὐ τοὺς καὶ ὁπηοῦν μετρίους ; Philostr. *Ep.* 39, καλὸς εἶ, κἂν μὴ θέλῃς, καὶ πάντας ἕλκεις τῷ ἀμελουμένῳ, ὥσπερ οἱ βότρυες καὶ τὰ μῆλα καὶ εἴ τι ἄλλο αὐτόματον καλόν ; Athan. *Or. cont. Gentes* 30 on men leaving the way of truth, on which they have been set διὰ τὰς ἔξωθεν αὐτοὺς ἑλκούσας ἡδονὰς τοῦ βίου; Ael. *N. A.* vi. 31). It is associated with δέλεαρ, δελεάζω, in Plut. *Moral.* 1093 D, αἱ δ' ἀπὸ γεωμετρίας καὶ ἀστρολογίας καὶ ἁρμονικῆς δριμὺ καὶ ποικίλον ἔχουσαι τὸ δέλεαρ [ἡδοναὶ] οὐδενὸς τῶν ἀγωγίμων ἀποδέουσιν, ἕλκουσαι καθάπερ ἴυγξι τοῖς διαγράμμασιν. Philo says (i. 512), ἐπιθυμία μὲν γάρ, ὁλκὸν ἔχουσα δύναμιν, καὶ ἂν φεύγῃ τὸ ποθούμενον διώκειν ἀναγκάζει. Such seems to be the sense here, ἐκ being prefixed to denote the drawing out of the right place or relation or the drawing aside out of the right way : cf. ἐκκλίνω, ἐκπίπτω, ἐκστρέφομαι, ἐκτρέπομαι, and especially (though not in N.T.) ἐξάγω. The present tense of the participles expresses only the enticing and alluring action of the

¹⁵εἶτα ἡ ἐπιθυμία συλλαβοῦσα τίκτει ἁμαρτίαν, ἡ δὲ ἁμαρτία ἀποτελεσθεῖσα ἀποκυεῖ θάνατον. ¹⁶Μὴ πλα-

desire, antecedently to its being obeyed or resisted. Renderings of ἐξελκόμενος like "drawn astray," though in themselves more expressive than "enticed," would therefore involve an erroneous anticipation of the next verse. Cf. on this use of ἕλκω Creuzer in Plotin. de pulchr. pp. 249 ff.

15. εἶτα, next] Εἶτα, when historical (in Heb. xii. 9 it is logical), marks a fresh and distinct incident, whether immediate or, as in the parable of the Sower (Mk iv. 17; Lk. viii. 12), after an interval. Thus here it separates the temptation from the yielding to temptation implied in συλλαβοῦσα.

ἡ ἐπιθυμία, the desire] That is, either his desire generally, as the article in v. 14 suggests, or that particular desire of his which tempted him; not desire in the abstract.

συλλαβοῦσα τίκτει, conceiveth and bringeth forth] The double image distinguishes the consent of the will (the man) to the desire from the resulting sinful act, which may follow either instantly or at a future time. On the other hand the compact phrase adopted from the O.T. (Gen. iv. 1, 17 etc.) participle and verb brings thought and act together as a single stage between the temptations on the one hand and the death on the other: the sin dates its existence from the moment of consent, though it is by act that it is born into the world.

ἁμαρτίαν, a sin] This might of course be "sin": but the individual sense suits the passage better; each special desire has a special sin for its illegitimate offspring. The personified sin of this verse is neither momentary thoughts nor momentary deeds, but has a continuous existence and growth, a parasitical life: it is what we call a sinful state, a moral disease which once generated runs its course unless

arrested by the physician.

ἡ δὲ ἁμαρτία ἀποτελεσθεῖσα, and the sin, when it is fully formed] 'Αποτελεσθεῖσα is not exactly "full-grown," a sense for which there is no authority, but denotes completeness of parts and functions either accompanying full growth as opposed to a rudimentary or otherwise incomplete state, e.g. of the winged insect in contrast to the chrysalis and the grub (Plato Tim. 73 D; Pseud.-Plato Epinom. 981 C; Aristot. H. A. v. 19, p. 552 a 28; Generat. Animal. ii. 1, p. 732 a 32; iii. 11, p. 762 b 4), or possessed by beings of high organisation (Aristot. H. A. ix. 1, p. 608 b 7, man as compared with other animals ἔχει τὴν φύσιν ἀποτετελεσμένην). Similarly it is used of mental or moral accomplishment (Xen. Hipparch. vii. 4; Oecon. xiii. 3; Lucian Hermot. 8, ὃς ἂν ἀποτελεσθῇ πρὸς ἀρετήν). In virtue of its morbid life the sin goes on acquiring new members and faculties (cf. Rom. vi. 6; Col. iii. 5) till it reaches the perfection of destructiveness. It may be safely assumed that ἀποτελεσθεῖσα does not mean, as some suppose, the carrying out of a sinful thought into act, though purposes, desires, hopes, prayers are said ἀποτελεῖσθαι. The image requires in this place a sense applicable to a living being.

ἀποκυεῖ θάνατον, giveth birth to death] The precise force of ἀποκυέω, here and in v. 18, is not altogether certain. Τίκτω, which St James has just employed, is the usual literary word for the bearing of a son or daughter by the mother (only poets employ it of the father): it has reference to parentage, the relation of mother to child. 'Αποκυέω, as most commonly used, is the medical or physical word denoting the same fact, but chiefly as the close of pregnancy (κυέω): thus a person named is very

νᾶσθε, ἀδελφοί μου ἀγαπητοί.   ¹⁷πᾶσα δόσις ἀγαθὴ

rarely said ἀποκυεῖσθαι; while this verb is often applied to the young of animals, and in the case of human births the accompanying substantive is usually βρέφος or some other neuter form. Perhaps in consequence of this neuter and so to speak impersonal reference, ἀποκυέω seems further (though the evidence is scanty) to have been specially applied to cases of births abnormal in themselves or in their antecedents; as of Athene from the brain of Zeus (*Et. Mag.* 371, 35); of misshapen animals (Herodian i. 14, 1); or of one species from another (Phlegon *passim*) etc. Here there is no father. The birth of death follows of necessity when once sin is fully formed, for sin from its first beginnings carried death within.

For other images of the relation of sin to death see Gen. ii. 17; Ezek. xviii. 4; Rom. v. 12; vi. 21 (the nearest in sense to St James' language), 23; vii. 11, 13; 1 Cor. xv. 56; cf. 1 Jn v. 16.

16. μὴ πλανᾶσθε, *be not deceived*] Occurs similarly 1 Cor. vi. 9; xv. 33; Gal. vi. 7 : in each case the danger lies in some easy self-deception, either springing up naturally within or prompted by indulgent acceptance of evil examples without. The "wandering" forbidden is not wandering from right action, but from a right habit of mind concerning action. The middle sense "go not astray" is possible here, but the passive "be not led astray" is preferable (2 Tim. iii. 13; cf. 1 Jn iii. 7). Delusions like these, St James means to say, would not be possible to men fully embracing the fundamental truth "Every gift" etc.

ἀδελφοί μου ἀγαπητοί, *my beloved brethren*] So *v.* 19; ii. 5. The simple ἀδελφοί or ἀδελφοί μου recurs often in the Epistle.

17. The first part of this verse admits several constructions. The commonest makes ἄνωθεν the pre-

dicate, and καταβαῖνον κ.τ.λ. epexegetic, "every good gift (or, giving) etc. is from above, descending etc." : ἄνωθέν ἐστιν is however a weak and unlikely phrase; contrast ἐκ τῶν ἄνω εἰμί (Jn viii. 23) with ἄνωθεν ἐρχόμενος (iii. 31); ἦν δεδομένον σοι ἄνωθεν (xix. 11). This difficulty is removed by making ἄνωθεν dependent on καταβαῖνον etc., which is thus taken into the predicate : but the substitution of ἐστὶ καταβαῖνον for καταβαίνει either is unmeaning or enfeebles the sense; in iii. 15, οὐκ ἔστιν αὕτη ἡ σοφία ἄνωθεν κατερχομένη, the participle is adjectival or qualitative, as the next clause shews, while here a statement of fact is required. Both constructions are liable to a more fatal objection, incongruity with the context. The doctrine contained in them is clearly enunciated in the Apocrypha and still more by Philo, being an obvious inference from O.T. language; and little if at all less clearly by heathen writers; but it is out of place here. Though every good gift were from above, yet evil gifts might proceed from the same source; and if so, the good God might remain the tempter. A perception of the difficulty has led Bengel and others into forcing an impossible meaning upon πᾶσα δόσις ἀγαθή, "a gift (giving) altogether good," and then extorting from this translation the sense "nothing but good gifts."

The true construction was pointed out by Mr Thomas Erskine (*The unconditional freeness of the Gospel*, Edinburgh, 1829 [ed. 3] pp. 239 ff.). The predicate is ἀγαθή and τέλειον ἄνωθεν, "every giving is good and every gift perfect from above (or, from its first source), descending etc."; paraphrased by Mr Erskine, "there are no bad gifts, no bad events; every appointment is gracious in its design, and divinely fitted for that design." Ἄνωθεν is more completely appropriate to τέλειος than to ἀγαθός

καὶ πᾶν δώρημα τέλειον ἄνωθέν ἐστιν, καταβαῖνον ἀπὸ

(cf. *Symb. Antioch. Macrost.* ap. Athan. *de Synod.* 26, p. 740 D [732 B Migne], οὐδὲν γὰρ πρόσφατον ὁ χριστὸς προσείληφεν ἀξίωμα, ἀλλ' ἄνωθεν τέλειον αὐτὸν καὶ τῷ Πατρὶ κατὰ πάντα ὅμοιον εἶναι πεπιστεύκαμεν): but had its force been intentionally limited to τέλειον (as Mr Erskine apparently assumes), it would hardly have been placed at the end; and it makes excellent sense with both adjectives. On this view St James must mean by "every gift" every gift of God: the limitation is supplied by the context, and is further justified by the absolute use of ἡ ὀργή, [τὸ] θέλημα (see Lightfoot, *On Revision of the N.T.*, 105 f.), and by the converse use of δῶρον absolute for an offering of man to God (Mt. xv. 5; Mk vii. 11; Lk. xxi. 4 [true text]). Thus i. 5 and this verse complete each other: God's giving is gracious and ungrudging in respect of His own mind; it is good and perfect in respect of its work and destination: δόσις and ἀγαθή form the intermediate link.

δόσις...δώρημα, *giving...gift*] These cannot possibly be synonyms: rhetorical repetition of identical sense in other diction is incompatible with the carefully economised language of all writers of the N.T., and here the words are emphatically distinguished by means of πᾶσα, πᾶν, and the separate adjectives. The difference is probably double. Since δόσις is often not less concrete than δόμα, and δωρεά (as always in Acts) than δώρημα, the variety of termination might have had no significance. But it was easy to use either δόσις and δωρεά or δόμα and δώρημα; so that the contrast of forms and genders would be singularly clumsy if it was not intentional. Δόσις occurs elsewhere in the N.T. only in Phil. iv. 15, where it is verbal, δόσεως καὶ λήμψεως: so Ecclus. xli. 19; xlii. 7. It is also verbal in Philo (*Leg. Alleg.* iii. 20, p. 100; *de Cherub.* 25, p. 154),

being in the second place treated, like δωρεά, as a species of χάρις. In one passage (Rom. v. 15 f.) St Paul distinctly employs δωρεά in the same relation to δώρημα as χάρις to χάρισμα (cf. *Mart. Polyc.* xx. 2); and the other places where he uses δωρεά gain force if it is taken as qualitative or semi-verbal (Rom. v. 17; 2 Cor. ix. 15; Eph. iii. 7; iv. 7: so probably also Jn iv. 10; Heb. vi. 4). On this evidence, direct and indirect, the relation of "giving" (so the Geneva and "Bishops'" Bibles) to "gift" must be accepted as distinguishing δόσις from δώρημα.

Another difference, probably here subordinate, is independent of the termination. In the second passage cited above, and also *Leg. Alleg.* iii. 70, p. 126, Philo distinguishes the δῶρα and δόματα of the LXX. in Numb. xxviii. 2 by value, calling δῶρα "perfect good things," and stating that δόσις is a "moderate grace" (χάρις μέση), δωρεά a "better" grace: but this conception is otherwise unsupported. On the other hand δωροῦμαι, δωρεά, δώρημα usually imply free giving, sometimes with anticipation of a return, but still not as matter of barter; and Aristotle (*Top.* iv. 4, p. 125 a 17) chooses δόσις as an illustration of a "genus," δωρεά of a "species"; for δωρεά," he says, "is a δόσις without repayment" (ἀναπόδοτος). This secondary difference cannot be rendered concisely in English without exaggeration: and indeed δώρημα merely gives prominence to what in this context is already latent in δόσις. Moreover in good Attic writers δόσις when not used technically is chiefly applied to Divine benefits, e.g. several times in Plato: so Plutarch (*C. Mar.* 46, p. 433 A) represents Antipater of Tarsus as counting up the happinesses (μακαρίων) of his life at its end, καθάπερ φιλοχρήστου τῆς τύχης ἅπασαν δόσιν εἰς μεγάλην χάριν τιθέμενον.

τοῦ πατρὸς τῶν φώτων, παρ' ᾧ οὐκ ἔνι παραλλαγὴ ἢ

ἀγαθή, good] Ἀγαθός denotes properly what is good in operation and
result to things outside itself, utility
in the utmost generality (Mt. vii. 17
πᾶν δένδρον ἀγαθὸν καρποὺς καλοὺς
ποιεῖ), and hence beneficence where
there is a personal agent. So Ecclus.
xxxix. 33, "All the works of Jehovah
are good (ἀγαθά), and he (or, they)
will supply every need in its season."
"Good" gifts in particular (not de-
ceptive gifts of evil effect), and that
as given by God, are the subject of
a saying by our Lord (Mt. vii. 11;
Lk. xi. 13) which St James may have
had in view: but the conception is
widely spread.

τέλειον, perfect] As ἀγαθός expresses the character of the gifts,
derived from the Giver, so τέλειος
expresses the completeness of their
operation when they are not misused.
Philo says θέμις δὲ οὐδὲν ἀτελὲς αὐτῷ
χαρίζεσθαι, ὥσθ' ὁλόκληροι καὶ παντελεῖς
αἱ τοῦ ἀγεννήτου δωρεαὶ πᾶσαι (i. 173);
χαρίζεται δὲ ὁ θεὸς τοῖς ὑπηκόοις ἀτελὲς
οὐδέν, πλήρη δὲ καὶ τέλεια πάντα
(i. 447).

ἄνωθεν, from the beginning or from
their source] The commonest sense
"from above," found in various similar
passages, is harsh here in combination
with the adjectives, though the etymology may have dictated the choice
of the word, as specially appropriate
to the subject of the verse. It is
rather, as often, "from the beginning"
(so Lk. i. 3; Acts xxvi. 5; Gal. iv. 9);
or, with a slight modification, "from
their source," origin suggesting the
ground antecedent to origin. Nearly
similar is the use in Dion Cass. xliv.
37: ὅσοις δὲ ἄνωθεν ("from their
ancestry," as the context shews) ἐκ
πολλοῦ σπέρμα ἀνδραγαθίας ὑπάρχει;
Ps.-Demosth. p. 1125, πονηρὸς οὗτος
ἄνωθεν ἐκ τοῦ Ἀνακείου κάδικος; Athenag. de Res. 17, αὕτη γὰρ τῶν ἀνθρώπων
ἡ φύσις, ἄνωθεν καὶ κατὰ γνώμην τοῦ ποιή-
σαντος συγκεκληρωμένην ἔχουσα τὴν

ἀνωμαλίαν; Clem. Alex. Protrept. iv.
p. 50, χρυσός ἐστι τὸ ἄγαλμά σου,...λίθος
ἐστίν, γῆ ἐστιν ἐὰν ἄνωθεν νοήσῃς.
God's gifts are inherently good and
perfect in virtue of His nature.
καταβαῖνον, descending] Sc. "as
they do." This clause is explanatory
of ἄνωθεν. They are good and perfect,
because their source is good and
perfect.

τοῦ πατρὸς τῶν φώτων, the Father
of lights] In Greek literature and in
Philo πατήρ is sometimes hardly
more than a rhetorical synonym for
"Maker," usually coupled with a more
exact word such as ποιητής or δη-
μιουργός: but this lax use finds no
precedent in Scripture, and leaves the
sense imperfect here. God's relation
to finite things must include authorship; but the authorship required by
St James' argument must be combined with likeness, and a higher
perfection in the likeness. Every
light is an offspring of the perfect
and primal Light, and in some sense
bears His image: its character as a
light fits it to set forth that character
of God to which St James makes
appeal. Philo calls God "an archetypal Splendour (αὐγή), sending forth
numberless beams" (i. 156); "not only
Light, but also [a light] archetypal of
every other light, nay rather elder
and more original (ἀνώτερον) than an
archetype" (i. 632); and "the primary
most perfect Good, the perpetual
fountain of wisdom and righteousness
and every virtue," "an archetypal
exemplar of laws and Sun [? arche-
typal] of sun, intellectual [Sun] of
material [sun], supplying from His
invisible fountains streams of visible
light to all that we see" (ὁρατὰ φέγγη
τῷ βλεπομένῳ) (ii. 254).

The plural φῶτα has various applications, to lamps or torches, to
windows, and to days. In the O.T.
אוֹר, "light," and מָאוֹר, "a light" or
"a luminary," are distinguished (mark-

edly in Gen. i. 3 ff., 18; contrast 14 ff.). But the phrase אוֹרִים occurs once (Ps. cxxxvi. 7), the subject being the heavenly luminaries, and there the LXX. also has φῶτα (in place of the usual φωστῆρες), as it has again in Jer. iv. 23 with the same sense, but apparently not reading the Massoretic text. The next clause suggests that the luminaries of the sky were present to St James' mind, nor indeed could he have forgotten the chief of visible lights: it does not however follow that they alone were meant to be denoted by τῶν φώτων, which would more naturally include all lights, and that invisible as well as visible (see next verse and iii. 15, 17). The words "Father" and "lights" taken in their proper sense illustrate each other. Plutarch (ii. 930) uses the phrase πολλὰ τῶν φώτων quite generally, so far as appears, while his immediate subject is the moon.

παρ᾽ ᾧ, with whom] This peculiar use of παρά, too lightly treated by commentators, occurs in two other phrases of the N.T., both repeated more than once; παρὰ ἀνθρώποις ἀδύνατον ἀλλ᾽ οὐ παρὰ θεῷ, πάντα γὰρ δυνατὰ παρὰ [τῷ] θεῷ (Mk x. 27; with Mt. xix. 26; Lk. xviii. 27); οὐ γάρ ἐστιν προσωποληψία παρὰ τῷ θεῷ (Rom. ii. 11; and virtually Eph. vi. 9). In the Gospel saying παρὰ ἀνθρώποις is probably formed only in antithesis to παρὰ τῷ θεῷ, itself taken from the common or Alexandrine text of Gen. xviii. 14, μὴ ἀδυνατεῖ παρὰ τῷ θεῷ ῥῆμα, where the original reading (Dov, Hil. a deo, B being deficient here) seems to be παρὰ τοῦ θεοῦ, as the Hebrew suggests, followed by the best MSS. of Lk. i. 37. The usage probably comes from the Hebrew instinct of reverence which preferred "in the presence of God," "with God" (עִם) to "in God" (בְּ); so Ps. xxxvi. 10, παρὰ σοὶ πηγὴ ζωῆς; cxxx. 7, παρὰ τῷ κυρίῳ τὸ ἔλεος καὶ πολλὴ παρ᾽ αὐτῷ λύτρωσις; Job xxvii. 11, ἀναγγελῶ ὑμῖν τί ἐστιν

ἐν χειρὶ Κυρίου, ἅ ἐστι παρὰ Παντοκράτορι οὐ ψεύσομαι. Winer's reference (p. 492 Moulton) to the "metaphysical" conception of possession, power etc. (penes) is forced; and the frequent meaning "in the sight of" (v. 27) is still less applicable. In the only classical passage cited (Matthiae, Winer) Demosthenes uses παρά with depreciative circumlocution analogous to but not identical with the biblical diction, εἰ δ᾽ οὖν ἐστι καὶ παρ᾽ ἐμοί τις ἐμπειρία τοιαύτη (De Cor., p. 318), "if indeed any such skill does reside with me."

οὐκ ἔνι, can be no or there is no room for] Ἔνι is not a contraction of ἔνεστι, ἔνεισι, but simply ἐνί, the Ionic form of ἐν, retained in this Attic idiom like πάρα without the substantive verb: so P. Buttmann Gr. Gr. ii. 375; Winer-Moulton, p. 96; Lightfoot on Gal. iii. 28, where as in Col. iii. 11 the use is identical. The same force adds indignant irony to St Paul's question in 1 Cor. vi. 5, οὕτως οὐκ ἔνι ἐν ὑμῖν οὐδεὶς σοφὸς ὃς κ.τ.λ.; "is it impossible that there should be among you etc.?", as it adds playful irony to the suggestion in Plato's Phaedo (77 E), μᾶλλον δὲ μὴ ὡς ἡμῶν δεδιότων, ἀλλ᾽ ἴσως ἔνι τις καὶ ἐν ἡμῖν παῖς ὅστις τὰ τοιαῦτα φοβεῖται, "perhaps it is not impossible that even among us etc.": there is no reason to think that ἔνι ever becomes a bare equivalent of ἔστιν.

παραλλαγή, variation] Παραλλάσσω, παράλλαξις, παραλλαγή, are words of wide range, perhaps starting from the notion of alternation or succession attached to the adverb παραλλάξ, but in common use applied to all kinds of variations (different states of a single thing), and then all differences as between one thing and another; not to speak of several derivative senses. The various periodic changes of the heavenly bodies are doubtless chiefly intended here. In the North of Scotland the emperor Severus, says Dion Cassius (lxxvi. 13), τήν τε τοῦ ἡλίου

τροπῆς ἀποσκίασμα.   ¹⁸βουληθεὶς ἀπεκύησεν ἡμᾶς λόγῳ

παράλλαξιν καὶ τὸ τῶν ἡμερῶν, τῶν τε νύκτων καὶ τῶν θερινῶν καὶ τῶν χειμερινῶν μέγεθος ἀκριβέστατα κατεφώρασεν. There is of course no reference to parallax in the modern sense, though it was known (παράλλαξις) to at least the later Greek astronomy. For the doctrine cf. Mal. iii. 6; Ps. cii. 25 ff.

τροπῆς, *change*] Though τροπή often means a solstice and sometimes also an equinox, this sense is excluded by the combination with "shadow," which must be intelligible through obvious phenomena without astronomical lore. Τροπή is a favourite word with Philo, usually coupled with μεταβολή, denoting any change undergone by any object. Some passages approach this verse, as i. 80, "When the mind has sinned and removed itself far from virtue, it lays the blame on things divine (τὰ θεῖα), attributing to God its own change (τροπή)"; i. 82, "How shall a man believe God? If he learn that all other things change (τρέπεται), but He alone is unchangeable (ἄτρεπτος)"; ii. 322, "It is unlawful that he [the high priest, Num. xxxv. 25] should have any defilement whatever attaching to him, either owing to deliberate act or in virtue of a change in the soul without purpose (κατὰ τροπὴν τῆς ψυχῆς ἀβούλητον: cf. βουληθείς in v. 18)."

St James may have had chiefly in view either night and day (cf. Bas. *Hex. Hom.* ii. p. 20 B, καὶ νὺξ σκίασμα γῆς ἀποκρυπτομένου ἡλίου γινόμενον), or the monthly obscurations of the moon, or even the casual vicissitudes of light due to clouds.

ἀποσκίασμα, *shadow*] Either the shadow cast by an object (more commonly σκίασμα, as several times in Plutarch, τὸ σκίασμα τῆς γῆς, the shadow cast by the earth on the moon in an eclipse), or a faint image or copy of an object. On the strength of this second sense some late writers

supposed St James to mean "not a trace (ἴχνος) of change": but usage gives them no support, and shadow no less than change must form part of the primary image. The genitive doubtless expresses "belonging to change," "due to change" ("shadowing by turning," Geneva).

The whole verse may be compared with 1 Jn i. 5 ff.: here temptation to evil, there indifference to evil, is declared impossible for the Perfect Light. But here the name Father introduces an additional conception, illustrated in the next verse.

A few lines may be quoted from a striking Whitsun Day sermon of Andrewes on the present verse (p. 752, ed. 1635). "Yet are there varyings and changes, it cannot be denied; we see them daily. True: but the point is *per quem*, on whom to lay them. Not on God. Seems there any recess? it is we forsake Him, not He us: it is the ship that moves; though they that be in it think the land goes from them, not they from it. Seems there any variation, as that of the night? it is *umbra terrae* makes it: the light makes it not. Is there anything resembling a shadow? a vapour rises from us, makes the cloud, which is as a penthouse between, and takes Him from our sight: that vapour is our lust; there is the *apud quem*. Is any tempted? it is his own lust doth it: that entices him to sin, that brings us to the shadow of death: it is not God; no more than He can be tempted, no more can He tempt any. If we find any change the *apud* is with us, not Him: we change; He is unchanged. Man walks in a vain shadow: His ways are the truth; He cannot deny Himself." [iii. p. 374.]

18. The details of this verse are best approached by asking to whom it refers. Does St James mean by ἡμᾶς "us" men, the recipients of God's word of reason; or "us" sons of Israel (Jew

and Christian not distinguished), the recipients of God's word of revelation generally; or "us" Christians, the recipients of God's word of the Gospel? Several considerations appear to shew decisively that he meant mankind generally. *First*, the natural sense of κτισμάτων: a chosen race or Church would surely have been called a firstfruit of "men" (as Apoc. xiv. 4: cf. Jam. iii. 9), not of God's "creatures"; the force of κτισμάτων is pointed by ἀπεκύησεν ("gave...birth"). *Second*, the connexion with vv. 12—17, which evidently refer to God's dealings with men generally: a statement applicable only to Christians, or Jews and Christians, could not have been affixed to them with such close structure of language, or without at least some word of clear distinction. *Third*, the absence of articles with λόγῳ ἀληθείας: a Jew, much more a Christian, could not fail to call the revelation made to him "the word of [the] truth"; St James never indulges in lax omission of articles; and the sense excludes explanation of the omission by a specially predicative emphasis. *Fourth*, a comparison with v. 21: if, as we shall find, τὸν ἔμφυτον λόγον can mean only "the inborn word," not any word proclaimed from without, there is a strong presumption that the "word of truth" of the earlier verse is the same. This conclusion is free from difficulty except on the assumption that St James could not call an inward voice of God "a word of truth," which will be examined below; and no other words of the verse favour, even in appearance, a more restricted reference.

βουληθείς, *of set purpose*] Βούλομαι and θέλω, though largely coincident in sense, and often capable of being interchanged, never really lose the distinction indicated by Ammonius, *De diff. verb.* p. 31, βούλεσθαι μὲν ἐπὶ μόνου λεκτέον τοῦ λογικοῦ, τὸ δὲ θέλειν καὶ ἐπὶ ἀλόγου ζώου, and again (p. 70), θέλειν καὶ βούλεσθαι ἐὰν

λέγῃ τις, δηλώσει ὅτι ἀκουσίως τε καὶ εὐλόγως ὀρέγεταί τινος (quoted though not accepted by W. Dindorf in Steph. *Thes.*). Θέλω expresses the mere fact of volition or desire, neither affirming nor denying an accompanying mental process: βούλομαι expresses volition as guided by choice and purpose. Hence βουλή, "counsel," agrees exactly in sense with βούλομαι, and the derivative βουλεύομαι differs only by accentuating deliberation of purpose still further: accordingly βουλεύομαι is substituted for βούλομαι in inferior MSS. of Acts, v. 33; xv. 37; 2 Cor. i. 17.

A distinction the inverse of this has been for many years traditional, founded on a part of Buttmann's acute but not quite successful exposition of Homeric usage in the *Lexilogus* (194 ff. E.T.). He observed that θέλω is applied to "a desire of something the execution of which is, or at least appears to be, in one's own power"; while βούλομαι expresses "that kind of willingness or wishing in which the *wish* and the *inclination* toward a thing are either the only thing contained in the expression, or are at least intended to be particularly marked": and he *assumed* purpose or design to be involved in the former kind of desire. But the observation does not sustain the inference. The cases in which we naturally speak simply of volition are just those in which action either follows instantly or is suspended only by another volition of the same agent: while the separation of wish and inclination from fulfilment exactly corresponds with the separation of the mental process leading to a volition from the volition itself, which is not in strictness formed till action becomes possible. This view is in like manner illustrated by two accessory observations. In Homer the gods are said βούλεσθαι, not θέλειν, although their action is unimpeded. Buttmann explains this peculiarity by a respect-

ἀληθείας, εἰς τὸ εἶναι ἡμᾶς ἀπαρχήν τινα τῶν αὐτοῦ
κτισμάτων.

18.   αὐτοῦ] ἑαυτοῦ

ful intention to emphasize "the inclination, the favour, the concession"; but it seems rather due to a feeling that the volitions of gods are always due to some provident counsel (Διὸς δ' ἐτελείετο βουλή). On the other hand the antithesis ἂν οἵ τε θεοὶ θέλωσι καὶ ὑμεῖς βούλησθε (Demosth. *Olynth.* ii. 20, p. 24, cited by Dindorf) probably rests on the contrast between the absoluteness of the Divine volitions and the human need of deliberation before decision. Again the meaning of inclination latent in βούλομαι is often extended so as to include preference or relative inclination: but as a rule preference implies comparison, and comparison belongs to the mental antecedents of volition, not to volition itself.

Βουληθείς, like βουλόμενος, might doubtless mean "of His own will," i.e. spontaneously, without compulsion or suggestion from without: but such a sense is feeble in this context. On the other hand it cannot by itself express graciousness of will, as some have supposed. If we give βούλομαι its proper force, an adequate sense is at once obtained. Man's evil thoughts of God are inconsistent with a true sense of his own nature and destiny, as determined for him from the beginning by God's counsel. Thus the words "that we might be a kind of firstfruits of his creatures" would by themselves shew why St James might place the Divine counsel or purpose in the forefront. But there is much reason for thinking that βουληθείς further refers to the peculiarity of man's creation in the Mosaic narrative, as having been preceded by the deliberative words "Let us make man," etc. It is morally certain that the rest of the verse is a paraphrase of what had been said about the creation in God's image: and if so,

St James, in recalling God's purpose concerning man, might naturally point to the mysterious language of Genesis which seemed to invest man's creation with special glory on this very ground as well as on the other. It is at least certain that the same interpretation was placed on these words of Genesis by several of the Fathers (Philo's explanation is quite different), and that without any apparent dependence on St James. It is probably implied in Tertullian's remarkable fifth chapter *against Praxeas* (e.g. Nam etsi Deus nondum Sermonem suum miserat, proinde eum cum ipsa et in ipsa Ratione intra semetipsum habebat tacite *cogitando et disponendo* secum quae per Sermonem mox erat dicturus ; cum Ratione enim sua *cogitans atque disponens* Sermonem eam efficiebat quam sermone tractabat). The language of others is quite explicit. Macarius Magnes (*Fragm. Hom. in Gen.*, Duchesne *De Macario Magnete*, p. 39): καὶ τὰ μὲν ἄλλα κτίσματα ῥήματι μόνῳ παρῆκται. ὁ δὲ ἄνθρωπος ἔσχεν ἐξαίρετόν τι κατὰ τὴν ποίησιν παρὰ ταῦτα. Βουλῆς γὰρ προηγουμένης ἐκτίσθη, ἵνα ἐκ τούτου δειχθῇ ὅτιπερ κτίσμα τίμιον ὑπάρχει· τὸ γὰρ Ποιήσωμεν ἄνθρωπον κατ᾽ εἰκόνα ἡμετέραν καὶ καθ᾽ ὁμοίωσιν οὐδὲν ἕτερον δείκνυσιν ἢ ὅτι συμβούλῳ ἐχρήσατο ὁ πατὴρ τῷ μονογενεῖ αὐτοῦ τῷ υἱῷ ἐπὶ τῇ τούτου κατασκευῇ κ.τ.λ....βουλῆς γὰρ ἐνέργεια τὸ πᾶν [p. 1397 B—D, Migne].

ἀπεκύησεν ἡμᾶς, *gave us birth*] i.e. at the outset, antecedently to growth. We are His children, made in His likeness. See note on *v.* 15.

λόγῳ ἀληθείας, *by a word of truth*] This phrase is evidently capable of various senses, according to context. In O.T. (Ps. cxix. 43; Prov. xxii. 21 *bis*; Eccl. xii. 10) it is a word of truth uttered by men in the common ethical sense, words of veracity or of faithful steadfastness. In 2 Cor. vi. 7, ἐν λόγῳ ἀληθείας, it means "utterance of truth" in speaking such things as are true and recognised as true; the matter of it having been previously called ὁ λόγος τοῦ θεοῦ (ii. 17; and esp. iv. 2, τῇ φανερώσει τ. ἀληθείας). This message of truth as a whole is called ὁ λόγος τῆς ἀληθείας Eph. i. 13; 2 Tim. ii. 15. In this last sense St James is understood by those who assume him to refer here directly to the Gospel. As seen above, this agrees neither with the absence of articles nor with the context. We must at least see whether the words cannot naturally bear a meaning which connects them with the original creation of man.

It is at first sight tempting to have recourse to the Jewish conception of the Creation as accomplished by ten Words of God ("And God said"). So *Aboth* v. 1, "By ten Sayings the world was created," and reff. in Taylor; Aristob. *ap.* Euseb. *Pr. Ev.* xiii. p. 664 says that "Moses has spoken of the whole creation (γένεσιν) of the world as θεοῦ λόγους." In this case λόγ. ἀλ. would be the actual words described as spoken. But it is not easy to see how they could be called λόγ. ἀλ., and moreover this sense, while it would suit well with ἔκτισεν or ἐποίησεν, does not harmonise with ἀπεκύησεν.

We must therefore seek the explanation rather in the distinctive feature of man's creation in Gen. ii. 7, the special imbreathing from God Himself, by which man became, in a higher sense than the animals, "a living soul." But how was this a word, a word of truth? The answer is given by looking back from the word of truth in the special Christian sense. St Peter (i. 23) speaks of Christians as ἀναγεγεννημένοι not by (ἐκ) a corruptible seed but an incorruptible, διὰ λόγου ζῶντος θεοῦ καὶ μένοντος: he goes on to quote Is. xl. 6—8 on the abidingness of the word of the Lord, and adds that this ῥῆμα

is τὸ εὐαγγελισθὲν εἰς ὑμᾶς: in other words, the essence of the Gospel was an utterance (ῥῆμα) of God's Word or speech to mankind. Here the abiding word of God stands to the new birth, or renewal, in the same position as λόγ. ἀλ. in St James to the original Divine birth, and the word is called a seed. This large view of God's revelation is, next, what we find in e.g. Ps. cxix., where the spiritual conception of God's law, which pervades the psalm (and of which we shall find much in St James), is exchanged occasionally for a similar conception of His "word" or utterance (*v.* 142 compared with 160), the word which abideth for ever in heaven. And now thirdly St James looks back beyond the Law to the original implanting of a Divine seed in man by God. By this Divine spark or seed God speaks to man, and speaks truth. This is the conception of Eph. iv. 24, τὸν κατὰ θεὸν κτισθέντα...τῆς ἀληθείας, and Col. iii. 10, εἰς ἐπίγνωσιν κατ' εἰκόνα τοῦ κτίσαντος αὐτόν. And so Aug. *De Gen. ad lit.* iii. 30 enquiring wherein consists the image of God says "Id autem est ipsa ratio vel mens vel intelligentia, vel si quo alio vocabulo commodius appellatur. Unde et Apostolus dicit, Renovamini etc."; and again (32) "Sicut enim post lapsum peccati homo in agnitione Dei renovatur secundum imaginem ejus qui creavit eum, ita *in ipsa agnitione creatus est*, ante quam delicto veterasceret, unde rursum in eadem agnitione renovaretur." Here the human *agnitio* is correlative to the Divine λόγος. Philo (*De opif.* 28, p. 20) says γεννήσας αὐτὸν (Adam) ὁ πατὴρ ἡγεμονικὸν φύσει ζῶον οὐκ ἔργῳ μόνον ἀλλὰ καὶ τῇ διὰ λόγου χειροτονίᾳ καθίστησι τῶν ὑπὸ σελήνην ἁπάντων βασιλέα. Thus the distinctly perceived word of truth of the Gospel enables St James to look back to the creation, and regard that too not only as a Divine birth, but as a Divine birth in virtue of a Divine seed which

¹⁹"Ἴστε, ἀδελφοί μου ἀγαπητοί. ἔστω δὲ πᾶς ἄνθρωπος ταχὺς εἰς τὸ ἀκοῦσαι, βραδὺς εἰς τὸ λαλῆσαι,

was also a Word of truth, the means by which all other words of truth were to enter man. [See on 1 Pet. *l.c.*]

εἰς τὸ, *in order that*] It is needless here to consider the debated question whether εἰς τὸ with infinitive following a verb denotes always purpose, or sometimes only result ("so that"). Here Divine purpose is clearly meant (cf. iii. 3): the relation of man to the world is part of God's plan, and cannot indeed be separated from His purpose respecting man himself.

ἀπαρχήν τινα τῶν αὐτοῦ (v. ἑαυτοῦ) κτισμάτων, *a kind of firstfruits of his creatures*] Here again the phrase has force at all three stages of revelation. It is manifestly true of Christians (cf. Rom. xi. 16): true also of Israel, as Jer. ii. 3 ἅγιος Ἰσραὴλ τῷ κυρίῳ, ἀρχὴ (וְרֵאשִׁית) γενημάτων αὐτοῦ; and again Philo *de const. princ.* 6 (ii. 366) τὸ σύμπαν Ἰουδαίων ἔθνος... τοῦ σύμπαντος ἀνθρώπων γένους ἀπενεμήθη οἷά τις ἀπαρχὴ τῷ ποιητῇ καὶ πατρί; and lastly of the human race (cf. Rom. viii.)

κτισμάτων] Wisdom ix. 2, καὶ τῇ σοφίᾳ σου κατεσκεύασας [κατασκευάσας] ἄνθρωπον ἵνα δεσπόζῃ τῶν ὑπὸ σοῦ γενομένων κτισμάτων. Amb. *Hex.* vi. 75, Sed jam finis sermoni nostro sit, quoniam completus est dies sextus et mundani operis summa conclusa est, perfecto videlicet homine in quo principatus est animantium universorum, et summa quaedam universitatis, et omnis mundanae gratia creaturae.... Fecerat enim hominem, rationis capacem, imitatorem sui, virtutum aemulatorem, cupidum caelestium gratiarum.

19. Ἴστε and ἔστω δέ] So read for Ὥστε and ἔστω without δέ, which is Syrian only, the connexion between the clauses not being perceived.

Ἴστε may be either indicative or imperative. But St James (iv. 4) has

the other form οἴδατε in indicative; and probably used this shorter and sharper form for distinction, to mark the imperative; this being also the best sense. The N.T. writers commonly use οἴδατε; but ἴστε occurs in two other places (Eph. v. 5; Heb. xii. 17), both of which gain by being taken imperatively, the former in particular.

Here St James repeats positively what he has said negatively in *v.* 16. In *vv.* 13—15 he was combating error; and then he finally says Μὴ πλανᾶσθε as introductory to his fundamental doctrine of 17, 18. That doctrine being now set forth, he a second time calls attention to it on the positive side, as the basis of what he is going to say. "Know it well, my beloved brethren (the old address repeated). And on the other hand" (δέ, with tacit reference to the acquiescence in evil hinted at in *v.* 13).

πᾶς ἄνθρωπος] There is force in ἄνθρωπος with reference to *v.* 18. The expression is not equivalent to πᾶς, but everyone of the human race, that race which is God's offspring and endowed by Him with a portion of His own light.

ταχὺς εἰς τὸ ἀκοῦσαι] There are two grounds for this admonition: (1) suggested by λόγῳ ἀληθείας (see *v.* 21); (2) the love of violent and disputatious speech was to be a special object of attack in the Epistle (*c.* iii.). The admonition itself is common enough among moralists (Greek exx. in Wetstein, Theile, etc.), and especially in Ecclus. as v. 11—13; iv. 29 (reading ταχὺς with אⁿ*, not τραχύς); xx. 5 ff. etc., and indeed in O.T. (Prov. xiii. 3 etc.). But in this connexion the sense must be more special, as also *v.* 20 shews; and the reference must be to speaking in God's name or on God's behalf. What is desired is a quick and attentive ear to catch

βραδὺς εἰς ὀργήν, ²⁰ὀργὴ γὰρ ἀνδρὸς δικαιοσύνην θεοῦ
οὐκ ἐργάζεται. ²¹διὸ ἀποθέμενοι πᾶσαν ῥυπαρίαν καὶ
περισσείαν κακίας ἐν πραΰτητι δέξασθε τὸν ἔμφυτον

what God has spoken or is speaking,
to be alive to any λόγος ἀληθείας of
His, rather than to be eager to dictate
to others about His truth and will
in a spirit of self-confidence and
arrogance.

Then he goes on in a secondary
way to βραδὺς εἰς ὀργήν, because this
arrogance of magisterial speech was
closely mixed up with violence of
speech, zeal for God being made a
cloak for personal animosities.

20. ὀργὴ γὰρ ἀνδρός, *for a man's
wrath*] Not "the wrath of man."
It is not exactly the broad distinction
of human as against Divine wrath,
which would require ἀνθρώπου or τῶν
ἀνθρώπων; but a single man's anger,
the petty passion of an individual
soul (cf. τ. ἰδίας ἐπιθυμίας, v. 14).
Contrast Rom. xii. 19, τῇ ὀργῇ, the
one central universal anger, which is
only a particular form of the universal
righteousness.

δικαιοσύνην θεοῦ οὐκ ἐργάζεται, *worketh no righteousness of God*] Not
"the righteousness of God," but no
righteousness which is a true part
and vindication of God's righteousness. The late text has οὐ κατεργάζεται
by a natural correction: this would
more distinctly express result. Result
is of course included in ἐργάζεται, but
the main point is that a man's anger
is not a *putting in force*, a *giving
operation to*, any true righteousness
of God, as it professed to be.

21. διό clearly marks the connexion of the verses, shewing that
19 f. must be so understood as to
prepare for δέξασθε and the accompanying words.

ῥυπαρίαν καὶ περισσείαν, *defilement
and excrescence*] These illustrate
each other, being cognate though not
identical images. περισσεία is by no

means to be confounded with the
semi-medical περίσσωμα, as it were
the refuse of the body. The proper
or usual sense of περισσεία is simply
abundance, superfluity; usually in a
good sense as overflow; sometimes in
a bad sense, as beyond measure.

The special image here is evidently
rank and excessive growth. So Philo
interprets περιτέμνεσθε τ. σκληροκαρ-
δίας as τ.περιττὰς φύσεις τοῦ ἡγεμονικοῦ
which are sown and increased by the
unmeasured impulses of the passions
(*De vict. offer.* ii. 258); also βλασται
περιτταί...τ. βλαβερὰν ἐπίφυσιν (*De
somn.* i. 667); and other passages have
the idea without the word. For the
contrast to the original proper growth
see Ps.-Just. *De Monarch.* i.: τῆς
ἀνθρωπίνης φύσεως τὸ κατ' ἀρχὴν συζυ-
γίαν συνέσεως καὶ σωτηρίας λαβούσης
εἰς ἐπίγνωσιν ἀληθείας θρησκείας τε τῆς
εἰς τὸν ἕνα καὶ πάντων δεσπότην, παρ-
εισδῦσα εἰς εἰδωλοποιίας ἐξέτρεψε
βασκανία τὸ ὑπερβάλλον τῆς τῶν ἀνθρώπων μεγαλειότητος, καὶ πολλῷ χρόνῳ
μεῖναν τὸ περισσὸν ἔθος ὡς οἰκείαν
καὶ ἀληθῆ τὴν πλάνην τοῖς πολλοῖς
παραδίδωσι.

Whether St James has trees particularly in view may be doubted, but he
probably means simply "excrescence."
The violent speech was not, as it was
supposed to be, a sign of healthy life:
it was a mere defilement and excrescence on a man considered in his
true character as made in God's
image.

κακίας, *malice*] It might be quite
general, "evil"; but it seems here to
have the proper sense of "malice":
what was called "holy anger" was
nothing better than spite.

πραΰτητι, *meekness*] The word is
contrasted with κακίας: the temper
full of harshness and pride towards

men destroyed the faculty of perceiving whatever God spoke.

τὸν ἔμφυτον λόγον, *the inborn word*] A simple phrase, made difficult by the context. Heisen has 120 pages on it. Its proper meaning is "inborn," or rather "ingrown," "congenital," "natural" (often coupled with φυσικός). It is used in opposition (Heisen 671) to διδακτός, ἐπικτήτος, ἐπείσακτος, etc. This agrees with the derivation. Φύω or φύομαι is to grow, or causatively, to make to grow, as of a living being putting forth fresh growings (growing teeth, beard, etc.), or a higher being creating that which grows, or a parent producing offspring. So ἐμφύομαι almost always is to be inborn in, to grow as part of. Where the causative use occurs (with one peculiar figurative exception Ael. *N. A.* xiv. 8 of eels fixing their teeth in a bait), it is always said of a higher power (God, nature, fate) who causes some power or impulse to grow up in a man or other living being from birth. Occasionally there is a secondary ingrowth, a "second nature," as we say; and both verb and adjective have this sense too. Thus Clem. *Str.* vi. 799, λαμβάνει τοίνυν τροφὴν μὲν πλείονα ἡ ἐγκεντρισθεῖσα ἐλαία διὰ τὸ ἀγρίᾳ ἐμφύεσθαι, i.e. "grows into" a wild olive, not "is grafted into," which would be mere tautology after ἐγκεντρισθεῖσα. Also ἔμφυτος Herod. ix. 94 of Evenius, καὶ μετὰ ταῦτα αὐτίκα ἔμφυτον μαντικὴν εἶχεν, i.e. he had a Divine gift of prophecy, not as a receiver of prophecies, but as the possessor of a power within himself. Such passages as these are useless for shewing that the word can mean implanted. So also passages in which God's bestowal of the gift is spoken of in the context. Thus Ps.-Ign. *Eph.* 17, διὰ τί λογικοὶ ὄντες οὐ γίνόμεθα φρονιμοί; διὰ τί ἔμφυτον τὸ περὶ θεοῦ παρὰ χριστοῦ λαβόντες κριτήριον εἰς ἀγνοίαν καταπίπτομεν, ἐξ ἀμελείας ἀγνοοῦντες τὸ χάρισμα ὃ εἰλήφαμεν ἀνοήτως ἀπολλύμεθα; Similarly Barn.

ix. 9, οἶδεν ὁ τὴν ἔμφυτον δωρεὰν τῆς διδαχῆς αὐτοῦ θέμενος ἐν ἡμῖν: where τ. διδαχῆς cannot be doctrine or revelation imparted to us, but an inward Divine teaching to interpret allegory, as is shewn by the parallel vi. 10, εὐλογητὸς ὁ κύριος ἡμῶν, ἀδελφοί, ὁ σοφίαν καὶ νοῦν θέμενος ἐν ἡμῖν τ. κρυφίων αὐτοῦ: and still more the corrupt passage i. 2, οὕτως (or, οὗ τὸ) ἔμφυτον δωρεᾶς πνευματικῆς χάριν εἰλήφατε (<τῆς before δωρ. C).

It is therefore impossible to take τ. ἔμφυτον λόγον as the outward message of the Gospel. He could never have used in that sense a word which every one who knew Greek would of necessity understand in the opposite sense. It may be that the idea of reception (δέξασθε) is transferred from the external word : but in any case it has an intelligible meaning. The word is there, always sounding there; but it may be nevertheless received or rejected. This notion of the reception of a word already within is like κτήσεσθε τὰς ψυχάς (Lk. xxi. 19), or κτᾶσθαι τὸ σκεῦος (1 Th. iv. 4). There is special force in ἔμφυτον contrasted with ῥυπαρίαν καὶ περισσ. : these are unnatural, accidental ; the voice of the word within is original and goes back to creation. This sense (Schulthess and as against the wrong sense Heinsius *in loc.*) has ancient authority. Oecum. (? e Did. Al.) τὸν ἔμφυτον λόγον καλεῖ τὸν διακριτικὸν τοῦ βελτίονος καὶ τοῦ χείρονος, καθ᾽ ὃ καὶ λογικοὶ ἐσμὲν καὶ καλούμεθα. Cf. Athan. *Or. c. Gent.* 34, ἐπιστρέψαι δὲ δύνανται ἐὰν ὃν ἐνεδύσαντο ῥύπον πάσης ἐπιθυμίας ἀπόθωνται καὶ τοσοῦτον ἀπονίψωνται ἕως ἂν ἀπόθωνται πᾶν τὸ συμβεβηκὸς ἀλλότριον τῇ ψυχῇ, καὶ μόνην αὐτὴν ὥσπερ γέγονεν ἀποδείξωσιν, ἵν᾽ οὕτως ἐν αὐτῇ θεωρῆσαι τὸν τοῦ πατρὸς λόγον, καθ᾽ ὃν καὶ γεγόνασιν ἐξ ἀρχῆς δυνηθῶσιν. κατ᾽ εἰκόνα γὰρ θεοῦ πεποίηται καὶ καθ᾽ ὁμοίωσιν γέγονεν...ὅθεν καὶ ὅτε πάντα τὸν ἐπιχυθέντα ῥύπον τῆς ἁμαρτίας ἀφ᾽ ἑαυτῆς ἀποτίθεται, καὶ μόνον τὸ κατ᾽

λόγον τὸν δυνάμενον σῶσαι τὰς ψυχὰς ὑμῶν. ²²Γίνεσθε
δὲ ποιηταὶ λόγου καὶ μὴ ἀκροαταὶ μόνον παραλογιζό-

εἰκόνα καθαρὸν φυλάττει, εἰκότως δια-
λαμπρυνθέντος τούτου ὡς ἐν κατόπτρῳ
θεωρεῖ τὴν εἰκόνα τοῦ πατρὸς τὸν λόγον,
καὶ ἐν αὐτῷ τὸν πάτερα, οὗ καί ἐστιν
εἰκὼν ὁ σωτήρ, λογίζεται κ.τ.λ. See
also 33 fin., διὰ τοῦτο γοῦν καὶ τῆς περὶ
θεοῦ θεωρίας ἔχει τὴν ἔννοιαν, καὶ αὐτὴ
ἑαυτῆς γίνεται ὁδός, οὐκ ἔξωθεν, ἀλλ' ἐξ
ἑαυτῆς λαμβάνουσα τὴν τοῦ θεοῦ λόγου
γνῶσιν καὶ κατάληψιν. Also *Vit. Anton.*
20 (812 AB).

τὸν δυνάμενον σῶσαι τὰς ψυχὰς
ὑμῶν] The simplest sense is right.
The contrast is between life and death,
the "soul" being the living principle;
as Mt. xvi. 25 etc., but esp. Lk. vi. 9.
[See note on 1 Peter i. 9.]
This life-giving power as ascribed
to the inborn word becomes intelligible if we consider it as differing at
different ages of the world according
to the stages of experience and of
revelation. It is always the *testi-
monium animae naturaliter Chris-
tianae* (cf. Rom. i. 19 ff.), but the
testimony becomes enlightened and
enriched as time goes by. To
Christians the inborn word speaks
with the increased force and range
derived from the Gospel: but what
St James is referring to here is not
the original reception of the Gospel
as a word from without, but the renewed reception of the word within
whatever its message may be: it is
the original capacity involved in the
Creation in God's image which makes
it possible for man to apprehend a
revelation at all. Cf. also Deut. xxx.
14 and St Paul's comment on it in
Rom. x. 6 ff.
22. Thus far we have had the
relation of hearing to speaking, and
hearing has been commended before
speaking. But the formalistic spirit
of the Jewish Christians could give
this too a wrong turn, as though
hearing were all that were needed.

There remained another antithesis,
hearing and doing, and to this
St James turns by way of precaution.

γίνεσθε, *shew yourselves*] i. e. in
hearing, to prove that you hear
rightly.

ποιηταί, *doers*] Cf. Rom. ii. 13;
and Jam. himself *vv.* 23, 25; iv. 11.
So with τ. νόμου 1 Macc. ii. 67. It is
founded on our Lord's sayings Mt. vii.
24 etc., the close of the Sermon on
the Mount, just as τέλειοι in *v.* 4 expresses the close of its first chapter
(v. 48) on the Old and New Law.

ποιηταὶ λόγου] Not the Word
whether external or internal, but any
word that has authority. It is almost
adjectival, "word-doers," as we say
"law-abiding," "law-breakers."

ἀκροαταί] used in N.T. only in the
same passages, Rom. ii. 13 and Jam. i.
23, 25. It expresses listening, but is
specially used of the disciples or
hearers of philosophers; and probably
also in Judea, where the attendance
on the rabbinical schools was strongly
inculcated.

Cf. R. Shimeon son of Gamaliel in
Aboth i. 18, "All my days I have
grown up amongst the wise, and have
not found aught good for a man but
silence: not *learning but doing* is the
groundwork, and whoso multiplies
words occasions sin." So also v. 20,
"There are four characters in college-
goers. He that goes and does not
practise, the reward of going is in
his hand. He that practises and does
not go, the reward of practice is in
his hand. He that goes and practises
is pious. He that goes not and
does not practise is wicked." And
again v. 18, "There are four characters in scholars. Quick to hear
and quick to forget, his gain is cancelled by his loss. Slow to hear and
slow to forget, his loss is cancelled by
his gain. Quick to hear and slow to

μένοι ἑαυτούς. ²³ὅτι εἴ τις ἀκροατὴς λόγου ἐστὶν καὶ
οὐ ποιητής, οὗτος ἔοικεν ἀνδρὶ κατανοοῦντι τὸ πρόσωπον
τῆς γενέσεως αὐτοῦ ἐν ἐσόπτρῳ, ²⁴κατενόησεν γὰρ

forget is wise. Slow to hear and quick
to forget; this is an evil lot." But
St James uses the common language
in a wider sense.

παραλογιζόμενοι] The word occurs
Col. ii. 4, where the context rather
suggests "delude by false reasoning."
But it is very doubtful whether the
word has that force. It has two chief
meanings, not to be confused, from
two meanings of λογίζομαι, to mis-
reckon, cheat in reckoning, and so
cheat in any way; and to misinfer,
draw a wrong conclusion from the
premises, but without implication of
evil intent. It is used several times
in LXX. for simple beguiling, though by
words. Lightfoot refers to Dan. xiv.
[Bel and D.] 7. Cf. Ps. Salom. iv. 12,
14 (παρελογίσατο ἐν λόγοις ὅτι οὐκ
ἔστιν ὁρῶν καὶ κρίνων), 25.

23. κατανοοῦντι, taking note of]
Not merely to see passively, but to
perceive : as Plato (Soph. 233 A) οὐ
γάρ πω κατανοῶ τὸ νῦν ἐρωτώμενον,
"I do not catch the question." Cf.
Mt. vii. 3; Acts vii. 31, etc.

τὸ πρόσωπον τῆς γενέσεως αὐτοῦ, the
face of his creation] Not altogether
easy. The phrase must be taken with
τ. τροχὸν τ. γενέσεως (iii. 6), but I
speak only of the simpler case here
presented. Here it is often understood as "his natural face" (A.V.),
lit. the face of his birth, with which
he was born, i.e. his bodily face. But
if such a meaning were intended, no
such circuitous and obscure phrase
would have been used ; τ. πρόσωπον
αὐτοῦ would have been enough, no
other face being mentioned. Also the
image so presented has no force: if it
is merely a case of hasty looking or
intent looking, all that is said in v. 24
is otiose.

The γένεσις is his birth strictly, in

antithesis to later degeneracy; but
the face is the invisible face, the re-
flexion of God's image in humanity.
St James is still consistently referring
to Gen. i. The face which a man
beholds when he receives the Divine
word is the representation of what
God made him to be, though now
defaced by his own wrong doings.
So Eustathius in Od. xix. 178, καὶ
οὕτω μὲν ἡ Πηνελόπη ὀκνεῖ διορθοῦσθαι
τὴν φύσιν, καὶ περιττοτέρα φαίνεσθαι
αὐτῆς, καὶ τ. εἰκόνα τοῦ ἐκ γενέσεως
προσώπου διαγράφειν εἴτε μεταγράφειν,
where the contrast is between Pe-
nelope's natural face and its disfigure-
ment by artificial cosmetics.

There is special fitness in the word
because it is used in LXX. for תּוֹלְדוֹת
and מוֹלֶדֶת, and has thus (from Gen.
ii. 4; v. 1) given Genesis its Greek
name. In itself the word is neuter in
force, and in Greek philosophy it
rather represents natural processes as
governed by necessity, not by Divine
will. But to a Christian Jew the only
γένεσις could be that of the Penta-
teuch, Psalms and Prophets, the
beginnings of things as coming from
the hand of God ; so that it virtually
carries with it the association of our
word "creation"; and it is to be observed that κτίσις, though found in
Apocr. for "creation," is never so
used in LXX. proper, though κτίζω (as
well as ποιέω) is; there being no
Hebrew substantive meaning "creation." Cf. 2 Macc. vii. 23, ὁ τ. κόσμου
Κτίστης, ὁ πλάσας ἀνθρώπου γένεσιν
καὶ πάντων ἐξευρὼν γένεσιν.

24. κατενόησεν, he takes note of]
The verb as before: he sees himself
and knows that it is himself that he
sees, the new man κατὰ θεὸν κτισθέντα.
The aorist denotes the instantaneous

ἑαυτὸν καὶ ἀπελήλυθεν καὶ εὐθέως ἐπελάθετο ὁποῖος ἦν.
²⁵ ὁ δὲ παρακύψας εἰς νόμον τέλειον τὸν τῆς ἐλευθερίας

and quickly passing character of the
seeing.

ἀπελήλυθεν, *is gone away*] He went
away and remains away : a contrast to
παραμείνας. It was a passing glance,
not taken up into his life, but re-
linquished.

εὐθέως ἐπελάθετο, *straightway forgetteth*] Again the aorist because
the forgetting was a single and immediate act.

ὁποῖος ἦν, *what manner of man he
was*] I.e. his original image antecedent to change and becoming. Cf.
Apoc. iv. 11, διὰ τὸ θέλημά σου ἦσαν
(not εἰσίν) καὶ ἐκτίσθησαν, where ἦσαν
perhaps expresses the Divine idea,
realised visibly in κτίσις.
On the whole thought of the verse
cf. Origen *Hom. in Gen.* i. § 13,
"Semper ergo intueamur istam imaginem Dei, ut possimus ad ejus similitudinem reformari. Si enim ad
imaginem Dei factus homo, contra
naturam intuens imaginem diaboli,
per peccatum similis ejus effectus est;
multo magis intuens imaginem Dei,
ad cujus similitudinem factus est a
Deo, per verbum et virtutem ejus
recipiet formam illam quae data ei
fuerat per naturam." Also Athan.
(*Or. cont. Gent.* ii. p. 3) speaks of man
as having nothing to hinder him from
attaining to the knowledge concerning the Divinity, for by his own purity
(καθαρότητος) he always contemplates
the image of the Father, the God-
Word, in whose image also he is made,
...ἱκανὴ δὲ ἡ τ. ψυχῆς καθαρότης ἐστὶ
τὸν θεὸν δι' ἑαυτῆς κατοπτρίζεσθαι, as
the Lord also says, Blessed are the
pure, etc." See also the passage cited
above on *v.* 21.
So also virtually (though confusedly)
Oecum., but supposing the word to be
the Mosaic Law (διὰ τ. νόμον μανθά-
νοντες οἱοὶ γεγόναμεν) and again speaking of a spiritual (νοητόν) mirror.

25. παρακύψας, *looketh into*] The
notion of a steady gaze has been im-
ported into the word from the context,
and prematurely. It seems never to
have any such meaning. Κύπτω and
all its compounds express literally
some kind of stretching or straining
of the body, as up, down, or forward.
Παρακύπτω is the stretching forward
the head to catch a glimpse, as
especially through a window or door,
sometimes inwards, oftener outwards.
When used figuratively, as here, it
seems always to imply a rapid, hasty,
and cursory glance. So Luc. *Pisc.* 30,
κἄπειδὴ μόνον παρέκυψα εἰς τὰ
ὑμέτερα, the speaker says to the philosophers : "As soon as ever I had
merely looked into your world, I
began to admire you, etc."; Bas. *Ep.*
lxxi. § 1, εἰ δὲ ὁ δεῖνα ἄρτι παρακύψαι φιλοτιμούμενος πρὸς τ. βίον τ.
Χριστιανῶν : "If so and so making it
his ambition just now to cast a glance
at the life of Christians, and then
thinking that his sojourn with us
confers on him some dignity, invents
what he has not heard, and expounds
what he has not understood": where
all turns on the slightness and super-
ficiality of the acquaintance ; Philo,
Leg. ad Gai. 8, p. 554, ποῦ γὰρ τοῖς
ἰδιώταις πρὸ μικροῦ θέμις εἰς ἡγεμονικῆς
(imperial) ψυχῆς παρακύψαι βουλεύ-
ματα; Ach. Tat. ii. 35 [cf. Jacobs,
p. 593] of beauty that παρακύψαν
μόνον οἴχεται; D. Cass. lxii. 3, Boadicea
of the Romans, ἐξ οὗπερ ἐς τὴν
Βρετανίαν οὗτοι παρέκυψαν, "from the
time that these men put their heads
into Britain"; lxvi. 17, of emperors
who partly reigned together, each of
them believed himself to be emperor
ἀφ' οὗ γε καὶ ἐς τοῦτο παρέκυψεν, "from
the time that he put his head into
this," i.e. began at all to reign (lii. 10
is not quite so clear); Demosth. *Phil.*
i. 24 (p. 46 fin.) auxiliary troops παρα-

καὶ παραμείνας, οὐκ ἀκροατὴς ἐπιλησμονῆς γενόμενος

κύψαντα ἐπὶ τὸν τ. πόλεως πόλεμον, πρὸς ᾿Αρτάβαζον καὶ πανταχοῖ μᾶλλον οἴχεται πλέοντα: they just shew themselves for the war, and then sail off. St James could not have used such a word to contain within itself steady looking, and it must therefore have a meaning analogous to Lk. ix. 62, putting hand to the plough, the stress being on παραμείνας. It answers to κατενόησεν ἑαυτόν. [See on 1 Pet. i. 12.] νόμον τέλειον τὸν τῆς ἐλευθερίας, a perfect law, even that of liberty] Here the word has become a law, but a perfect law, just as they are interchanged in Ps. cxix. The starting point is language such as we find in that Psalm, also Ps. xix. 7: but Christ's word in the Sermon on the Mount (Mt. v. 48), itself founded on Deut. xviii. 13, is the main source, that being the sum and climax of Mt. v., the subject of the new or rather subjacent Law. (On the recognition of the heathen as having a law and covenant see Isa. xxiv. 5 and Delitzsch and Cheyne.) Thus St James refers at once to the Gospel and to what was before the Law (cf. Rom. ii. 14 as to the heathen): his "perfect Law" unites both. It is perfect, as expounded by our Lord, because it deals not with single acts but with universal principles.

τὸν τῆς ἐλευθερίας] In what sense? Irenaeus thinks of free-will: but that is not in the context. In LXX. ἐλευθερία is never used in any such figurative or ethical sense. The nearest approach in sense is in Ps. cxix. 32, 44 f., 96 (בחב, רחב, "broad," πλατύνω, πλατυσμός, πλατεία), where the reception of God's law is represented as giving spacious room in which to walk, removing the narrowing bondage of petty personal desires (cf. Wordsworth's Ode to Duty). The idea of the Law as a source of freedom was not strange to the later

Jews: so Aboth iii. 8 (R. Nechoniah Ben Ha-Kanah), "Whoso receives upon him the yoke of Thorah, they remove from him the yoke of royalty and the yoke of worldly care," etc. (p. 60); also Perek R. Meir (=Aboth vi.) 2 (R. Joshua Ben Levi), "It (the Bath Kol) saith, And the tables were the work of God, and the writing was the writing of God, graven upon the tables (Ex. xxxii. 16); read not charuth 'graven' but cheruth 'freedom,' for thou wilt find no freeman but him who is occupied in learning of Thorah" (p. 114, with Taylor's note); and also Philo, Q. omn. prob. lib. 7 (ii. 452), ὅσοι δὲ μετὰ νόμου ζῶσιν ἐλεύθεροι: but he has also the Stoic language about the freedom of the wise man: cf. Sacr. Ab. et Cain, 37 (i. 188). But St James seems to mean more than ethical result; rather the character of the law, as positive not negative ("Thou shalt love...") and depending on expansive outflow, not on restraint and negation.

καὶ παραμείνας, and there continueth] The first meaning is to "stay where one is": then to "stay with a person loyally": also absolutely to "persevere," esp. in contrast to others who fall away. Diod. Sic. (ii. 29), contrasting the Greeks with the Chaldaeans and their hereditary lore says: παρὰ δὲ τοῖς ῞Ελλησιν ὁ πολὺς ἀπαράσκευος προσιὼν ὀψέ ποτε τῆς φιλοσοφίας ἅπτεται, καὶ μέχρι τινὸς φιλοπονήσας ἀπῆλθε, περισπασθεὶς ὑπὸ βιωτικῆς χρείας, ὀλίγοι δὲ παντελῶς ἐπὶ φιλοσοφίαν ἀποδύντες ἐργολαβίας ἕνεκεν παραμένουσιν ἐν τῷ μαθήματι. The idea then probably is "perseveres in" the law, not perseveres looking at it, nor abides beside it. So Ps. i. 2, καὶ ἐν τ. νόμῳ αὐτοῦ μελετήσει ἡμέρας καὶ νυκτός.

γενόμενος, shewing himself] As γίνεσθε in v. 22.

ἀκροατὴς ἐπιλησμονῆς...ποιητὴς ἔργου,

ἀλλὰ ποιητὴς ἔργου, οὗτος μακάριος ἐν τῇ ποιήσει
αὐτοῦ ἔσται. ²⁶Εἴ τις δοκεῖ θρησκὸς εἶναι μὴ χαλινα-

a hearer that forgetteth...a doer that worketh] The first genitive *must* be adjectival: not exactly an adjective "a forgetful hearer," but a hearer in contrast to a doer, and so characterised by forgetting. This sense of a characteristic, or even something stronger, is always to be traced in these Hebraistic genitives in Greek. In like manner ἔργου is quasi adjectival, and so without the article: with the article it would have to be in the plural.

μακάριος] not εὐλογητός. "Happy" in the sense "to be envied." He may have delight in it or he may not : the state itself is good and desirable : if he is in a right mind, he cannot but delight in it. This μακάριος hardly goes back to the Sermon on the Mount (it comes nearer Jn xiii. 17): rather it is to be referred, if any whither, to the Psalms, not least to Ps. i.

ἐν τῇ ποιήσει, *in his doing*] Not διὰ τὴν π. Not a reward, but a life. His action is the action that is right and therefore μακαρία. It refers back to ποιητής.

26. δοκεῖ, *seemeth*] Sc. to himself, as often.

θρησκός, *religious*] An interesting but extremely rare word. Not known except here and in Lexicographers ; Latt. *religiosus*. The derivation is probably directly from τρέω, and it seems to mean one who stands in awe of the gods, and is tremulously scrupulous in what regards them. The actual renderings in Lexx. are strange: Hesych. ἑτερόδοξος, εὐγενής (?) ; *Et. Mag.* and Suid. ἑτερόδοξος ; *Et. Gud.* ὁ ἑτερόδοξος, αἱρετικός. Oecum. (Did.), having previously said that θρησκεία denotes something more than faith, a knowledge of secret things (κρυφίων), interprets θρησκός as "one who knows and exactly keeps the things hidden

(ἀπορρήτων) in the Law." We get more help from other glosses in Hesych. θρέξατο ἐφυλάξατο, ἐσεβάσθη ; θρεσκή ἁγνή, πάντα εὐλαβουμένη ; θρεσκός περιττός, δεισιδαίμων. None can come from this passage : so that they attest other lost passages, all having the idea of cautious observance of religious restrictions, sometimes spoken of with praise, sometimes with blame. This exactly answers to the proper meaning of *religiosus*, as of *religio* which is properly the gathering up of oneself in awe, and consequent scrupulousness. It thus belongs to an early stage of what we now call religion, containing indeed elements which are and must be permanent, but still as a whole narrow and immature, not including faith in God or love of God. Now this was just the spirit of much of the later Judaism, notwithstanding its opposition to the spirit of the prophets and of much else in the O.T., and it was apparently getting the better of the Jewish Christians. Men prided themselves on a special religiousness because (as in the Gospels) they made clean the outside of the cup and of the platter and tithed mint and cummin. Thus the word, though not here used in an evil sense, is used probably in a limited sense, in the sense which these persons would use for themselves. θρησκός would be the word which they would choose to express their ideal man.

These two concluding verses of c. i. bring together the two points of Christian conduct, which he has been dwelling on since *v.* 19. From 19 to 21 he taught slowness to speak and so here he teaches the bridling of the tongue. From 22 to 25 he taught doing as against barren hearing : and so here and in *v.* 27 he gives illustrations of rightful doing.

γωγῶν γλῶσσαν ἑαυτοῦ ἀλλὰ ἀπατῶν καρδίαν ἑαυτοῦ,
τούτου μάταιος ἡ θρησκεία. ²⁷θρησκεία καθαρὰ καὶ

26. ἑαυτοῦ bis] αὐτοῦ

χαλιναγωγῶν γλῶσσαν ἑαυτοῦ, *bridling his tongue*] A very common
figure, worked out more fully in iii. 2 ff.

ἀπατῶν καρδίαν ἑαυτοῦ, *deceiving his
heart*] This answers to παραλογιζό-
μενοι ἑαυτούς in *v.* 22. He again, as in
20, implies that the unbridledness of
tongue aimed at was one which was
defended as the speech of uncom-
promising zeal.

μάταιος, *vain, to no purpose*] At
once unreal in itself and ineffectual.
Cf. ματαία ἡ πίστις ὑμῶν (1 Cor. xv. 17).
It is much used in the O.T. for the
futility of idols and idolatry (and
hence in N.T., Acts xiv. 15 ; cf. 1 Pet.
i. 18), and so Jer. x. 3, τὰ νόμιμα τ.
ἐθνῶν μάταια. But still more Isa. xxix.
13 (repeated by our Lord Mt. xv. 8 f.;
Mk vii. 6 f.), μάτην δὲ σέβονταί με, etc.
(LXX. not Heb.); especially applicable
here to a depravation of the true religion.

θρησκεία, *religion*] A far commoner
word than θρησκός, and probably of
wider sense, but still a word of very
limited history. It occurs twice in
Herod. ii. 18, 37, both times with
reference to the Egyptians, first about
an abstinence from certain flesh, and
the second time (ἄλλας τε θρησκίας
ἐπιτελέουσι) about white robes, circumcision, shaving, frequent washings,
etc., all cases of *personal* ceremonial
(so also θρησκεύω ii. 64). It is apparently absent, as also θρησκεύω,
from Attic literature : but like many
words found in Herod. came into use
in late days. It is doubtful whether
there is any earlier instance than this,
except Wisd. xiv. 18, 27 (-εύω xi. 16;
xiv. 16), all of worship of idols or
lower creatures. In N.T. in a good
sense, τ. ἡμετ. θρησκείας, Acts xxvi. 5,
which illustrates the use of εἴ τις...
θρησκός : and in St Paul (Col. ii. 18)
θρ. τ. ἀγγέλων (also 23, ἐθελοθρησκεία).

It has a more positively bad sense in
Philo, *Quod deter. pot.* 7 (i. 195), where
a man who uses purifications or
lavishes wealth on temples and heca-
tombs and votive offerings is called
θρησκείαν ἀντὶ ὁσιότητος ἡγούμενος.
But shortly afterwards Clem. Rom.
uses it freely in a good sense (xlv. 7),
τῶν θρησκευόντων τ. μεγαλοπρεπῆ καὶ
ἔνδοξον θρησκείαν τ. ὑψίστου, and lxii. 1,
περὶ μὲν τῶν ἀνηκόντων τῇ θρησκείᾳ
ἡμῶν, the virtuous life "suitable to
our worship" of God, as just expounded by a prayer. And still more
strongly Melito, p. 413 Otto, οὐκ ἐσμὲν
λίθων θεραπευταί, ἀλλὰ μόνον θεοῦ τοῦ
πρὸ πάντων...καὶ τ. χριστοῦ αὐτοῦ...
ἐσμὲν θρησκευταί : where θρησκευταί is
equal to or better than θεραπευταί.
And so often in the Fathers and other
later writers. What is commonly said
that θρησκεία means only ritual is not
exact. θρησκεία is simply reverence
of the gods or worship of the gods,
two sides of the same feeling. The
reverence gives rise to ceremonial
rites, not of worship but of abstention,
which are often called θρησκεία. The
worship was expressed in ritual acts,
which sometimes are called θρησκεία,
esp. in the plural θρησκεῖαι. But the
fundamental idea is still what under-
lies both. Besides, however, the exx.
already cited, there are others which
especially connect it with Jewish
ceremonial religion, as 4 Macc. v. 6, of
refusal to eat pork or things offered to
idols. Thus St James is still using
the word preferred by the Jewish
Christians, not that which he would
have chosen independently.

27. θρησκεία καθαρὰ καὶ ἀμίαντος,
a pure and undefiled religion] It is
not ἡ καθ. καὶ ἀμ. θρ. He does not
say or mean that what follows includes
all that can be called pure and undefiled religion.

ἀμίαντος παρὰ τῷ θεῷ καὶ πατρὶ αὕτη ἐστίν, ἐπισκέπτεσθαι ὀρφανοὺς καὶ χήρας ἐν τῇ θλίψει αὐτῶν, ἄσπιλον
ἑαυτὸν τηρεῖν ἀπὸ τοῦ κόσμου.

Why these particular words, καθαρά and ἀμίαντος, rather than ἀληθινή or some such word? Because he is still keeping in view the pretension made on behalf of the vain religion, viz. that it was pure and free from pollution. This alone would suffice to shew that St James had chiefly in view ceremonial θρησκεία, the washings and purifications of late Judaism, multiplying Levitical ordinances. These terms which you claim, he means, for your vain θρησκεία do really belong to something very different (Lk. xi. 41).

παρά] In His sight, in His presence, and so in His eyes.

τῷ θεῷ καὶ πατρί] The two names are probably combined with reference both to what has preceded and to what is going to follow. The false religion spoke much of God, but forgot that He was also Father. A true sense of being His children would lead to a different conception of Him and of the kind of service acceptable to Him. And again, to think of Him as Father was to think of men as brethren; a point of view forgotten in this θρησκεία which set no store on such brotherliness as is involved in the visiting of orphans and widows.

ἐπισκέπτεσθαι, to visit] The word is often used in O.T. of God visiting individual persons or His people: but no case like this. Ecclus. vii. 35 has it of visiting the sick, and so Test. Sim. i; Mt. xxv. 36, 43 (the latter ἐν φυλακῇ as well as ἀσθενοῦντα): and it seems an ordinary Greek usage as Xen. Cyr. v. 4. 10; Mem. iii. 11. 10; Plut. Mor. (ii. 129 c, τ. φίλους ἀσθενοῦντας); Luc. Philops. 6.

The word must doubtless then be taken literally: not the mere bestowal of alms, but the personal service. The Bible represents God as specially taking thought for the fatherless and widow, as their "father," Ps. lxviii. 5 (cf. Deut. xxvii. 19; Isa. i. 17; Ecclus. iv. 10). In contrast Mk xii. 40 (|| Lk. xx. 47), the devouring widows' houses is a mark of the scribes.

ἄσπιλον, unstained] Quite a late word, apparently not extant before N.T. The force of the word here is that after St James has noticed the acts of brotherly care towards orphans and widows, he returns to the claim of purity, as though to point out that there was indeed a purity and undefiledness in the strictest sense to be pursued, not from fictitious and artificial pollutions, but from a power able to infect and pollute the inward self.

ἀπὸ τοῦ κόσμου, from the world] The use of κόσμος here is remarkable. The word can hardly be used neutrally here, as though St James meant only that the κόσμος contained things that might bring moral defilement. The κόσμος is evidently thought of as itself defiling. The same comes out yet more strongly in iv. 4, and probably also in the difficult iii. 6. We are used to this language as conventional. But it needs investigation as to its strict meaning and origin. There is nothing of the kind in the first three Gospels or in the Acts or (strange to say) the Apocalypse or Hebrews: very abundant in St John's Gospel and first Epistle; and 1 Jn. ii. 15 furnishes a remarkable parallel to iv. 4. It is not very clear in St Paul (2 Cor. vii. 10), ὁ κ. οὗτος [1 Cor. iii. 19; v. 10; vii. 31; Eph. ii. 2] being, at least partly, a different conception; but it is found in 2 Peter, distinctly in ii. 20, τὰ μιάσματα τ. κόσμου (cf. ἄσπιλον), and indirectly i. 4; ii. 5 (bis); iii. 6. Thus it is clear in St John's Gospel and Epistle, 2 Peter, and St James. There is nothing to be made of the common Greek sense

II. ''Αδελφοί μου, μὴ ἐν προσωπολημψίαις ἔχετε

as the visible universe, or the order of it. This physical sense seems to belong to some places where the word is used, but not to those where the word κόσμος is in any sense evil. The conception must be Jewish: can it be traced back to the O.T.? Certainly not the Greek word from the LXX., for there it has only the "order" or "ornament" meanings. In the Apocr. it is the world, but not in an evil sense. In the LXX. its place is apparently taken by οἰκουμένη, which represents the Heb. תֵּבֵל, a curious ancient word, always used without the article, meaning apparently at first the fruitful soil of the earth, and then as a virtual synonym of "earth," but esp. earth as the habitation of men. Sometimes, like "world," it is naturally transferred to the collective races of men. Hence we get an intermediate sense in Ps. ix. 8, where God appears as judging תֵּבֵל in righteousness, and the phrase is repeated in the later psalms, xcvi. 13; xcviii. 9. But it acquires a more distinctly bad sense in the early chapters of Isaiah, xiii. 11; xiv. 17 (21); xviii. 3; xxiv. 4 (see foll. *vv.* for sense); xxvi. 9, 18. In these passages it means the sum of the fierce surrounding heathen nations, the powers of the heathen world at once destructive and corruptive (xxvi. 9), and see Cheyne's note, who calls attention to two points: "(1) the Jews are in constant intercourse with the heathen; (2) they suffer, not merely by their political subjugation, but by the moral gulf between themselves and the heathen." Thus תֵּבֵל is virtually the ideal Babylon of the prophets and still more of the Apocalypse. Delitzsch (Isa. xxvi. 18) rightly calls it a κόσμος: and conversely we may say that the N.T. κόσμος probably came from this source.

To Jewish Christians scattered through the Empire, to the Christians of Ephesus (1 Jn), the contact with the heathen world would be a perpetual source of moral danger, and they would be tempted to all sorts of risks from trying to avoid collisions with it. Its injurious effects would be many; but their prevailing characteristic would be defilement. In St John, and perhaps to some extent here, we have the paradox of the holy people itself becoming the world, by putting on in other forms the maxims and practice of an outer world. At all events the evil is conceived of as residing not in anything physical, but in a corrupt and perverted society of men. This is probably always the true ethical sense of "world." Thus the two clauses answer to each other in respect of the outward objects of the two forms of pure religion: the one is a duty of communication with men for good, the other a duty of avoiding such evil as comes from communication with men.

The whole verse has doubtless a paradoxical shape, though this is explained by the latent antithesis to the spurious θρησκεία. But in any case the conception is that of Isa. lviii. 3—7 (esp. 6); Zech. vii. 4—10.

It closes the paragraph 19—27 with a general statement as to religion, corresponding to *vv.* 17, 18, which form a general statement as to theology concluding the first section.

II. 1. *ἀδελφοί μου*] The preface being ended St James turns to the special points of practice which he had directly in view. He makes no further exordium, but breaks at once in medias res with this personal appeal, putting ἀδ. μου in the forefront. It does not occur again at the beginning of a sentence till the close (v. 19).

In what follows in this verse three points of construction require con-

τὴν πίστιν τοῦ κυρίου ἡμῶν Ἰησοῦ Χριστοῦ τῆς δόξης;

2. Χριστοῦ] Χριστοῦ,

sideration: the mood and general force of μὴ...ἔχετε; the nature of the genitive τοῦ κυρίου in connexion with τὴν πίστιν; and the construction and consequent interpretation of τῆς δόξης.

μὴ ἐν προσωπολημψίαις ἔχετε] This is often, naturally enough, taken as an imperative: but this gives a rather tame sense, and gives no exact sense to ἐν πρ. ἔχετε, and especially to the position of ἐν πρ. as coming before ἔχετε. It is more natural to take it as an interrogative appeal to their consciences: "Can you really think ἐν προσωπολημψίαις that you are having or holding the faith etc."

The plural -αις probably expresses "in (doing) acts of." When words having an abstract sense are in the plural, the meaning is either *different kinds* (as "ambitions"= different kinds of ambition) or different concrete acts or examples. The abstract has no number strictly speaking: but a plural at once implies a number of singulars to make it up, and (apart from kinds) things concrete can alone be numbered.

προσωπολημψίαις, *acts of partiality*] This group of words has a Hebrew origin. פָּנִים נָשָׂא, "to receive the face of," is much used in different books of the O.T. for receiving with favour an applicant, whether in a good or bad sense. The exact force of the phrase is not clear. נָשָׂא has not the strong sense "accept," "welcome," but rather either simply "take" or "lift up," and some accordingly adopt "lift up." Against this Gesen. *Thes.* 915 f. (cf. Hupfeld on Ps. lxxxii. 2) has argued with much force: but he has not succeeded in explaining the precise manner in which "taking the face of" comes to have the required meaning. From the sense of receiving a particular person with favour would naturally come the perversion, the receiving with undue favour, i.e.

favouritism, partiality. In some of the passages the partiality is spoken of as due to bribes: but this is an accident: the partiality itself is what the phrase denotes. It is variously rendered by the LXX. as λαμβάνω πρόσωπον, προσδέχομαι πρ., θαυμάζω πρ. etc. The N.T. has λαμβ., θαυμ., βλέπω εἰς. From the commonest rendering were formed a group of compound words, προσωπολήμπτης Acts x. 34; ἀπροσωπολήμπτως 1 Pet. i. 17; προσωπολημπτέω Jam. ii. 9; and προσωπολημψία here and three times in St Paul. They are doubtless words of Palestinian Greek.

ἔχετε τὴν πίστιν τοῦ κυρίου ἡμῶν κ.τ.λ.] The two most obvious senses of the genitive here are the subjective, the faith which our Lord Himself had, and the objective, the faith in Him. The former is not a likely sense to be meant without some special indication of it: the latter is not supported by any clear parallels, and (taken thus nakedly) gives a not very relevant turn to the sentence. The true sense is doubtless more comprehensive, and answers to an idea widely spread in the N.T.; "which comes from Him, and depends on Him," "the faith which He taught, and makes possible, and bestows": it is a faith in God, enlarged and strengthened by the revelation of His Son; the faith in God which specially arises out of the Gospel and rests on Him of whom the Gospel speaks. It thus *includes* a faith *in* Christ: but this is only the first step on the way to a surer and better faith in God. "He that hath seen me hath seen the Father." This is the probable sense always where πίστις is followed by Ἰησοῦ or similar words. Even Mk xi. 22, ἔχετε πίστιν θεοῦ, is not so much "Have faith in God" as "Have faith from God. Trust on, as men should do to whom God is a reality."

τοῦ κυρίου ἡμῶν] It is impossible to determine precisely how much meaning St James put into these words. But they do not differ from St Paul's formula, and probably to say the least go much beyond what the disciples meant by κύριος in the days of the ministry. They must be taken with i. 1.

τῆς δόξης, who is *the Glory*] Δόξης is very difficult in this position. Some take it with πίστιν, changing the meaning of πίστιν: Have ye the faith in respect of glory? equivalent to, Do ye take the same view of true glory and dignity? This gives a fair sense; but imports an unnatural force into πίστιν, and leaves the transposition of τ. δόξης inexplicable, besides disturbing the connexion between τ. πίστιν and τ. κυρίου etc. The other interpretations, "faith in the glory," "glorious faith," are evidently impossible.

Another favourite way is to take it with τ. κυρίου (so A.V.). The possibility of two genitives, ἡμῶν and τ. δόξης, cannot be denied : so in 1 Tim. iv. 2 δαιμονίων and ψευδολόγων are probably independent genitives governed by διδασκαλίαις: also Acts v. 32 (T.R.); 2 Cor. v. 1; Phil. ii. 30; Mt. xxvi. 28: (Winer-Moulton 239). But τ. κυρίου τ. δόξης is itself a phrase at once so compact and so nearly unique (1 Cor. ii. 8; cf. ὁ θεὸς τ. δόξης Ps. xxix. 3, and probably thence Acts vii. 2) that the division of it into two distant parts is not probable, and can only be taken as a possible interpretation.

It is needless to examine the combination with Χριστοῦ, or with the whole phrase τ. κυρίου ἡμῶν 'I. X.

There remains the possibility of not taking it as directly dependent on any preceding words, but in apposition to 'I. X., "our Lord Jesus Christ, *who is* the Glory": so Bengel. Several passages of the Epistles give a partial confirmation. Rom. ix. 4, ἡ δόξα seems to be the glory of the Divine presence (O.T.); 1 Cor. xi. 7, a man

is said to be εἰκὼν καὶ δόξα θεοῦ, which may be taken with *v*. 3, κεφαλὴ δὲ γυναικὸς ὁ ἀνήρ, κεφαλὴ δὲ τοῦ χριστοῦ ὁ θεός; Eph. i. 17, ὁ θεὸς τοῦ κυρίου ἡμῶν 'I. X. ὁ πατὴρ τῆς δόξης, where the two clauses seem to stand in precise parallelism and it seems impossible to give the second an intelligible sense except it means that the Son was Himself the Glory; Tit. ii. 13, τὴν μακαρίαν ἐλπίδα καὶ ἐπιφάνειαν τῆς δόξης τοῦ μεγάλου θεοῦ καὶ σωτῆρος ἡμῶν X. 'I., where it is on the whole easiest to take X. 'I. as in apposition to τ. δόξης τ. μεγάλου θεοῦ κ. σωτῆρος ἡμῶν. Illustrative passages are 2 Cor. iv. 6; Heb. i. 3 (ἀπαύγασμα τ. δόξης, He who is an effulgence of the Father's glory being thereby Himself the Glory); possibly 1 Pet. iv. 14; also Apoc. xxi. 11, 23, where note the parallelism to καὶ ὁ λύχνος αὐτῆς τὸ ἀρνίον. [See Add. Note.]

But was there anything to lead to such a representation? The O.T. speaks much of the כָּבוֹד of the Lord. From this and from the late dread of connecting God too closely with lower things arose the Jewish conceptions of the Glory יְקָרָא, and the Shechinah. See Weber 160 on the Glory as in Heaven; 179 ff. on the Glory and the Shechinah, and the relation of the Shechinah to the Word in the Targums (cf. Westcott, *Introd.*⁶ 152); and 182 ff. the combination of both conceptions (Word and Shechinah) in the Shechinah in Talmud and Midrash. Now the Word of the Targums is the true antecedent of the Logos in St John, much more so than the Logos of Philo; and it would be only natural that the other great conception which linked God to men, that of the Glory, should be transferred to Christ as the true fulfiller of it.

The force then of the title here would probably be that the faith of Christ as the Glory was peculiarly at variance with this favouritism shewn to the rich: since He who represented the very majesty of heaven

²ἐὰν γὰρ εἰσέλθῃ εἰς συναγωγὴν ὑμῶν ἀνὴρ χρυσοδακ-

was distinguished by His lowliness and poverty : cf. Phil. ii. 5 ff. ; 2 Cor. viii. 9. As St James (iii. 9) rebukes the cursing of men who are made in the likeness of God, so here he rebukes the contemptuous usage of poor men, even such as the Incarnate Glory of God Himself became.

2. εἰς συναγωγὴν ὑμῶν, into your (place of) assembly] The word means either the assembly or the building which held the assembly, and either makes sense : in Jn vi. 59, xviii. 20 it is the assembly clearly.

Two subjects of historical interest, the thing and the word, demand notice. As regards the thing synagogue see Plumptre in Smith's Dict.; Schürer ii. § 27. The date when the synagogue-system arose is unknown. It is remarkable that there are no clear traces of it in the Apocrypha ; yet probably there is a reference in Ps. lxxiv. 8 (Maccabaean). But it was widely spread in the first century in all places where Jews were to be found.

The name "synagogue." The origin is doubtless in the LXX., but in a confused way. There are two chief words in O.T. (cf. Schürer l.c. [and Hort, Christian Ecclesia]) for kindred meanings, קָהָל, "congregation," and עֵדָה, "assembly": in this sense עֵדָה is almost always rendered συναγωγή, קָהָל ἐκκλησία about 70 times, συναγωγή about half as many, other words very rarely. Probably ἐκκλησία was chosen for קָהָל, because both words express the calling or summoning of a public assembly (convocation) by a herald. Both עֵדָה and συναγωγή are somewhat more general words. But the difference in usage was very slight. They stand side by side in Prov. v. 14 (where see Delitzsch), also (Heb.) Exod. xii. 6 ; and [ἐξ]εκκλησιά-ζειν συναγωγήν occurs several times ;

also συνήχθησαν...ἐκκλησία (sic) 2 Ezra x. 1, and ἐπισυνήχθη ἐκκλησία 1 Macc. v. 16. This O.T. double use recurs in Apocrypha, especially Ecclus. and 1 Macc. The late traces of ἐκκλησία shew that it must have survived, apparently as the body of men making up a congregation, the religious community so to speak ; and also as the community of the whole nation (Mt. xvi. 18), as in the O.T. (For the Hebrew words used see Schürer l.c.) The late use of συναγωγή was apparently limited to the individual buildings, or to the congregation as assembled in them. There is some evidence of its being employed to denote some religious associations among the Greeks (see Harnack cited below), but probably this had nothing to do with the selection. It is very common for Jewish synagogues in N.T.; three times in Josephus ; also Philo, Q. omn. prob. lib. 12 (ii. 458), "The seventh day is reckoned holy, on which abstaining from other works, καὶ εἰς ἱεροὺς ἀφικνούμενοι τόπους, οἱ καλοῦνται συναγωγαί, they sit in ranks according to age, the younger below the older, placed for listening with the fitting order."

Now, as far as evidence goes, the Christian usage was to adopt ἐκκλησία both for single congregations and for a whole community. For the building it is not used in the apostolic age, though it was afterwards. On the other hand the Christian use of συναγωγή is very limited : see a long note in Harnack Hermas Mand. xi. 9. He shews how rarely and as it were etymologically only it was used by ordinary Christian writers, and it at last became definitely the synagoga contrasted with ecclesia as in Augustine ; and in earlier writers it sometimes is used in a depreciatory sense like our "conventicle." What however especially concerns us here is

τύλιος ἐν ἐσθῆτι λαμπρᾷ, εἰσέλθῃ δὲ καὶ πτωχὸς ἐν
ῥυπαρᾷ ἐσθῆτι, ³ἐπιβλέψητε δὲ ἐπὶ τὸν φοροῦντα τὴν
ἐσθῆτα τὴν λαμπρὰν καὶ εἴπητε Cὺ κάθου ὧδε καλῶς,
καὶ τῷ πτωχῷ εἴπητε Cὺ στῆθι ἢ κάθου ἐκεῖ ὑπὸ τὸ
ὑποπόδιόν μου, ⁴οὐ διεκρίθητε ἐν ἑαυτοῖς καὶ ἐγένεσθε

3. ἢ κάθου ἐκεῖ] ἐκεῖ ἢ κάθου   4. οὐ διεκρίθητε...πονηρῶν;] διεκρίθητε...πονηρῶν.

the evidence for its use among Jewish
Christians, see Lightfoot, *Phil.* 190:
Epiph.(xxx.18)states that the Ebionites
call their church συναγωγήν and not
ἐκκλησίαν; and Jer. *Ep.* 112. 13 says
of the Ebionites, "To the present day
through all the synagogues of the E.
among the Jews there is a heresy
called of the Minaei" etc. This makes
it very likely that Jewish Ebionites
inherited the name from the purer
days of Jewish Christianity, and that
St James does here distinctly mean
"synagogue": and since he elsewhere
(v. 14) speaks of τ. πρεσβυτέρους τῆς
ἐκκλησίας, i.e. the living congregation,
the difference of word suggests that
here the building is meant.

χρυσοδακτύλιος] Not known elsewhere. The adjective was doubtless
chosen to express that the wearing of
gold rings, probably a multitude of
them (τῶν δακτυλίων πλῆθος ἔχων, Luc.
Nigr. xiii.), was characteristic of the
kind of man.

ἐσθῆτι λαμπρᾷ contrasted with ῥυπαρᾷ ἐσθῆτι] The two words are
strictly opposed, as often ; practically
new glossy clothes and old shabby
clothes. Λαμπρός has nothing to do
with brilliance of colour, being in fact
often used of white robes. Artemi-
dorus (ii. 3 s. *fin.*), after enumerating
the omens from garments of all sorts
of colours, concludes ἀεὶ δὲ ἄμεινον
καθαρὰ καὶ λαμπρὰ ἱμάτια ἔχειν καὶ
πεπλυμένα καλῶς ἢ ῥυπαρὰ καὶ ἄπλυτα,
πλὴν τῶν τὰς ῥυπώδεις ἐργασίας ἐργαζο-
μένων.

3. ἐπιβλέψητε δὲ ἐπί, *and ye look
with favour on*] Ἐπιβλέπω ἐπί is
often used in LXX. of God looking
with favour on men; not apparently

of men on men. But Aristotle (*Eth.
Nic.* iv. 2, p. 1120 b 6) says (in giving)
τὸ γὰρ μὴ ἐπιβλέπειν ἐφ᾽ ἑαυτὸν ἐλευ-
θερίου, to pay no regard to oneself
and one's own interest.

καλῶς, *in a good place*] Ael. *V. H.*
ii. 13, καὶ δὴ καὶ ἐν καλῷ τ. θεάτρου
ἐκάθητο; xiii. 22, Ptolemy having
built a temple for Homer αὐτὸν μὲν
καλὸν καλῶς ἐκάθισε, κύκλῳ δὲ τὰς
πόλεις περιέστησε τ. ἀγάλματος.

στῆθι ἢ κάθου] It is uncertain
whether to read στῆθι ἢ κάθου ἐκεῖ
ὑπὸ τὸ ὑποπόδιον (B ff), or στῆθι ἐκεῖ
ἢ κάθου ὑπὸ τὸ ὑποπόδιον. Probably
the former, notwithstanding the want
of verbal balance. Stand anywhere
contrasted with sit in a particular
humble place.

ὑπὸ τὸ ὑποπόδιόν μου, *below my foot-
stool*] Ὑπό might be "down against,"
i.e. close up to, with the accessory
sense of lowness. But more probably
"below" in the sense of in a lower
place, as Plutarch *Artax.* v. (i. 1013 E)
καθεζομένων τῆς μὲν ὑπ᾽ αὐτόν, τῆς δὲ
μητρὸς ὑπὲρ αὐτόν.

4. No καὶ before οὐ; perhaps omit
οὐ (B* ff) which gives the same sense,
substituting affirmation for question.

διεκρίθητε ἐν ἑαυτοῖς, *divided in
your own minds*] As i. 6; explained
by Mt. xxi. 21, ἐὰν ἔχητε πίστιν καὶ μὴ
διακριθῆτε, appearing in Mk xi. 23 as
καὶ μὴ διακριθῇ ἐν τῇ καρδίᾳ αὐτοῦ ἀλλὰ
πιστεύῃ ὅτι κ.τ.λ.; cf. Acts x. 20;
Rom. iv. 20; xiv. 23 (ὅτι οὐκ ἐκ
πίστεως): cf. Jude 22. The idea is
that the singleness and strength of
faith is split up and shattered by the
divided mind, professing devotion to
God yet reaching away to a petty and
low standard. Ἐν ἑαυτοῖς is in anti-

H. J.   4

κριταὶ διαλογισμῶν πονηρῶν; ⁵Ἀκούσατε, ἀδελφοί μου
ἀγαπητοί. οὐχ ὁ θεὸς ἐξελέξατο τοὺς πτωχοὺς τῷ

thesis to what follows: the wrong-doing to others is traced back to its root within, just as in iv. 1.

κριταὶ διαλογισμῶν πονηρῶν, *judges swayed by evil deliberations*] The genitive is not unlike i. 25. The idea seems to be "judges swayed by evil deliberations or thinkings": contrast Prov. xii. 5, λογισμοὶ δικαίων κρίματα. διαλογισμός is a very elastic word. In Mt. xv. 19 διαλογισμοὶ πονηροί (∥ Mk. vii. 21, οἱ διαλογισμοὶ οἱ κακοί) stand at the head of the evil things that come forth from the heart, and probably mean malicious evil plottings (cf. 1 Tim. ii. 8, χωρὶς ὀργῆς καὶ διαλογισμοῦ), answering apparently to the single Hebrew word מְזִמָּה, properly only a thought, device, but usually an evil device. In various places of St Luke it is used of the plotting of the Pharisees and the imperfect faith of the disciples. Probably the mere suggestion that they made themselves κριταί contained a reproach: cf. iv. 11: they broke the command of the Sermon on the Mount (Mt. vii. 1). But further the office of a true judge is to divide, to sever right from wrong: but here the division was dictated not by justice according to the facts, but by evil divisions within their own minds (cf. Rom. xiv. 10, 13), by evil calculations, as we might say. Contrast Lk. xiv. 12 ff. Such moral distraction is a form of διψυχία, and opposed to the singleness of faith.

5. ἀκούσατε, *hearken*] An imperative like ἴστε in i. 19, but with a sharper tone, as of a warning prophet: cf. especially Isa. li. 1, 4, 7. It introduces an appeal to a truth that could not be denied by any who accepted Christ's Gospel. It is softened at once by ἀδελφοί μου ἀγαπητοί, of which ἀγαπ. here occurs for the last time (previously in i. 16; i. 19, where likewise there are appeals to accepted but practically belied truths).

οὐχ ὁ θεὸς ἐξελέξατο, *did not God choose*] What choice by God is meant here? In our Lord's apocalyptic discourse Mt. xxiv. 22 (with ∥ˢ) He spoke of the shortening of the days of tribulation for the elect's sake, and Mk adds οὓς ἐξελέξατο, which is virtually implied in the verbal ἐκλεκτούς. The conception doubtless is that the infant church or congregation of Christians owed their hearing and reception of the Gospel to God's choice. Here as elsewhere it is not a simple question of benefit bestowed on some and refused to others: those on whom it is bestowed receive it for the sake of the rest: they are God's instruments for the diffusion of His truth and salvation. This choice of Christians by God from among heathenism or unbelieving Judaism is spoken of by St Paul 1 Cor. i. 27 f. (a passage much resembling this) and Eph. i. 4. It is implied in various places where ἐκλεκτός or ἐκλογή is spoken of. Both words occur often in St Paul, ἐκλογή in 2 Pet. i. 10, and ἐκλεκτός especially in 1 Pet. viz. i. 1; ii. 4, 6, 9, where St Peter carries it back to two passages of Isaiah, one xxviii. 16 LXX. only (cf. Prov. xvii. 3 LXX.) properly "well-tried"; the other xliii. 20, where as in neighbouring chapters and some Psalms it refers to Israel as the object of God's choice. But ἐξελέξατο itself stands in a still more fundamental passage, Deut. xiv. 1, 2. [See further on 1 Peter *ll. cc.*]

St James does not however refer directly to Christians but to the poor. The reference is doubtless to the special manner in which Christ's own preaching was addressed to the poor. The Gospel was not intended to be confined to them; but they were to be its first and its strictly primary recipients, the recipients who would

κόσμῳ πλουσίους ἐν πίστει καὶ κληρονόμους τῆς βασιλείας ἧς ἐπηγγείλατο τοῖς ἀγαπῶσιν αὐτόν; ⁶ὑμεῖς δὲ
ἠτιμάσατε τὸν πτωχόν.   οὐχ οἱ πλούσιοι καταδυνα-

best shew its true character. "Blessed
are ye poor" are the first words of
the Sermon on the Mount: πτωχοὶ
εὐαγγελίζονται is the culminating mark
of Christ's true Messiahship, founded
about Isa. lxi. 1, which is quoted in
full in the words spoken in the synagogue at Nazareth which head the
ministry in St Luke (iv. 18), as the
Sermon on the Mount does in
St Matthew.

τοὺς πτωχοὺς τῷ κόσμῳ, *the poor in
the eyes of the world*] Τῷ κόσμῳ
might be taken as "in relation to the
world": but more probably 'in the
eyes of "the world"' (cf. 1 Cor. i. 18, τ.
ἀπολλυμένοις κ.τ.λ.; 2 Cor. x. 4 δυνατὰ
τῷ θεῷ; Acts vii. 20 ἀστεῖος τ. θεῷ).
Cf. Lk. xvi. 15 τὸ ἐν ἀνθρώποις ὑψηλόν,
said to the φιλάργυροι Pharisees.
"The world" is used in the same
sense as before, here as judging by an
external and superficial standard.

πλουσίους ἐν πίστει, to be *rich in
virtue of faith*] Not "as being," but
"to be" expressed more explicitly in
Eph. i. 4 by εἶναι ἡμᾶς ἁγίους καὶ
ἀμώμους κ.τ.λ.
The meaning is not "abounding in
faith," which would weaken the force
of πλουσίους in this connexion, but
"rich in virtue of faith": their faith
of itself constituted them not only
powerful, able to move mountains,
but rich: see 2 Cor. vi. 10; viii. 9;
Apoc. ii. 9; iii. 18; and esp. 1 Pet.
i. 7.   The explanation is that the use
and enjoyment of riches contain two
elements, the thing used and enjoyed,
and the inward power of using and
enjoying it; and this inward power
is so intensified and multiplied by a
strong and simple faith in God that
it so to speak extracts more out of
external poverty than can without it
be extracted out of external riches.

Cf. Ps. xxxvii. 16 and in spirit the
whole Psalm; *Test. Gad* 7, ὁ γὰρ
πένης καὶ ἄφθονος, ἐπὶ πᾶσι Κυρίῳ εὐ-
χαριστῶν, αὐτὸς παρὰ πᾶσι πλουτεῖ, ὅτι
οὐκ ἔχει τὸν πονηρὸν περισπασμὸν τῶν
ἀνθρώπων.

κληρονόμους τῆς βασιλείας, *heirs of
the kingdom*] The kingdom of heaven
is what in the Sermon on the Mount
is especially pronounced to belong to
the poor. The Gospel preached to
them is the Gospel of the kingdom.
In Lk. xii. 32 we have "Fear not, little
flock; for it is your Father's good
pleasure to give you the kingdom";
and less distinct passages abound.
The combination κληρον. τ. βασιλ. occurs in Mt. xxv. 34 and in St Paul
(1 Cor. vi. 9 f.; xv. 50; Gal. v. 21: cf.
Eph. v. 5), but not in connexion with
the poor. The conception of inherit-
ance is common however in similar
contexts, and especially in the O. T.
It is involved in the conception of
sonship, as Gal. iv. 7.

ἧς ἐπηγγείλατο τοῖς ἀγαπῶσιν αὐτόν,
*which He promised to them that love
Him*] This corresponds exactly to the
use of the same phrase with τὸν στέφανον τ. ζωῆς in i. 12. Even with that
peculiar phrase derivation from the
Apocalypse was seen to be unlikely:
much more this commoner phrase from
Apoc. i. 6; v. 10. The promise referred
to is probably Dan. vii. 18, 27, though
our Lord's language may possibly be
meant, or may at least give definite-
ness to the older language. Τοῖς
ἀγαπῶσιν is, as before, the general
Deuteronomic term expressing fulfilment of the new and perfect Law.

6. ὑμεῖς δέ] in the strongest contrast.
ἠτιμάσατε] Sc. in that act. Not
merely failed to give him honour, but
treated him with dishonour. So Prov.
xiv. 21; xxii. 22; and cf. 1 Cor. xi. 22.

4—2

στεύουσιν ὑμῶν, καὶ αὐτοὶ ἕλκουσιν ὑμᾶς εἰς κριτήρια;
⁷οὐκ αὐτοὶ βλασφημοῦσιν τὸ καλὸν ὄνομα τὸ ἐπικληθὲν

οὐχ οἱ πλούσιοι, do not the rich] What follows shews that rich men not Christians are meant. But this does not force us to take the rich and poor of *v.* 2 as other than Christians. Within the Christian body there were both classes: but further the whole body was bound to regard itself emphatically as a band of poor men in the face of the wealth and power of the encompassing heathen or even Jewish world. The whole passage reminds us that the name Ebionites for the Jewish Christians of Palestine has nothing to do with an imaginary Ebion, but is simply the *Ebionim*, the Poor Men.

καταδυναστεύουσιν ὑμῶν, oppress you] Δυναστεύω is to "be a potentate," "have" or "exercise mastery," either absolutely or over some one in particular: sometimes in a neutral sense, sometimes with a bad sense "lord it over." Καταδυναστεύω expresses the same more strongly, violent exercise of mastery, tyranny. It occurs in Xen. and often in late Greek: much in LXX, chiefly for עָשַׁק, to oppress; as the poor Ezek. xviii. 12; xxii. 29; (LXX. Amos viii. 4); also Wisd. ii. 10. The case is usually (always in LXX.) the accusative, but the genitive occurs Diod. Sic. xiii. 73 fin. and Symm. apparently (Ps. lxiv. 4), cf. Wyttenb., as often happens with compounds into which κατά enters.

καὶ αὐτοὶ ἕλκουσιν ὑμᾶς, and are not they the men that drag you] Not "drag you in person," as is shewn by *v.* 7. The pretext of law covered violent usage: cf. σύρω Acts viii. 3; xvii. 6. [Swete on Ps.-Pet. iii.]

εἰς κριτήρια, into courts of justice] Here the meaning can hardly be "suits," though κριτήρια may mean this. Better, as sometimes, courts of justice, though we should have expected ἐπί rather than εἰς.
It can hardly be doubted that this

means judicial persecutions, whether formally on the ground of being Christians, we cannot tell for that time. No definite law against Christians is likely to have then existed. But if they had become objects of dislike, it was easy to find legal pretexts.

7. οὐκ αὐτοὶ βλασφημοῦσιν, are not they the men who abuse] Βλασφημέω carries with it nothing of our sense of "blaspheme" as containing some extreme irreverence towards God. It is simply abusive and scurrilous language whether directed against God or men. Very rare in LXX. It comes here from Isai. lii. 5 where the word is נָאַץ, properly expressive of contempt, usually rendered παροξύνω (even with τὸ ὄνομα) or some such word (one derivative is once βλασφημία, Ezek. xxxv. 12).

τὸ καλὸν ὄνομα, the honourable name] Worthy of admiration, not contempt and contumely. Καλός is what is good as seen, as making a direct impression on those who come in contact with it; contrast ἀγαθός which is good in result.

τὸ ἐπικληθὲν ἐφ' ὑμᾶς, by the which ye are called] From the LXX. of Amos ix. 12 (quoted Acts xv. 17) literally following the Hebrew, but also Jer. xiv. 9. The phrase is adopted for its vividness. The name was as it were laid upon them, stamping them with a special allegiance.

What name does he mean? Probably Χριστός or Χριστιανός, as 1 Pet. iv. 14, 16; cf. Acts xxvi. 28. That is, the watchword, as seen in the Acts, was "Jesus is Christ": and so in the more important and significant name of the two the whole sense became concentrated. If the Epistle was indeed addressed first to Antioch, it is an interesting fact that there the disciples were first called Christians.

ἐφ᾽ ὑμᾶς; ⁸εἰ μέντοι νόμον τελεῖτε βασιλικὸν κατὰ τὴν

It matters little for St James' meaning whether the name was chosen by Christians themselves or given by others in reproach (Tac. *Ann.* xv. 44, quos per flagitia invisos vulgus Christianos appellabat). It would soon be willingly accepted: and if this had not taken place when St James wrote, it would at least contain the καλὸν ὄνομα Χριστός. [See Lightfoot, *Ignatius* vol. I. p. 400.]

8. μέντοι, *indeed, really*] Not an easy use of this particle, which occurs Jn five times; 2 Tim. ii. 19; Jud. 8. In St John and St Paul it clearly has its commonest (adversative) sense "however," "howbeit," and perhaps also in St Jude. Hence commentators naturally try to find the same sense here. A sharp and intelligible adversativeness is obtained by supposing St James to be replying to an imagined plea of the Jewish Christians that they were shewing their love to their neighbours by their civility to the man with the gold rings. It is hardly credible however that so absurd a plea, of which there is not the least hint in the text, should be contemplated by St James; and it is difficult to find any other way of satisfactorily justifying an adversative sense. It seems more likely that μέντοι retains its original force of a strong affirmation, which is not confined to answers to questions, though they furnish the commonest examples. It is virtually little more than a strengthened μέν, and a δέ naturally follows. It thus becomes equal to "if you indeed," "if you really." This kind of sense is common in Xen. especially the *Memorabilia* (as i. 3. 10 with εἰ; i. 4. 18 with ἤν; see Kühner : also his Gr. ii. 694 f.: cf. Sturz *Lex. Xen.* iii. 114 f.). The force of the particle seems to lie in an implied reference to a contradiction between the respect of persons and a virtue specially claimed, namely fulfilment of the Law. Thus just as

St James had rebuked the unreal ἀκρόασις, the unreal θρησκεία, the unreal πίστις, so here he rebukes an unreal keeping of the law.

τελεῖτε, *fulfil*] As Rom. ii. 27. In both places the peculiar word was probably chosen to express that it is not a direct *performance*, but a virtual fulfilment: cf. Rom. ii. 14 f.

νόμον...βασιλικόν, *a royal law*] The order shews that either βασιλικόν is accessory ("a law, a royal *law*"), or has a special force, a law which well deserves to be called "royal." But in what sense royal? Probably not in the vague figurative sense common in Greek to denote anything specially high or worthy (sometimes βασιλικὸς καὶ θεῖος); nor again in the Greek application to laws, perhaps starting from Pindar's famous νόμος πάντων βασιλεύς (on which see Thompson *Gorg.* 484 B), of which the most interesting for our purpose are in Xen. *Oec.* xiv. 6 f. and Ps.-Plat. 317 C. Probably one of two senses, either fit to guide a king, a law such as a true king would take for his own government as Ps. lxxii., Zech. ix. 9, and the Gospels in so far as they set forth our Lord as a king;—or, more probably perhaps, a law which governs other laws, and so has a specially regal character. This sense gains in probability if taken with the context. St James does not deny that there was an obedience to a law of some rank or other. When our Lord rebuked the Pharisees (Mt. xxiii. 23), it was for tithing herbs on the one hand and leaving τὰ βαρύτερα τ. νόμου, judgment, mercy, and faith, on the other, adding "these ought ye to have done etc."; thereby implying the existence of less weighty parts of the law. So here the law, fulfilling which was made a boast, was not denied, but with it was contrasted by implication the neglect of the higher and more fundamental law of love.

γραφὴν 'Αγαπήςεις τὸν πληςίον coy ὡς ςεαγτόν, καλῶς ποιεῖτε·
⁹εἰ δὲ προσωπολημπτεῖτε, ἁμαρτίαν ἐργάζεσθε, ἐλεγχόμενοι ὑπὸ τοῦ νόμου ὡς παραβάται. ¹⁰Ὅστις γὰρ
ὅλον τὸν νόμον τηρήσῃ, πταίσῃ δὲ ἐν ἑνί, γέγονεν

One of the two commandments, of which our Lord had said that on them hung all the Law and the Prophets, might well be called royal.

There is no difficulty in thus applying so wide a term as νόμος to a single precept, since the precept itself was so comprehensive. Thus in Rom. xiii. 8 ff. the separate commandments are called ἐντολαί, but this the sum of them is called a νόμος, and by one not improbable interpretation τὸν ἕτερον νόμον.

κατὰ τὴν γραφήν, *according to the Scripture*] Doubtless the O.T. (Lev. xix. 18): the saying had a double sanction, Scripture, and the Lord's ratification of it.

καλῶς ποιεῖτε, *ye do well*] This has no sarcasm, as some suppose: simply "ye do well" (cf. *v.* 19; Mk vii. 37; Acts x. 33; 1 Cor. vii. 37 f.; 2 Pet. i. 19; 3 Jn 6). "I do not complain of you for seeking to fulfil a law, but for neglecting the true value of one law as compared with another: if you are fulfilling a law of the high kind, you are indeed doing well."

9. προσωπολημπτεῖτε, *ye have respect of persons*] Apparently a ἅπαξ λεγόμενον.

ἁμαρτίαν ἐργάζεσθε] A strong phrase, which must mean more than "ye commit sin." Probably a reminiscence of Mt. vii. 23 (Sermon on the Mount), where those who say "Lord, Lord" are at last addressed, "I never knew you, depart from me οἱ ἐργαζόμενοι τὴν ἀνομίαν" (from Ps. vi. 8). St James never uses ἄνομος, ἀνομία; and ἁμαρτία is often used as virtually a synonym, though the conceptions are different. Moreover (see *v.* 10) it is quite possible that he refers to a willingness to treat this conduct as no sin at all.

ἐλεγχόμενοι, *convicted, shewn to be guilty.*

τοῦ νόμου] The definite concrete law of Moses.

παραβάται, *transgressors*] Cf. Rom. ii. 25, 27; Gal. ii. 18. Παραβάτης is not used in LXX.; though παραβαίνω much (and παράβασις once), chiefly of covenants but also of laws and commandments, just as in classical usage: the strict sense is to "overstep." The point is that the sticklers for law are marked as essentially "law-breakers," and that on the shewing of legality itself. Probably there is no reference to such places in the Law itself as Exod. xxiii. 2; Deut. xvi. 19: otherwise the following γάρ would lose force.

10. ὅλον τὸν νόμον τηρήσῃ, *keep the whole law*] The subjunctives τηρήσῃ... πταίσῃ are certainly right according to the best MSS. It is the only quite certain N. T. example of ὅστις or ὅς with subjunctive without ἄν, though it has some good authority in Mt. x. 33 (*not* xviii. 4). But it certainly occurs occasionally in good Greek authors. There is no real difference of sense, though ἄν marks the indefiniteness more explicitly. See Kühner ii. 205f., better than Winer-Moulton 386.

This is probably said with reference to the plea that the whole Law had been observed. The verse seems to be a reminiscence of our Lord's answer, Mk x. 21, ἕν σε ὑστερεῖ; Lk. xviii. 22, ἔτι ἕν σοι λείπει (cf. Mt. xix. 21, εἰ θέλεις τέλειος εἶναι), said after an enumeration of the commandments of the second table, and the profession that they had been kept. The selling of goods and giving to the poor there corresponds antithetically to the neglect of the poor here.

πάντων ἔνοχος. ¹¹ὁ γὰρ εἰπών Μὴ μοιχεγϲηϲ εἶπεν καί
Μὴ φονεγϲηϲ· εἰ δὲ οὐ μοιχεύεις φονεύεις δέ, γέγονας
παραβάτης νόμου. ¹²οὕτως λαλεῖτε καὶ οὕτως ποιεῖτε
ὡς διὰ νόμου ἐλευθερίας μέλλοντες κρίνεσθαι. ¹³ἡ γὰρ

τηρήσῃ] No longer τελέσῃ. The
more formal word is appropriate here.
πταίσῃ, trip or stumble] As iii. 2 bis.
It is incipient falling (Romans xi. 11):
cf. Deut. vii. 25. Common in Philo.

γέγονεν πάντων ἔνοχος, is become
(makes himself) guilty of all] Ἔνοχος
is used with genitive or dative of
crimes, or punishments, or, as here,
precepts. Properly speaking it means
simply "bound by," "subject to,"
"coming under."
The force of πάντων is determined
by ἑνί: it is all separate points or
items that make up the Law.
Various Jewish writings contain sayings like this verse (Schöttg. 1016 ff.);
as Shabbath (R. Jochanan): "If a man
do all (of the 39 works prescribed by
Moses), but omit one, he is guilty for
all and each." There is nothing in
the O. T. exactly answering to this :
but Deut. xxvii. 26, after the various
specific curses on Mt Ebal, ends with
"Cursed be he that confirmeth not
(all) the words of this law to do them,"
where the LXX. and Samar. insert
πᾶσιν, and St Paul (Gal. iii. 10) so
quotes the passage. The insertion is
partially supported by Deut. xi. 32
(taken with vv. 26, 28) as Delitzsch
points out. The same principle of
the Law being one whole is implied in
Mt v. 18 f., ἰῶτα ἓν ἢ μία κερέα...μίαν
τ. ἐντολῶν τούτων τ. ἐλαχίστων.

11. ὁ γὰρ εἰπών κ.τ.λ.] It is very
unlikely that the two commandments
are chosen at random, as though both
were unconnected with προσωποληψ-
ψία. If this were the case, there would
be no clear and coherent course of
thought. It is quite possible that
Μὴ μοιχεύσῃς implies that such sins
as adultery were really avoided and
condemned by those who dishonoured

the poor; and that they made their
condemnation of fleshly sins an excuse
for indulgence towards spiritual sins.
At all events Μὴ φονεύσῃς is directly
connected with the matter in hand,
because murder is only the extreme
outcome of want of love to neighbours
or brethren. Our Lord (Mt. v. 21—
26) had carried back murder to the
expression of anger (cf. Jam. i. 19 f.),
and though St Paul (Rom. xiii. 8, 9)
had carried back all commandments
of the second table alike to love of
the neighbours, the 6th was evidently
the most direct expression of the
principle common to all, for (v. 10)
"love worketh no ill to a neighbour."

12. οὕτως λαλεῖτε καὶ οὕτως ποιεῖτε,
so speak ye, and so do] The two chief
spheres of shewing forth love or its
absence. We have had them paired
already in i. 19—21 contrasted with
22—25, i. 26 contrasted with 27; and
are now going to have them on a
larger scale, in inverted order, ii. 14—
26 contrasted with iii. 1—12. Both
are exemplified in the treatment of
the poor in the synagogues, the contemptuous language accompanying the
loveless acts.
ὡς διὰ νόμου ἐλευθερίας, as by a law
of liberty] This use of διά with κρίνεσθαι is singular, though disguised by
the ambiguity of "by," which denotes
κατά with acc., or ὑπό with gen. (cf.
Jn vii. 51, "Doth our law judge a
man ?"), as well as διά with gen. Apparently it comes from Rom. ii. 12,
ὅσοι ἐν νόμῳ ἥμαρτον διὰ νόμου κριθή-
σονται, where it apparently means "on
terms of," "in a state depending on,"
and corresponds to some other peculiar
uses of διά by St Paul, as διὰ γράμ-
ματος καὶ περιτομῆς (Rom. ii. 27); δι'
ἀκροβυστίας (iv. 11); διὰ προσκόμματος

κρίσις ἀνέλεος τῷ μὴ ποιήσαντι ἔλεος· κατακαυχᾶται

(xiv. 20); (?) διὰ δόξης (2 Cor. iii. 11); (?) δι᾽ ἐπαγγελίας (Gal. iii. 18). Thus the sense would seem to be not that the law of liberty is the standard or the instrument by which they are to be judged, but that they are to be judged as men who have lived in an atmosphere, as it were, of a law of liberty, and subject to its conditions. The two conceptions are closely related, but διά seems to lay stress chiefly on the present state rather than on the future judgment. It is probably for this reason that διὰ νόμου ἐλ. stands before μέλλοντες.

A law of liberty, exactly as i. 25: viz. Christ's Law, as distinguished from the Mosaic. The transition from the Mosaic Law in vv. 10, 11 to the Christian Law here corresponds precisely to the transition in the Sermon on the Mount from the one jot or tittle, one of these least commandments of Mt. v. 18 f., to "Except your righteousness etc." of Mt. v. 20, where the exceeding righteousness of the Christian disciple consists not in the performance of a greater number of positive precepts than the Scribes and Pharisees, but in the inner subjection of the spirit to the law of love, taking possession not of individual acts or abstinences, but of the whole life. The whole passage implies that under the unity of the external law there lies a much deeper unity of the spiritual law. If the whole external law was broken by the murderous conduct of a man who kept himself clean from adultery, much more was wrong done to the whole spiritual and free law of love by the attempt to keep any part of conduct exempt from it.

13. ἡ γὰρ κρίσις] To be interpreted by κρίνεσθαι: the Divine judgment: cf. v. 9.

ἀνέλεος τῷ μὴ ποιήσαντι ἔλεος, without mercy to him that hath shewed no mercy] The requital is in kind, cf. Mt. vii. 1, 2, and the parable of the Two Debtors, Mt. xviii. 21—35, esp. 33. Here not love but mercy or pity is named. It is quite possible that St James is not thinking exclusively of the treatment of the poor in the synagogue, but going on to a wider range of kindred conduct (cf. i. 27), and the absence of tenderness which is a common mark of the Pharisaical or perverted religious spirit. But in any case the word is in place, for while love is the universal fundamental attitude between man and man according to the Divine plan of the world, the characteristic form which love takes when directed to the poor is pity. To suffer with their suffering is the test of its reality.

κατακαυχᾶται, glorieth against] This is the true as well as the common reading: another ancient reading is κατακαυχάσθω, and another, less attested, κατακαυχᾶσθε. The abrupt introduction of this apophthegm gave rise to various conjunctions, δέ the best attested, also (T. R.) καί, also quoniam or "for."

The verb itself recurs iii. 14, and is found Rom. xi. 18; also three times in LXX., scarcely at all elsewhere. The sense of the image will depend on the interpretation of ἔλεος and κρίσεως. The opposition of the two words is singular, because they are coupled in the O. T., Ps. ci. (c.) 1; (LXX. xxxiii. (xxxii.) 5); virtually Hos. xii. 6; Mic. vi. 8; Zech. vii. 9. In these places κρίσις, מִשְׁפָּט, means the quality by which justice is done, as by an actual or virtual judge. ἔλεος is in like manner coupled with righteousness, and with truth. The same combination with ἔλεος appears Mt. xxiii. 23 (with faith added), these being the weightier matters of the law neglected by the Scribes and Pharisees. This cannot however be St James' sense. Except as applied to God's judgment, he never uses κρίνω, κρίσις, κριτής in a good sense; but always as governed

ἔλεος κρίσεως.   ¹⁴ Τί ὄφελος, ἀδελφοί μου, ἐὰν
πίστιν λέγῃ τις ἔχειν ἔργα δὲ μὴ ἔχῃ; μὴ δύναται ἡ

by "Judge not that ye be not judged."
Here, as the previous ἡ κρίσις suggests,
there must be at least some reference
to the Divine judgment on its con-
demnatory side, as κρίμα iii. 1, and
κριθῆτε v. 9. The image then probably
is that κρίσις comes so to speak as the
accuser before the tribunal of God,
and ἔλεος stands up fearlessly and as
it were defiantly to resist the claim.
Is it then human or Divine ἔλεος, the
plea of the mercy that has been shewn
in life or the Divine mercy resisting
the Divine condemnation? Probably
neither without the other: the two
mercies are coupled as in Mt. v. 7, in
the Lord's Prayer, and the Two
Debtors.

There is a somewhat similar use of
καυχῶμαι (not κατακαυχ.) in Ecclus.
xxiv. 1, 2. Schneckenburger well refers
for a similar virtual καύχησις to 1 Cor.
xv. 55. On the general sense cf. Or.
Sib. ii. 81, 'Ρύεται ἐκ θανάτου ἔλεος,
κρίσις ὅππστ᾽ ἂν ἔλθῃ.

It is however probable that in so
far as St James contemplates this
sense of the defying of judgment by
mercy, it is only as a particular case
of a universal truth. That is, he may
mean that this final triumph of mercy
proceeds from the previous and inherent superiority of mercy to κρίσις,
human as well as Divine, answering
to the superiority of mercy to sacrifice
(Mt. ix. 13; xii. 7). Mercy is greater
and better than human κρίσις in this
narrower sense (an echo of κριταὶ διαλογισμῶν πονηρῶν in v. 4), just as the
Gospel is greater and better than the
Law: and they who recognise and act
on this truth become recipients of the
Divine mercy, and have passed beyond
condemnation by the Divine judgment
in so far as it is embodied in the Law.

Unless this sense is present, it is
difficult to account for the absence
of δέ. Since there is no conjunction,

this clause can hardly be merely anti-
thetical to the preceding, but must
supply its foundation: the quoniam
gives the truer connexion, though not
the whole of it.

14. We now come to the section
on faith and works.

ἀδελφοί μου]   Marking a fresh
appeal, though closely connected with
what precedes.

ἐὰν πίστιν λέγῃ τις ἔχειν, if a man
say he hath faith]   We have already
had (i. 22 ff.) hearing without doing:
here we have believing without doing.
We have also had a spurious θρησκεία:
here we have a spurious πίστις. The
profession of a πίστις has been already
presumed in ii. 1, where St James
implies that the true faith of Jesus
Christ was absent or defective. Our
Lord in St Luke's account of the
explanation of the Parable of the
Sower (viii. 13) had spoken of a temporary believing, which fell away in
time of πειρασμός. The expression of
it is "Lord, Lord"; and the ἔργα μὴ
ἔχῃ here exactly answers to Lk. vi. 46
(καὶ οὐ ποιεῖτε ἃ λέγω), just as the
listening to words without doing in
i. 22 f. answers to Mt. vii. 24, 26.
The hearing the word, which is also
spoken of in the Parable of the Sower,
is the first step of reception; and
belief marks another step: the failure
may take place at either stage.

It is to be observed that here at
least St James does not say ἐὰν πίστιν
ἔχῃ τις but ἐ. π. λέγῃ τις ἔχειν: it is not
faith without works but the profession
of faith without works that thus far
is pronounced unprofitable.

There is no reason for referring this
spurious claim to faith to a Jewish
origin. There is no clear evidence
for anything answering to it among
the Jews. It would on the other
hand be a natural accompaniment
of a slackening Christian devotion.

πίστις σῶσαι αὐτόν; ¹⁵ἐὰν ἀδελφὸς ἢ ἀδελφὴ γυμνοὶ
ὑπάρχωσιν καὶ λειπόμενοι τῆς ἐφημέρου τροφῆς, ¹⁶εἴπῃ
δέ τις αὐτοῖς ἐξ ὑμῶν Ὑπάγετε ἐν εἰρήνῃ, θερμαίνεσθε

"Faith" or "believing" was emphatically the Christian watchword, hardly less prominent in the first three Gospels than in St Paul or St John. And the corruption of the Christian type of religion would need reprobation by the authority of one in St James' position quite as much as the corruption of so much of the Jewish type of religion as the Jewish Christians retained. The question of justification introduces a fresh element; but we do not reach that till *v.* 21.

ἡ πίστις] Naturally "the faith," "that faith," the faith which is compatible with the absence of works. The phrase doubtless implies that there was something to which the name might in some sense be given; though it is not what St James recognises as genuine faith.

σῶσαι] As i. 21.

15. This verse shews the connexion with what precedes. The examples of deficient works to which St James at once flies are taken from the treatment of the poor, quite as much as all that has been said about places in the synagogues.

ἀδελφὸς ἢ ἀδελφή] The explicit notice of both sexes brings out two degrees, as it were, in the helplessness which craved the sympathy and support of Christians. The women, as in the special example of the widows in i. 27, would have all the needs and difficulties of the men, and the additional needs and difficulties falling naturally to their sex, especially in ancient times.

The term "brother" "sister," repeated from i. 9, calls attention to the special ties between those who by believing in the Son had acquired a closer and deeper tie of brother-

hood as alike children of the Father. There was a true sense in which it was applied to all mankind: but in those days when the little community was surrounded by a more or less hostile population, the specially Christian sense had peculiar force. Christ too had in this connexion spoken of His own brethren, Mt. xxv. 35 f., 40, 42 f.

γυμνοί, *naked*] In the conventional sense of Scripture, as needing clothing, corresponding to the next phrase on the need of food.

ὑπάρχωσιν] Ὑπάρχω denotes not simple being, but being in a state or condition as distinguished from what is temporary or accidental: it is used properly with reference to antecedent states. Often it means what one is by nature: but that specially strong force comes from the context. The prior continuity is the main thing. Hence what is implied here is that not some casual poverty but habitual poverty is meant.

λειπόμενοι, *in lack of*] With the gen. just as in i. 5. In this sense of outward destitution Just. Mart. uses it absolutely. *Ap.* i. 67, οἱ ἔχοντες τοῖς λειπομένοις πᾶσιν ἐπικουροῦμεν; and again, καὶ αὐτὸς ἐπικουρεῖ ὀρφανοῖς τε καὶ χήραις, καὶ τοῖς διὰ νόσον ἢ δι' ἄλλην αἰτίαν λειπομένοις.

Omit ὦσιν after λειπόμενοι; the participle instead of λείπωνται continues the indication of ὑπάρχωσιν, expressing a habitual condition, not an accidental want of food.

τῆς ἐφημέρου τροφῆς] Simply the food needed day by day, daily food.

16. εἴπῃ δέ τις αὐτοῖς ἐξ ὑμῶν] He first begins indefinitely, "if a man say to them," and then after αὐτοῖς adds ἐξ ὑμῶν, implying that such a speech would really be the speech

καὶ χορτάζεσθε, μὴ δῶτε δὲ αὐτοῖς τὰ ἐπιτήδεια τοῦ
σώματος, τί ὄφελος; ¹⁷οὕτως καὶ ἡ πίστις, ἐὰν μὴ ἔχῃ

expressive of the temper of their own minds, though only one here or there might have the boldness to put it into these words.

'Υπάγετε ἐν εἰρήνῃ, *Go in peace*] A common Jewish farewell (Judg. xviii. 6 etc.: and used by our Lord Lk. vii. 50 etc.): here a dismissal, a sending away, in euphemistic and seemly form.

θερμαίνεσθε καὶ χορτάζεσθε, *be ye warmed and filled*] These words are usually taken as imperatives. Plumptre ingeniously suggests that they are indicatives; the unreal assertion that the poor are warmed and fed being a repetition of the unreal assertion that they had faith when they shewed such a lack of love. But it is difficult to get this sense out of the words as actually put into the mouth of the speaker, not as another's description of his act. We must therefore keep to the imperative sense. It is not a mere substitution for the optative, "I hope you may somehow get warmed and fed," but an exhortation to go and get for themselves the means of doing this. It reminds us to a certain extent of "Send the multitude away that they may buy for themselves victuals" (Mt. xiv. 15 and parallels). Not that there is any clear reflexive force in the middle, which is probably rather a passive, or at least not distinguishable from such: but it does lie in the use of the imperative. The use of the present tenses, not aorists, goes with ὑπάρχωσιν and λειπόμενοι, as marking the reference to a continuous state, "get your food and clothing now and always."

θερμαίνω, χορτάζω. Two strong words seem to be purposely chosen. "Warming" (Heb. and LXX.) is spoken of as an effect of clothes: Job xxxi. 20; Hag. i. 6 (cf. 1 Kin. i. 1). Plut.

Symp. 691 D speaks of the same garment as warming in winter, cooling in summer. Galen, *V. M. S.* ii. (ap. Wetst.) speaks of it as a common incorrect custom to speak of a thing as warming, because it hinders chilling.

χορτάζω, originally of pasturing cattle, is used in late Greek of feeding men: but usually, perhaps always, with the sense of feeding to the full, satisfying.

Thus the warm garments and satisfying food correspond to ἐν εἰρήνῃ.

μὴ δῶτε δέ, *and yet ye give not*] Transition to the full plural. Though one alone might be ready to speak the words, the general line of conduct was common to a large number.

τὰ ἐπιτήδεια τοῦ σώματος, *the things needful to the body*] 'Επιτήδειος is properly what is convenient or fitting, useful. But τὰ ἐπιτήδ. by usage are ordinary necessaries, sometimes called τὰ ἀνάγκαια ἐπιτήδεια.

Τοῦ σώματος has force in relation to the following comparison (οὕτως καί). It is an appeal to an example from the obvious realm "of the body."

17. οὕτως καί, *even so*] What is the precise comparison? i.e. what is it that in *vv.* 15, 16 is compared to faith as being liable to be dead? The result spoken of is that the body is, as a matter of fact, chilled and starved if it has not necessaries. Presently, in *v.* 26, St James says, in a similar comparison about the deadness of faith without works, that the body without spirit is dead. One is tempted to assume that he meant the love or beneficence is dead if it contents itself with words. But there would be no real image there, merely a repetition of the dead faith in a particular application. Moreover τί ὄφελος points not to the unreality of the beneficence but to the absence of result in the way of starvation

ἔργα, νεκρά ἐστιν καθ' ἑαυτήν. ¹⁸ἀλλ' ἐρεῖ τις Cὺ
πίστιν ἔχεις ; κἀγὼ ἔργα ἔχω. δεῖξόν μοι τὴν πίστιν
σου χωρὶς τῶν ἔργων, κἀγώ σοι δείξω ἐκ τῶν ἔργων μου

18. ἔχεις ;] ἔχεις

prevented. Apparently the comparison is to the words spoken : they
are dead words inasmuch as they
produce no effect on the supposed
need. This is Grotius' explanation,
and although not altogether satisfactory, it seems to be the best.
Most commentators overlook the need
of explanation altogether. Wetstein
quotes from Plaut. *Epidic.* i. 2. 13 f.
A man asks another for money: the
reply is "If I had it, I certainly would
not refuse it"; and then comes the
rejoinder, Nam quid te igitur rettulit
Beneficum esse oratione, si ad rem
auxilium *emortuum* est ?

ἔχῃ ἔργα, *have works*] A remarkable phrase, but very expressive of
St James' true meaning. The works
are not something added on to the
faith, but elements of it, parts of
itself.

νεκρά ἐστιν, *is dead*] Again the
same, not merely "useless" or "un-
acceptable" but "dead." It is no
question of faith *v.* works, but whether
faith *is* faith if it has no works.

καθ' ἑαυτήν, *in itself*] This brings
out the same yet more emphatically,
"in and by itself," not merely in
relation to other things, not merely
in its utility, so to speak; but in its
own very and inherent nature.

18. ἀλλ' ἐρεῖ τις, *But some one
will say*] An extremely difficult
verse. The natural way of taking
ἀλλ' ἐρεῖ τις is as the words of an
objector, and then it is difficult to
see how the next words could be put
into an objector's mouth. It is then
suggested that the τις is virtually
St James himself, like "so that a
man shall say etc." (Ps. lviii. 11) as
often wrongly interpreted (the true
meaning being "men shall say"); but
this is very unnatural from every

point of view. Accordingly it is
often now supposed that a third
person is introduced, mainly on
St James' side. This however only
lessens, by no means removes, the
difficulty. (1) It is very unlike
St James to favour the broad positive
statement addressed to those whom
he is rebuking, "Thou hast faith, and
I have works"; (2) ἀλλ' ἐρεῖ τις is a
most unlikely phrase for introducing
one who is more for than against the
writer; and (3) the supposed speaker
disappears thenceforward, and it is
difficult to see what good purpose
would be served by this momentary
introduction.

Not only the most natural but the
only natural way to understand ἀλλ'
ἐρεῖ τις is as introducing an objector,
one of the persons rebuked (τις...ἐξ
ὑμῶν), as in 1 Cor. xv. 35 (cf. Rom.
ix. 19; xi. 19). Indeed it is difficult
otherwise to understand the σύ of
v. 19, ὦ ἄνθ. κενέ of 20, and βλέπεις
of 22, but especially 20. In 24 there
is a return to the plural in ὁρᾶτε, but
the intermediate singular 2nd person
singles out someone for rebuke, who
can be no other than the τις of 18,
for the τις of 16 belongs exclusively
to the illustration.

A very fair and, to say the least,
not improbable sense may then be
obtained by taking Σύ to ἔχω alone
as put into the objector's mouth,
the rest of the verse being taken as
St James' own reply; and further by
taking Σύ πίστιν ἔχεις by itself as a
question. Questions of this kind are
very common in St James, and 19 is
best so interpreted. The sense will
then be "Thou, James, hast thou faith,
that thing which thou slightest in me ?
I for my part as well as thou (κἀγώ)
have works"; that is, "I do not allow

τὴν πίστιν. ¹⁹σὺ πιστεύεις ὅτι εἷς θεὸς ἔστιν ; καλῶς
ποιεῖς· καὶ τὰ δαιμόνια πιστεύουσιν καὶ φρίσσουσιν.

19. θεὸς ἔστιν] ὁ θεός ἐστιν

that I have no works, I have works
(sc. works of the law) in addition to
my faith: can you conversely say that
you have faith in addition to your
works?" St James' reply then attacks
the notion that faith and works are
two separate things. All turns on
χωρίς, which does not mean simply
"without," but "apart from," "separated from." "Shew me," he says,
"thy faith apart from the works, the
works that properly belong to it and
should characterise it"; implying that
this is an impossibility; "and I will
shew thee by my works the faith, the
faith belonging to them and inspiring
them." That is, he turns the tables,
and pleads that it is he alone, not
the antagonist, who can shew both.
The form δεῖξόν μοι...κἀγώ σοι δείξω
occurs Theoph. Ant. i. 2, Ἀλλὰ καὶ
ἐὰν φῆς Δεῖξόν μοι τὸν θεόν σου, κἀγώ
σοι εἴποιμι ἄν Δεῖξόν μοι τὸν ἄνθρωπόν
σου κἀγώ σοι δείξω τὸν θεόν μου;
where two impossibilities are set
against each other : but in St James
the κἀγώ σοι is positive, not merely
contingent on the other shewing.
The whole is little more than a paraphrase of "By their fruits ye shall
know them."

19. σὺ πιστεύεις, thou believest,
dost thou not ?] The sense is not
very different whether we take it as
indicative or interrogative : but interrogative is more forcible.

ὅτι εἷς θεὸς ἔστιν, that there is
(exists) one God] MSS. much divided.
The best attested readings are εἷς
θεὸς ἔστιν and εἷς ὁ θεός ἐστιν (or,
inverted, in the common form, εἷς
ἐστὶν ὁ θεός). The second (and third)
would mean "that God is one." Cf.
Deut. vi. 4 etc. On the whole it is
more probable that St James is not
singling out the detached affirmation
of unity, but taking all together the

first article in the creed of Jew and
Christian alike, an article not first
only but fundamental. The meaning
apparently is "you claim to have a
belief detached from works, though
you claim likewise to have works
independently : well, what is that
belief ? Take it in its simplest and
most fundamental form, the belief
that there is One God. A belief
without works necessarily consists in
belief in a proposition ; belief not in
One God, but that there is One God.
Well, so far so good : thou doest
well."

καὶ τὰ δαιμόνια πιστεύουσιν, the devils
also believe this] Καί is of course not
"and" but "also," they as well as
thou.

πιστεύουσιν] Sc. this, believe that
this is true.

τὰ δαιμόνια] Here as in the Gospels
we must not think simply of "powers
of evil," as such, but of the πνεύματα
πονηρά or ἀκάθαρτα by which those
called demoniacs were possessed.
The reference is probably to the
Gospel narratives, "What have we to
do with thee, Jesus of Nazareth ? Art
thou come to destroy us? We know
thee who thou art, the Holy One of
God" (Mk i. 24 etc.).

φρίσσουσιν, shudder] Properly the
same as the Latin horror, the standing
of hair on end with fear. Specially
used of awe of a mysterious Divine
power, as often of the adepts in the
Greek mysteries. Cf. Plat. Phaedr.
251 A, πρῶτον μὲν ἔφριξε καί τι τῶν τότε
ὑπῆλθεν αὐτὸν δειμάτων, εἶτα προσορῶν
ὡς θεὸν σέβεται. It is something at
once more distant and more prostrate
than worship. Cf. Ast on the above
p. 449 and Wytt. on Plut. ii. 26 B.
An Orphic fragment quoted by Clem.
Alex. Str. v. 724 and Euseb. P.E.
xiii. 13 (Hermann pp. 453 f.) on God :

²⁰θέλεις δὲ γνῶναι, ὦ ἄνθρωπε κενέ, ὅτι ἡ πίστις χωρὶς τῶν ἔργων ἀργή ἐστιν; ²¹Ἀβραὰμ ὁ πατὴρ ἡμῶν οὐκ ἐξ

Δαίμονες ὃν φρίσσουσι, θεῶν δὲ δέδοικεν ὅμιλος; an oracle ap. Lact. de ira Dei xxiii. (and in Latin Aug. Civ. Dei xix. 23), Wolff Proph. Orac. p. 143:

Ἐς δὲ θεὸν βασιλῆα καὶ εἰς γενετῆρα προπάντων,
ᵃὍν τρομέει καὶ γαῖα καὶ οὐρανὸς ἠδὲ θάλασσα
Ταρτάριοί τε μυχοὶ καὶ δαίμονες ἐκφρίσσουσιν;

and a magical invocation (Ὀνειροπομπὸς Ἀγαθοκλεῦς(sic) in A. Dieterich Papyrus magica Mus. Lugd. Bat. p. 800: Lips. 1888), Θώθ, ὃν πᾶς θεὸς προσκυνεῖ καὶ πᾶς δαίμων φρίσσει. There is thus no force of "and yet" in καί before φρ.: it is rather "their belief" is so strong and undeniable that it ends in a kind of strong homage. It is a proof that they believe, not something done in spite of it.

Thus the force of the clause lies on the word δαιμόνια (cf. δαιμονιώδης iii. 15). A belief such as this, even though its contents are so true and important as a belief in One God, cannot be a very Divine thing when it can be shared by the δαιμόνια.

The whole then turns on the real nature of the belief or faith supposed, and Bede seems to have understood it rightly, when, taking up language of Augustine, he says: "Sed nec Deum credere et contremiscere magnum est, si non et in eum credatur, hoc est si non ejus in corde amor teneatur. Aliud est enim credere illi, aliud credere illum, aliud credere in illum. Credere illi est credere vera esse quae loquitur: credere illum credere quod ipse sit Deus: credere in illum est diligere illum. Credere vera esse quae loquitur multi et mali possunt, credunt enim esse vera, et nolunt ea facere, quia ad operandum pigri sunt. Credere autem ipsum esse Deum, hoc et daemones potuerunt. Credere vero in Deum soli novere qui diligunt

Deum, qui non solo nomine sunt Christiani sed et factis et vita." (For reff. to Aug. see Pearson Creed p. 16.)

20. θέλεις δὲ γνῶναι, but wilt thou gain the knowledge] He is now going to prove his point by reference to Scripture. The words are equivalent to "Do you ask me what proof I have that..."

ὦ ἄνθρωπε κενέ, O vain man] Ἄνθρωπε probably in contrast to δαιμόνια, a being who shouldest have such a much better faith than δαιμόνια can.

Κενός (by itself) is not at all common as applied to men: it denotes pretentiousness, hollowness accompanying display. Thus Epictet. ii. 19. 8, "But if I am κενός, especially at a banquet, I astonish the visitors by enumerating the writers (on a particular subject)"; iv. 4. 35, κενόν, ἐφ᾽ οἷς οὐ δεῖ ἐπαιρόμενον. Plutarch Sertor. xxvi. (581 F), "to despise Mallius ὡς κενοῦ καὶ ἀλαζόνος," Moral. 81 B, agriculturalists like to see ears of corn bending down, but those that are lifted by lightness κενοὺς ἡγοῦνται καὶ ἀλαζόνας; and so of youths intending to philosophise, those who are most κενοί and deficient in βάρος θράσος ἔχουσι, and a gait and walk and countenance full of scorn and contempt. The use of ἄνδρας κενούς (lit. empty) in Judg. ix. 4 does not help. Probably the sense is rather analogous to the Greek sense than identical. It is doubtful whether personal arrogance is intended here. Rather the unreality of the kind of faith professed, a faith which had no inner core to it.

ὅτι ἡ πίστις χωρὶς τῶν ἔργων] Probably as before (v. 18) this faith separated from the works belonging to it.

ἀργή, worthless] So best mss., not νεκρά, which comes from v. 26; ἀργός is worthless, i.e. either not working, idle,

ἔργων ἐδικαιώθη, ἀνενέγκας Ἰσαὰκ τὸν υἱὸν αὐτοῦ ἐπὶ τὸ θυσιαστήριον; ²²βλέπεις ὅτι ἡ πίστις συνήργει τοῖς ἔργοις

lazy, or producing no works in the
sense of results, hence useless, fruit-
less, ineffectual, as 2 Peter i. 8, οὐκ
ἀργοὺς οὐδὲ ἀκάρπους; and perhaps Mt.
xii. 36, πᾶν ῥῆμα ἀργόν. This sense
would suit the context: but as there
is an apparent contrast to συνήργει in
v. 22, it is better to refer it rather to
the act of working than to the result.
Τῶν ἔργων are the concrete works
capable of being spoken of separately;
so that there is no tautology, the working being thought of with reference
to the agent, and ἀργή here meaning
"inactive," putting forth no powers.

21. St James comes now to his examples to prove his point.

Ἀβραὰμ ὁ πατὴρ ἡμῶν] These words
stand first, before οὐκ, in the sense
"Take Abraham our father for instance, was not he," etc. "Abraham
our father" in a combination of senses,
as the father of the old Israel (Mt. iii.
9, etc.), as the father of the new Israel
which had arisen out of the old Israel
(claimed by Stephen, Acts vii. 2), and
above all as the father of those who
have shewn faith (Rom. iv. 11, 12, 16;
Gal. iii. 7 ff.). The context seems to
shew that this last is chiefly meant.
Abraham's example is important for
this purpose just because he was the
typical instance of faith.

οὐκ ἐξ ἔργων] The words do not
express whether he means that works
had a share in it, or that works alone
were concerned: but the former sense
alone can be reconciled either with
the general argument or with the
quotation in v. 23.

ἐδικαιώθη] This word is manifestly
to be interpreted in the first instance
by its O.T. usages. The active voice
δικαιόω represents the Piel and Hiphil
of צדק, both causative, to cause to be
צדיק (δίκαιος), just as δικαιόω as applied
ethically to persons is properly to
make δίκαιος. The passive voice δι-

καιοῦσθαι is one of the representatives
of the Kal of the same verb, to be
צדיק or δίκαιος, a word chiefly though
not exclusively used in Job (see especially Isa. xliii. 9, 26; xlv. 25), and
sometimes rendered δίκαιός εἰμι, or in
English "to be righteous." So far all
is etymologically clear: the active is
to make righteous, the passive to be
made righteous. But then comes the
question, does צדיק or δίκαιος or righteous mean always simply a quality in
a man without reference to the recognition of it? Certainly not. Various
passages (e.g. Ps. cxliii. 2) express or
imply the sense of being righteous in
God's sight, and this is almost the
only sense of the active, chiefly with
the force "defending the cause of,"
"pleading for the righteousness" or
"innocence of." The same senses
reappear freely in Ecclus. So in N.T.:
Mt. xii. 37; Lk. vii. 29; x. 29; xvi. 15;
xviii. 14 (not to count ἐδικαιώθη ἡ
σοφία etc., Mt. xi. 19; Lk. vii. 35); besides all the passages in St Paul, and
also Acts xiii. 39 where St Paul is the
speaker.

Leaving then for the present St Paul
out of sight, that we may not disturb
St James' argument, we have naturally here the sense "Did not Abraham
appear righteous in God's sight on the
ground of works?"

ἀνενέγκας κ.τ.λ.] From a combination of Gen. xxii. 2 (ἀνένεγκον) and 9, ἐπέ-
θηκεν αὐτὸν ἐπὶ τὸ θυσιαστήριον. There
is sometimes doubt when ἐπὶ stands
before τὸ θυσιαστήρ. whether it means
"to" or "upon": but here doubtless,
as the Hebrew suggests, it is "upon,"
as Mt. v. 23; 1 Pet. ii. 24. The meaning is that this act was distinctly a
work. The faith in God which Abraham felt was carried out in a piece
of conduct which tried it to the utmost.

22. βλέπεις, thou perceivest] It is

αὐτοῦ καὶ ἐκ τῶν ἔργων ἡ πίστις ἐτελειώθη, ²³καὶ ἐπληρώθη ἡ γραφὴ ἡ λέγουσα Ἐπίϲτεγϲεν δέ Ἀβραάμ τῷ θεῷ,
καὶ ἐλογίϲθη αὐτῷ εἰϲ Δικαιοϲύνην, καὶ φίλος θεοῦ ἐκλήθη.

so obvious, when looked at, that there
is no room for doubt.

ἡ πίστις, the faith] Sc. in this case:
the faith in antithesis to the works
was not separate from them but
wrought with them.

συνήργει, worked with] A bold
image. The faith not only was followed or accompanied by works—that
is expressed in τοῖς ἔργοις αὐτοῦ—but
itself worked with his works. Not
for faith plus works does St James
plead, but for faith at work, living,
acting in itself, apart from any value
in its results ; συνεργέω is properly to
be a συνεργός: not used in LXX., but
twice in Apocr. and in four other
places of the N.T.

καὶ ἐκ τῶν ἔργων, and by the works]
Ἐκ as before, in consequence of, by
effects proceeding from.

ἡ πίστις ἐτελειώθη, the faith was
made perfect] So long as the faith
was not exercised, it was in a manner
imperfect. It gained maturity and
completeness by being thoroughly
acted out. This is the only place
where St James uses this verb (common in N.T., especially Jn, 1 Jn,
Heb.), but τέλειος, as we have seen,
he has five times, and this nearly
answers to ἔργον τέλειον ἐχέτω in i. 4.
It is to be observed that the two
clauses are exactly complementary to
each other. The works received the
co-operation of a living power from
the faith : the faith received perfecting and consummation from the works
into which it grew.

23. καὶ ἐπληρώθη ἡ γραφὴ ἡ λέγουσα, and there was a fulfilment of
the Scripture which saith] The usual
phrase, as Lk. iv 21, etc. The Divine
word spoken is conceived of as receiving a completion so to speak in acts
or events which are done or come to
pass in accordance with it. This idea

of filling, or giving fullness to, is
always contained in the biblical use of
fulfilling, though not always in precisely the same sense. ἡ γραφή probably the individual saying of Scripture (ἡ γραφὴ αὕτη in Lk.).

The passage Gen. xv. 6 was the one
which most clearly expressed the faith
of Abraham and which at the same
time connected it with the accounting
it on the part of God as righteousness.
The words ἐλογίσθη αὐτῷ εἰς δικ. are
equivalent to saying ἐδικαιώθη (he, not
the faith). Philo, Leg. All. iii. 81
(p. 132) paraphrases them, Ἀβραάμ γέ
τοι ἐπίστευσε τῷ θεῷ, καὶ δίκαιος ἐνο-
μίσθη. The two passages are brought
together also in 1 Macc. ii. 52, Ἀβραὰμ
οὐχὶ ἐν πειρασμῷ εὑρέθη πιστός, καὶ
ἐλογίσθη αὐτῷ εἰς δικαιοσύνην; for the
πειρασμός doubtless refers to Gen. xxii.
1, ὁ θεὸς ἐπείρασε τὸν Ἀβραάμ.

καὶ φίλος θεοῦ ἐκλήθη, and (so) he
was called the friend of God] Probably the meaning is that this was
another result of the faith which he
shewed in the sacrifice of Isaac, the
first result being the fulfilling of the
words spoken of him with reference
to an earlier exhibition of faith. The
reference itself is doubtless mainly, if
not wholly, to Isa. xli. 8 (Heb. Sym.,
not LXX. ὃν ἠγάπησα) "who loved me,"
not "whom 1 loved" (see Cheyne);
2 Chr. xx. 7 (Heb. not LXX. τῷ
ἠγαπημένῳ σου; but v.l. τῷ φίλῳ
apud Field), and ἐκλήθη means not
"acquired the human title," but "was
Divinely stamped" with that unique
name. At the same time the name,
though doubtless originating in Isaiah
if not earlier, was widely spread, and
St James may have had Greek authority
for it. See the authorities in Lightfoot
on Clem. Rom. 10 (Clement refers to
it 17 also) ; and Rönsch in Hilg. Z. S.
1873 iv. 583 ff., and Wetst. Philo

²⁴ὁρᾶτε ὅτι ἐξ ἔργων δικαιοῦται ἄνθρωπος καὶ οὐκ ἐκ
πίστεως μόνον. ²⁵ὁμοίως δὲ καὶ 'Ραὰβ ἡ πόρνη οὐκ ἐξ

uses it, even substituting it once for
τοῦ παιδός μου in Gen. xviii. 17. Judith viii. 26=22 in lat. vg., "quomodo
pater noster Abraham tentatus est, et
per multas tribulationes probatus Dei
amicus factus est." Cf. Wisd. vii. 27;
Clem. Hom. xviii. 13; Recog. i. 32.
So also Lib. Jubil. 19, Ber. R. on
Gen. xiii. 8, etc.; and the name is still
in use among the Arabs, El Khalil.
Weil, cited by Rönsch 585, quotes
"When Abraham by Nimrod's command was to be thrown into the fire,
the heaven with its angels and the
earth with all the creatures therein
cried out with one voice, 'God of
Abraham, Thy friend, who alone on
earth adores Thee, is thrown into the
fire' etc." This various use shews by
the way that the occurrence of the
phrase in a Christian author is no
sufficient proof that he employed the
Epistle of St James.
  It is very doubtful whether the
name is etymological, though a writer
against the Jews called Molon, cited
by Alex. Polyhistor ap. Euseb. P. E.
9. 19, p. 420, says, ὃν δὴ μεθερμηνεύεσθαι
Πατρὸς φίλον; and Rönsch argues
that ח being changed into ה, רַחַם represents φίλος, though more properly
"one on whom God had mercy."
  24. ὁρᾶτε, ye see] St James now
turns from the "empty man" to the
brethren whom he was previously
addressing. Τοίνυν is spurious. Elsewhere in the N.T. ὁρᾶτε is always imperative, but in the sense "see to it,"
"beware," which will not do here. It
is not likely to be used in the sense
"take note," "observe," so that the
indic. is the most natural. The sense
must be "ye see by this example of
Abraham": otherwise ὁμοίως δὲ καί
has no force.
  ἐξ ἔργων δικαιοῦται] The same phrase
as in v. 21: but here the important
explanatory clause is added, καὶ οὐκ ἐκ

πίστεως μόνον; shewing that with him
it was no question of faith contrasted
with works, but of faith without works
contrasted with faith with works: the
faith as a ground of justification is
assumed as a starting point.
  25. ὁμοίως δὲ καί] This introduces
another example, not needing such
full exposition. Abraham the father
of the Jewish people was the first;
now St James cites a heathen, a
Canaanitess, as a type of the other
branch of Israelites and of Christians,
the proselyte Jews, the Gentile Christians; nay the first of all proselytes,
for her act took place at the very
entrance into the Promised Land.
In doing this, St James doubtless was
building on a Jewish traditional view.
Setting aside Heb. xi. 31, the remarkable introduction of Rahab's name in
Mt. i. 5 (as also Tamar, Ruth, Bath-
sheba) implies a tradition as to her
marriage to Salmon which marks her
out in a signal manner. See Wetst.
(i. 226) and better Wünsche Erl. der
Ev. 3 f. Thus Megilla 14 b, "Eight
prophets who were also priests are
descended from the harlot Rahab, etc."
(ten prophets and prophetesses according to Midrash, Ruth i.): another
Midrash says priests. Midr. Cant.
"As long as the Israelites do the will
of God, He brings every righteous
man whom He sees among the other
peoples, and joins him to Israel, as
came to pass with Jethro and Rahab."
  The precise purpose of adding ἡ
πόρνη (added also in Heb.) is not
clear. Perhaps her occupation is
meant to point to her heathen origin,
and as marking the extreme form of
a faith which was due to a change or
conversion, not part of an orderly and
continuous growth, as in Abraham or
Samuel.
  οὐκ ἐξ ἔργων ἐδικαιώθη] The force
of this lies in what is implied, that

ἔργων ἐδικαιώθη, ὑποδεξαμένη τοὺς ἀγγέλους καὶ ἑτέρα
ὁδῷ ἐκβαλοῦσα; ²⁶ὥσπερ τὸ σῶμα χωρὶς πνεύματος

26. ὥσπερ] + γὰρ

she was justified in virtue of her faith in that she embraced the belief in the one true God, and risked all on the belief. This very faith, he says, was not one barren of works: it shewed its strength by her willingness to risk her life to save the servants of the true God.

ὑποδεξαμένη, *hospitably entertained.*

τοὺς ἀγγέλους] Called κατασκόπους in Heb., and τοὺς κατασκοπεύσαντας Josh. vi. 25. The more favourable word is perhaps chosen to suggest that in receiving them she was as it were receiving angels.

ἑτέρᾳ ὁδῷ] Probably no more than "different from the way by which they came."

ἐκβαλοῦσα, *dismissed them*] So probably. The word is a stronger one than we should expect to find used, but the same thing happens in other places of the N.T., as Mt. ix. 38, Lk. x. 2, ἐργάτας; Jn x. 4, πρόβατα; Mt. xii. 35, ἐκ τ. ἀγαθοῦ θησαυροῦ τὰ ἀγαθά, etc.

26. γάρ is very doubtful: some authority for δέ: but no conjunction most likely. It is a general summing up, not standing in very near relation to *v.* 25, but referring alike to the whole passage from *v.* 14.

χωρὶς πνεύματος, *separated from (the) spirit*] Not spirit in the higher sense, but simply the breath of life. The body with the breath in it has all the difference from the body out of which the breath has departed that life has from death, although externally the body is nearly the same. So too the same contents of faith, that there is one God, or to go on to all that is contained in ii. 1, the faith of the Lord Jesus Christ the Glory, is a dead thing if it is separated from works, in other words, from active energy. The paradox must be intentional. The opposite is what most

would be tempted to say: but it would be only superficially true. True faith is a faith that aims at work and motion; false faith is virtually a corpse. He uses νεκρά here where he had said ἀργή before. The idea is much the same, but νεκρά expresses it by a strong image.

Now as regards the relation of this section to St Paul, the examples cited are certainly not enough to imply that St Paul had already written. St Paul mentions Abraham: but who could do otherwise in speaking of faith? St Paul does not mention Rahab; and though the Pauline author of Heb. does, it is not in connexion with justification or with any controversial purpose but simply as one of a series of examples of faith. It is remarkable that Philo, *de nobil.* 5 (ii. 442), first speaks strongly of Abraham (διὸ καὶ πιστεῦσαι λέγεται τῷ θεῷ πρῶτος, ἐπειδὴ καὶ πρῶτος ἀκλινῆ καὶ βεβαίαν ἔσχεν ὑπόληψιν, ὡς ἔστιν ἐν αἴτιον τὸ ἀνωτάτω καὶ προνοεῖ τοῦ τε κόσμου καὶ τῶν ἐν αὐτῷ), and then proceeds Ταύτην τὴν εὐγένειαν οὐ μόνον θεοφιλεῖς ἄνδρες ἀλλὰ καὶ γυναῖκες ἐζήλωσαν, and then gives as an instance Tamar, who appears in Mt. with Rahab, using language that might be applied at once to Rahab, how she was an inhabitant of Palestine, a woman brought up in a city full of many gods, full of images etc.: and then how out of deep darkness she was able to see a little dawn of light, and how she waxed strong unto piety, little heeding life if she were not to live nobly. Thus both examples might come quite naturally to St James simply from his Jewish education.

But the phrase ἐξ ἔργων ἐδικαιώθη, taken in its juxtaposition to faith, is very hard to explain without reference to St Paul. There is no real evidence for any similar Jewish language. Justification is not part of St James'

νεκρόν ἐστιν, οὕτως καὶ ἡ πίστις χωρὶς ἔργων νεκρά
ἐστιν.

III. ¹ Μὴ πολλοὶ διδάσκαλοι γίνεσθε, ἀδελφοί μου,
εἰδότες ὅτι μεῖζον κρίμα λημψόμεθα· ²πολλὰ γὰρ

original argument: but he brings it
in from *vv.* 21—24 in a way which
implies that he is arguing against
some actual plea. If he had been
intending to argue against St Paul
he would have used language which
struck at St Paul's doctrine. But
this he avoids. His language is
indeed formally inconsistent with
St Paul's, since St Paul altogether
declined to speak of any justification
by works. But this language of
St Paul may easily have been used,
even by men opposed to him, in a
manner at variance with his true
purpose. Such verbal contradictions
are sometimes inevitable for the expression of the fulness of the truth:
and laying aside the insoluble question whether St James personally
would have accepted every word that
St Paul used, or St Paul every word
that St James used, we are justified
in considering both, not merely to
have been needful as leaders of the
Church in the Apostolic age, but as
having contributed two forms of
teaching, each of which is perma-
nently necessary for the completeness
of truth.

III. 1. St James takes up now a
fresh point: wrong speech after wrong
action.

μὴ πολλοὶ διδάσκαλοι, *not many
teachers*] There is no need to correct
to πολυδιδάσκαλοι or otherwise. The
phrase is peculiar, but forcible and
clear enough as interpreted by the
context and by *vv.* 13 ff. It is assumed
that for the good of the community
there should be teachers, discharging
a special function for the rest (1 Cor.
xii. 29, μὴ πάντες διδάσκαλοι; cf. 28,
τρίτον διδασκάλους), and then implied
that many set up as teachers not from

a sense of responsibility but from a
vain or censorious spirit. Thus the
single notion "many teachers" practically involves the idea that the teaching arose from low personal motives.
The context would allow διδάσκαλοι
to be used vaguely, as if ordinary
social censoriousness were intended.
But it is hardly likely that this word
would have been chosen except with
reference to actual public teaching.
The sense is illustrated by the whole
of 1 Cor. xii.—xiv., but especially by
xiv. 26; though it is true that we
cannot conclude too rapidly from the
ways of Corinthian Greeks to the
Jews of the Dispersion. Still what
follows in the rest of the chapter is
strikingly analogous to much that St
Paul says in 1 Cor. about σοφία and
λόγος, and to the manner in which he
connects together the misuse of both.
The disputatiousness of Greeks may
well have had much in common with
the disputatiousness of Jewish Christians, more especially as many of
them were of Greek race.

This precise tendency has no distinct echo in the Gospels, except the
warning against idle words. Mt. xxiii.
8—10 refers rather to the honour of
rabbiship than to the pride of the
exercise of the office of teacher.

ἀδελφοί μου] This again introduces
a fresh point, softening off at the outset the sharpness of what St James
had to say.

εἰδότες] Not "taking note," "ob-
serving," but "knowing as ye already
do."

μεῖζον κρίμα λημψόμεθα, *shall receive greater judgment*] The word of
Christ on idle words (Mt. xii. 36 f.)
pronounced that account should be
given ἐν ἡμέρᾳ κρίσεως; "for by thy

5—2

πταίομεν ἅπαντες. εἴ τις ἐν λόγῳ οὐ πταίει, οὗτος
τέλειος ἀνήρ, δυνατὸς χαλιναγωγῆσαι καὶ ὅλον τὸ σῶμα.
³εἰ δὲ τῶν ἵππων τοὺς χαλινοὺς εἰς τὰ στόματα βάλ-

words...thou shalt be condemned (καταδικασθῇσῃ)."

κρίμα λημψόμεθα] This phrase occurs in a different context Mk xii. 40 || Lk. xx. 47, with περισσότερον for μεῖζον. There περισσότερον seems to mean that those who combined the pretensions of scribeship with these faults and vices should be condemned yet more than ordinary offenders. Here μεῖζον must have much the same force, but perhaps also a special reference to the just retribution involved in "Judge not that ye be not judged": that is, it seems to be implied that wrong judging was a characteristic of the much teaching. This seems to follow from γάρ in v. 2, which cannot be otiose. We all stumble and therefore come under judgment: but the judgment is greater if we have been taking on ourselves to judge others.

2. πολλὰ γὰρ πταίομεν ἅπαντες, For in many things we all stumble] Πταίω as before (ii. 10).

πολλά] Lies between πολύ and πολλάκις: it is "much" with the idea of plurality and repetition introduced: so Mt. ix. 14 v. l. (νηστεύομεν); Mk iii. 12 (ἐπετίμα); v. 10 (παρεκάλει), 38 (ἀλαλάζοντας), 43 (διεστείλατο), etc.

ἅπαντες] "one and all."

εἴ τις ἐν λόγῳ οὐ πταίει, If any stumbleth not in speech] Not μή but οὐ, = "succeeds in escaping stumbling," the two words being taken together. For the phrase cf. Ps. xxxix. 1, τοῦ μὴ ἁμαρτάνειν ἐν γλώσσῃ μου; Ecclus. xix. 16, καὶ τίς οὐχ ἥμαρτεν ἐν τῇ γλώσσῃ αὐτοῦ; (Cf. Philo de nom. mut. 1082 c; de Abr. 352 c.) The image was applied to the tongue by Zeno ap. Diog. Laert. vii. 26 (Wetst.), κρεῖττον εἶναι τ. ποσὶν ὀλισθεῖν ἢ τῇ γλώττῃ: cf. Eustathius in Od. viii. 171.

The previous sentence spoke of

moral stumbling of any kind. Here it becomes narrowed to speech: stumbling in speech is peculiarly easy and common: but the misuse of speech in pride and bitterness of teachership is something much worse than ordinary stumbling in speech. Here then St James drops for a while the subject begun in v. 1, to be taken up again in 13—18. The vicious teachership suggested to him the vicious use of the tongue in general, and so he launches out into this wider subject.

τέλειος ἀνήρ, a perfect man] The adjective as before, consecrated by Mt. v. 48. 'Ανήρ cannot have the sense that ἄνθρωπος would have, "one shewing the perfection of humanity": it is simply "one that is perfect."

δυνατὸς χαλιναγωγῆσαι καὶ ὅλον τὸ σῶμα, able to bridle the whole body also] The force of καί is that his stumbling not in speech arises from his bridling his tongue; and that a man who can bridle his tongue can also bridle his whole body. This may be in two senses, that the tongue is so difficult to bridle that it is an easier thing to bridle the whole body, and that in the bridling of the tongue the bridling of the body is virtually accomplished at the same time. The comparison to the horses' bridle in v. 3 and to the rudder in v. 4 and the whole language of 6 prevent the exclusion of the second sense, while the form of this sentence rather suggests the first. Probably St James meant both senses to be included.

The bridling of the tongue (already named i. 26) is naturally one of the commonest of images in various languages: but it is especially associated with μὴ ἁμαρτάνειν ἐν γλώσσῃ in Ps. xxxix. 1 (Heb. not LXX.).

3. εἰ δέ] True reading, not ἰδέ (or

λομεν εἰς τὸ πείθεσθαι αὐτοὺς ἡμῖν, καὶ ὅλον τὸ σᾶμα
αὐτῶν μετάγομεν· ⁴ἰδοὺ καὶ τὰ πλοῖα, τηλικαῦτα
ὄντα καὶ ὑπὸ ἀνέμων σκληρῶν ἐλαυνόμενα, μετάγεται
ὑπὸ ἐλαχίστου πηδαλίου ὅπου ἡ ὁρμὴ τοῦ εὐθύνοντος

as T.R. with a few ἰδού) derived from supposed parallelism to ἰδού in v. 4. The δέ is equivalent to the logical "now": the verse is really an inference from the force of the word χαλιναγωγῆσαι. St James has used it completely metaphorically of the whole body, when he might have said in general terms "keep in order": but it occurs to him that the word has a special force for his purpose because it is just through the mouth, the source of speech, that the process of bridling takes place.

τῶν ἵππων] Put first because horses are the direct subjects of comparison with τέλειος ἀνήρ: it thus is equivalent to "in the case of horses" though of course governed not only by τα στόματα but also by τοὺς χαλινούς: the mouths are the part of the horses into which we put the bits by which we mean to restrain them. This accounts for the two articles.

εἰς τὸ πείθεσθαι (not πρός), to make them obey us] St James doubtless means to express not merely result but purpose. The reason why the phrase is introduced is probably because St James is thinking how far control of the tongue goes towards producing control of the whole body.

μετάγομεν, we turn about] Μετάγω as commonly used means to "transfer" or "transport" in a strong sense, as prisoners to a strange land, or the power of government from one class to another. It is also used of turning men to a better mind (still transference) Plut. ii. 225 F; Epict. Ench. xxxiii. 3. Apparently here simply in the sense of leading not from one place to another but from one direction to another, though it is not satisfactory to have no clear authority for it.

Lexicons and commentaries pass the point over.

4. The example of the ships and rudders comes in by way of addition, apparently as suggested by the last words of v. 3.

τηλικαῦτα ὄντα καὶ ὑπὸ ἀνέμων σκληρῶν ἐλαυνόμενα, though they are so great, and though they are driven by rough winds] This is the most natural construction according to the form of the sentence. On the other hand it is somewhat singular that the size and the driving by winds, which would not be always rough, are coupled together; and it is possible that καί means not "and" but "even," "the ships, great as they are, even when they are being driven by rough winds, are turned about," etc.

πηδαλίου, rudder] From the Odyssey onwards.

ὁρμή, impulse] This might be either the impulse in the mind of the steersman or the impulse which his hand communicates to the helm: but the whole phrase would be rather feeble if referred to the mind only: moreover there would be almost a contradiction between the "impulsiveness" and the purpose (βουλή).

τοῦ εὐθύνοντος, the steersman] Εὐθύνω, first to make straight, is then used of any kind of guidance, shepherd of sheep, charioteer of chariot, steersman of ship (Plato etc.); and of the rudder itself (Luc. Dial. Mort. x. 10, εὔθυνε, ὦ πορθμεύ, τὸ πηδάλιον; Eur. Cyc. 15,

ἐν πρύμνῃ δ' ἄκρᾳ
αὐτὸς λαβὼν ηὔθυνον ἀμφῆρες δόρυ).

βούλεται, willeth] By a bold figure the deliberation and decision is transferred to the last point at which the steersman's action passes into that of

βούλεται· ⁵οὕτως καὶ ἡ γλῶσσα μικρὸν μέλος ἐστὶν καὶ
μεγάλα αὐχεῖ. ἰδοὺ ἡλίκον πῦρ ἡλίκην ὕλην ἀνάπτει·

the rudder by the movement of his
hand. Βούλομαι as before implies not
mere will but intention: the steersman
turns the helm this way or that
because he knows which way his
course lies. Rudders and steersmen
have furnished many images. This
combination of the horse's bridle and
the ship's rudder as illustrative of the
government of the tongue is found in
Ps.-Plat. *Axioch.* [? ap. Theoph. Simoc.
Ep. 70] and in Plutarch and Philo
[see Wetst. and Mayor].

5. Apparently a direct comparison
with *v.* 4. What is not easy is μεγάλα
αὐχεῖ (so better than μεγαλαυχεῖ).

μεγάλα αὐχεῖ, *hath great things
whereof to boast*] Αὐχέω is properly to
stretch the neck and hold up the
head in pride, and hence to speak
with proud confidence. Μεγαλαυχέω
seems always to be used in a disparaging sense, to denote "boastfulness." The difficulty is that the
comparison seems to require not great
pretension but great performance to
be ascribed to the tongue. Oecumenius has μεγάλα ἐργάζεται by way of
paraphrase, and something like this
is doubtless what we should expect.
It does not help much to say that the
pretension comes first, the performance next, viz. in the following verses.
The true solution lies probably in the
wider use of αὐχέω than of μεγαλαυχέω.
Though αὐχέω never loses the sense of
boast, it frequently, both in early and
late Greek, is used without sense of
unreality in the boast, and virtually
as equivalent to "having cause to
boast." The only question then is as
to the use of μεγάλα, which *prima
facie* has an adverbial force, "greatly."
Now αὐχεῖ used absolutely without
reference to any object could refer
only to boastfulness, pretence; and
μεγάλα as an adverb would only
accentuate this force, by the association with μεγαλαυχέω. But in late

Greek αὐχέω is not infrequently used
with the accusative of things boasted
of, where the classical usage would be
with dative with or without ἐπί. Thus
Aristid. i. 103, μόνοις δ' ὑμῖν ὑπάρχει καθαρὰν εὐγένειάν τε καὶ πολιτείαν αὐχῆσαι:
just as we use the verb "boast" transi-
tively: "that country boasts many
great cities." So here μ. αὐχεῖ doubtless means "hath great things whereof
to boast," or shortly "great are its
boasts" (i.e. the concrete subjects for
boasting, αὐχήματα, not the boastings,
αὐχήσεις). This sense is supported
by the analogy of κατακαυχᾶται in ii.
13, where the glorying of mercy
against judgment is no mere vain
boasting, but a true position proudly
held. It is thus quite doubtful
whether there is even an indirect
reference to arrogance of tongue.
What follows gives examples of the
"great things."

ἰδοὺ ἡλίκον (not ὀλίγον) πῦρ ἡλίκην
ὕλην ἀνάπτει, *Behold how much wood
is kindled by how small a fire*]
'Ηλίκος expresses magnitude in either
direction, *quantus* or *quantillus* (Luc.
Hermot. 5): the antithesis explains
that with πῦρ it means "how little,"
with ὕλην "how great." This is a
good example of St James' pregnant
enigmatic style, leaving much to the
reader's intelligence.

ὕλην] Etymologically = *silva*, and
answers fairly to both the English
words "wood" and "timber." It is
used either of dead wood or living,
and either will make sense here. But
it never means *a* wood, *a* forest. As
applied to living wood it is either
woodland as opposed to mountains
and cultivated plains, specially the
rough bushy skirts of the hills, or
brushwood. Thus Plat. *Polit.* 272 A
says, καρποὺς ἀφθόνους εἶχον ἀπό τε
δένδρων καὶ πολλῆς ὕλης ἄλλης. A
spark setting fire to the brush might
suggest the image, or it may be (as

⁶καὶ ἡ γλῶσσα πῦρ, ὁ κόσμος τῆς ἀδικίας ἡ γλῶσσα

often) simply a great mass of cut timber ready for the carpenter. The word is interesting on account of Plato's use, answering to *materia, materies.* [See Additional Note.] The image was probably taken from the Hebrew Proverbs of Ben Sira (transl. in Drusius ap. *Crit. Sacr.* viii. p. 1879) cf. Ecclus. xi. 32. "A burning fire kindles many heaps of corn." On which the Scholiast has "There is nothing which more devastates the world than an evil tongue: for a tongue of this kind, though it be not *very* evil, is the ruin of many just and pious men. (Example of Doeg.) Wherefore the wise Hebrews declare that in an evil tongue lurks deadly poison, and that because of it the world suffers chastisement," etc.

6. A very difficult verse. Οὔτως is spurious before ἡ γλῶσσα καθίσταται, and misleading also. It is impossible Greek to take ἡ σπιλοῦσα as predicate to the sentence ἡ γλῶσσα καθίστ. as though it were τὸ σπιλοῦν. The best punctuation is to take καὶ ἡ γλῶσσα πῦρ as a separate clause, " the tongue also is a fire," introductory to what follows. Then ὁ κ. τ. ἀδ. ἡ γλ. καθίστ. ἐν τ. μέλ. ἡμ.; then ἡ σπιλοῦσα... γεέννης, in which last clause references to fire appear again. Hence ἡ γλῶσσα (the 2nd) must be the subject, ὁ κόσμος τ. ἀδ. the predicate ; and the reason why ὁ κόσμος τ. ἀδ. is put first is because ἡ γλῶσσα must be put last in order to connect it distinctly with the following participles. Thus the arrangement of words is exactly analogous to that of i. 7, 8.

καὶ ἡ γλῶσσα πῦρ, *The tongue also is a fire*] Cf. Prov. xvi. 27 ; Ps. cxx. 4 ; Ecclus. xxviii. 21–23 ; also Ps. Sol. xii. 2.

ὁ κόσμος τῆς ἀδικίας, *the unrighteous world*] Certainly a difficult phrase. The article must of course have its full force, "*a* world of iniquity" cannot be right. Some take κόσμος as

"ornament": understanding it to mean that the tongue gives a specious and seductive colour or gloss to what is evil by means of plausible words. But though words might by a rather bold figure be called the adornment of iniquity, the tongue that utters them could not : nor has that sense any special force here. The commonest interpretation is to take it as "world" in the sense of universe, "that world of iniquity." The article here acquires a possible sense with the other construction, in apposition with πῦρ ; but not as the predicate after καθίσταται. The sense itself too is at once exaggerated and vague. It is not the comprehensiveness of the tongue within itself that the context refers to, but its power of acting upon what is without it.

There remains the "evil" sense of κόσμος, found already i. 27, and recurring iv. 4. To repeat very briefly. This sense of something called the κόσμος as not only containing evil elements but itself in some sense evil is chiefly found in Jn and 1 Jn, also 2 Pet.; perhaps not elsewhere (2 Cor. vii. 10 doubtful). It is *not* derived from the physical universe, but a Jewish image taken from the תֵּבֵל of the early chapters of Isaiah (cf. Ps. ix. 8 etc.), rendered οἰκουμένη in LXX., denoting the heathen nations around, the heathen world at once as destructive and as corruptive: hence it is human society in a corrupt and perverted state. As applied to the tongue then, the meaning is that the tongue is to the rest of the body what the corrupt society is to mankind, and especially to the Church as the representative of mankind in its true state. Thus τ. ἀδικίας may be compared to its use in Lk. xvi. 8, τὸν οἰκονόμον τῆς ἀδικίας and 9, μαμωνᾶ τ. ἀδ. and xviii. 6, ὁ κριτὴς τ. ἀδ.: the world which gives itself up to unrighteousness, which takes its form from unrighteousness

καθίσταται ἐν τοῖς μέλεσιν ἡμῶν, ἡ σπιλοῦσα ὅλον
τὸ σῶμα καὶ φλογίζουσα τὸν τροχὸν τῆς γενέσεως

and obeys it: somewhat similar are the genitives in i. 25. Much the same ultimate sense would be obtained by taking κόσμος as the sphere or region, the domain as it were in which unrighteousness obtains a footing. But this is not a natural sense of the word, which is more easily interpreted by the other passages of this Epistle referred to.

καθίσταται, *is constituted, shews itself, makes itself, acts the part of*] The exact force is shewn by iv. 4. Καθίστασθαι εἰς is to come into a certain state, or καθ. with nominative to become (contrast καθέστηκα to *have* become, to be). Thus Plut. ii. 2 E, trees if neglected στρεβλὰ φύεται καὶ ἄκαρπα καθίσταται, τυχόντα δὲ ὀρθῆς παιδαγωγίας ἔγκαρπα γίνεται καὶ τελεσφόρα (cf. 6 F).

ἐν τοῖς μέλεσιν ἡμῶν, *among our members*] Apparently not merely with reference to its action on the other members; but as being that one among the members which has this special power.

ἡ σπιλοῦσα, *that stainer of*] The article has the effect of giving a substantive force to the participle, as it were, the tongue that stainer of the body. The use of this word agrees with the interpretation just given of κόσμος, when compared with ἄσπιλος ...ἀπὸ τ. κόσμου in i. 27. The image however is difficult: in what sense can the tongue be said to stain the body? Apparently with reference to the idea that runs through chap. i. that there is a Divine image received by man at creation, a true ideal form derived from likeness to God, and that all moral evil is to be regarded in relation to this as (i. 21) a ῥυπαρία or defilement and a περισσεία or excrescence (unnatural growth). Still why "the body," for St James certainly regarded the Divine image as

(at least in the first instance) inward and spiritual? Probably because he regarded the body as the outward expression of the inward mind; and the external deformities of passion as true types as well as results of the invisible deformities from which they spring. Moreover the *action* of the tongue might be regarded as staining the *action* of the whole body, the total conduct of which the body is the organ. Cf. also Eccles. v. 5.

καὶ φλογίζουσα τὸν τροχὸν τῆς γενέσεως, *and it setteth on fire the wheel of man's creation*] Here we reach one of the hardest phrases in the Bible. To discuss it fully would take too long. We must be content to deal with the leading points. At the outset Grotius' suggestion that τροχόν should be read τρόχον, a running or course, must be set aside. The word, chiefly poetic, is never used figuratively; and at all events φλογίζουσα points to some physical image. The suggestion comes from too prosaic a dealing with the imagery of a prophet. Φλ. τ. τροχόν must mean "setting on fire the wheel."

But then what is τ. γενέσεως, and what wheel is meant? Attention was called eight years ago by Hilgenfeld (*ZWT.* 1873. 20; cf. *Einl.* 539 f.) to the certainly curious fact that Simplicius on Arist. *de caelo* ii. p. 91 B in allegorising Ixion's wheel says, "and he hath been bound by God τῷ τῆς μοίρας τροχῷ καὶ τῆς γενέσεως, ὃν ἀδύνατον μεταλλάξαι κατ' 'Ορφέα (what follows is hopelessly corrupt, but ends with τὰς ἀνθρωπίνας ψυχάς), clearly referring to an Orphic doctrine. The sense comes out more clearly, but with κύκλος for τροχός, in Procl. *Tim.* v. 330 A (on Plato's words τῇ ταὐτοῦ καὶ ὁμοίου περιόδῳ), "This is the one salvation of the soul which is held forth by the Creator, delivering it τοῦ

κύκλου τ. γενέσεως and from the great
error and from the ineffectual life,
namely the ascent of the soul to the
spiritual region (τὸ νοερὸν εἶδος) and
its flight from all things which cleave
to us ἐκ τῆς γενέσεως ; and lower down
(B)...ἀπὸ τῆς περὶ τὴν γένεσιν πλάνης,
ἧς καὶ οἱ παρ᾽ Ὀρφεῖ τῷ Διονύσῳ καὶ
τῇ Κόρῃ τελούμενοι τυχεῖν εὔχονται
  Κύκλου τ᾽ αὖ λῆξαι καὶ ἀναπνεῦσαι
  κακότητος.
There is somewhat similar language
in Procl. Tim. i. 32 E and Theol. Pl.
vi. 3 p. 351 ; cf. Verg. Aen. vi. 748,
Hos omnes ubi mille rotam volvere
per annos.   For γενέσεως we have
ἀνάγκης in the statement of Diog.
Laert. viii. 14, Vit. Pyth., "They
say that he was the first to declare
the soul κύκλον ἀνάγκης ἀμείβουσαν
ἄλλοτε ἄλλοις ἐνδεῖσθαι ζώοις.   So
more vaguely, without reference to
any one in particular, Chrys. Mt. lxxv.
728 C, περιφορὰν καὶ γένεσιν λέγοντες.
Also Philo de Somn. ii. 6, p. 664 of
Pharaoh's gold chain round Joseph's
neck, ἀγχόνην ἐπιφανῆ, κύκλον καὶ
τροχὸν ἀνάγκης ἀτελευτήτου,...οὐκ ἀκο-
λουθίαν καὶ τὸ ἑξῆς ἐν βίῳ καὶ τὸν
εἱρμὸν τῶν τῆς φύσεως πραγμάτων, ὡς
ἡ Θάμαρ, οὐ γὰρ κλοιός, ἀλλ᾽ ὁρμίσκος
αὐτῆς ὁ κόσμος (cf. de mut. nom. 23
p. 598).   In the first places cited the
reference is certainly to the Orphic or
Pythagorean doctrine of a cycle of
metempsychosis : Chrys. and Philo
are ambiguous.   Another passage of
Simplicius (Comm. in Epict. Ench.
p. 177 c) gives it a distinctly wider
sense, " The dissolution of compounds
and the change of simples one into
another is good for the whole ; since
the destruction of one is the origin
(γένεσις) of another ; and this is the
cause why τὸν τῆς γενέσεως κύκλον
remains imperishable (ἀνέκλειπτον).

But it is most improbable that
St James should use a phrase of this
origin to convey a doctrine with which
he can have had no sympathy.   The
Orphic doctrine would be entirely
alien to him (notwithstanding Hilgen-

feld's references to θρησκός), and the
vaguer doctrine hardly less.   Γένεσις
in this connexion was the word used
in late Greek philosophy to express
natural necessity; the necessary chain
of causation ; and it was especially
opposed to any religious view of the
world.

An equal improbability lies in the
mode of use: this setting on fire of
the τροχὸν τ. γενέσεως is evidently
spoken of as an evil thing ; but to a
believer in God this interruption of
the wheel of earthbound destiny
would be no subject for regret.   The
interpretation thus just inverts the
purport of the sentence.

Moreover it is difficult to think that
τῆς γενέσεως should recur in two places
of the Epistle (here and i. 23) in very
peculiar phrases, yet be entirely different in sense: for whatever sense
we give to γενέσεως with τὸ πρόσωπον,
it cannot possibly be destiny.

Another simpler image occurs in
various classical writers, partly again
in connexion with Ixion, that of human
life as a wheel rolling down hill over
all sorts of inequalities : thus Sil. Ital.
vi. 120.   But here too there is no
special force in the setting fire, and
τ. γενέσεως remains inexplicable.   The
same may be said of the vaguer
senses "course of life," "course of
nature."

The true clue is doubtless to be
found in τ. γενέσεως which we saw (on
i. 23) to refer to the original creation
of man.   It is not in classical but
in biblical language that we should
naturally expect to find the explanation.   Not the heathen godless genesis but the genesis of revelation, the
origin of the world in the will and
purpose of God, is denoted by the
word for St James.   It is the תלדת or
מלדת (see Gen. ii. 4 ; v. I), whence
Genesis has its Greek name.   Κτίσις
is not used in LXX. (though κτίζω is) :
see 2 Macc. vii. 23, ὁ τοῦ κόσμου
κτίστης, ὁ πλάσας ἀνθρώπου γένεσιν καὶ
πάντων ἐξευρὼν γένεσιν.   It thus is

καὶ φλογιζομένη ὑπὸ τῆς γεέννης. ⁷πᾶσα γὰρ φύσις

equivalent to what in modern language we call Creation. The phrase "the wheel of creation" is limited by the sense of the rest of the sentence to "the wheel of man's creation," i.e. the wheel of man's nature according to its original Divine purpose, just as τ. πρόσωπον τ. γενέσεως αὐτοῦ is "the face of his creation," the face reflecting the Divine image in which he was created.

What then is meant by the wheel? It can hardly be the detached wheel rolling uselessly along, as in the classical image. It must be the chariot-wheel of man as he advances on the way of life, fulfilling his appointed course. Probably, I do not say more, but probably there is an allusion to the wheel in the vision of Ezekiel (i. 15, 16 b, 19—21). This may sound fanciful till we remember that this vision of Ezekiel, called the Chariot by the later Jews, was in Jewish thought associated with the Creation. According to the imagery of the vision, the wheel might be the body and all its activities, by means of which the spirit moves upon the earth. This is represented as set on fire by the tongue, because its orderly Divinely-appointed motion is made violent and irregular by the passions which the tongue excites: it catches fire, and loses its power to fulfil its proper course. [See Additional Note.]

καὶ φλογιζομένη ὑπὸ τῆς γεέννης, and is set on fire by hell] The fire is not a fire from above but from beneath. This seems to be the true force of the reference to Gehenna, which usually in the N.T. appears simply as the place of punishment for evil (whether we mean by punishment retribution only, or retribution combined with purification), not excepting perhaps Mt. xxiii. 15, υἱὸν γεέννης, as itself so to speak a realm of evil. The fire lighted at the nether fires is a simpler and broader image, answering in some

degree to the lower wisdom of v. 15. Wetstein quotes the Targum on Ps. cxx. 2 (where the hot burning coals may be taken as describing either the operation of the tongue or its punishment, or indeed both, i.e. its *appropriate* punishment) Lingua dolosa... cum carbonibus juniperi, qui incensi sunt in gehenna inferne.

7. γάρ, *For*] The purpose of γάρ seems to be to introduce an explanation and justification of the strong language just used. From the word "bridle" in v. 2 St James has been led to the idea of a small agency exercising great power, and especially to the image of fire as representing the tongue : and now he proceeds to explain this, pointing first to its un-bridledness, and then to its strange inconsistency of action.

πᾶσα φύσις, *every nature*] Φύσις is often used periphrastically with the genitive, so that this might mean simply "all beasts and birds," etc. And it is also sometimes used for "kind." Thus Diod. Sic. i. 10, ἡ γῆ πάλιν ἐξ ἀρχῆς καινὰς ἤνεγκε τῶν ζώων φύσεις; Plut. ii. 636 E, ζώων δὲ πολλὰς φύσεις τοῦ κόσμου περιέχοντος, οὐδέν, ὡς εἰπεῖν, γένος ἄμοιρόν ἐστι τῆς ἐξ ᾠοῦ γενέσεως. But even in such places the original sense is latent, "many kinds" as dependent on "many natures." Here, at all events, the strict sense is required by τῇ φύσει τῇ ἀνθρωπίνῃ; for although ἀνθρωπίνη φύσις is occasionally, though very rarely, equivalent to "mankind," the periphrasis would have a rhetorical unnaturalness here, especially in the resolved form τῇ φ. τῇ ἀνθ. (not τῇ ἀνθ. φ.). The meaning doubtless is that the inherent nature of man, that nature which proceeds from the Divine image, has proved its kingship over the natures of different classes of animals, probably with reference to Gen. i. 28; ix. 2. The meaning cannot be that every kind, or the nature of every kind, of animals

θηρίων τε καὶ πετεινῶν ἑρπετῶν τε καὶ ἐναλίων δαμάζεται καὶ δεδάμασται τῇ φύσει τῇ ἀνθρωπίνῃ· ⁸τὴν
δὲ γλῶσσαν οὐδεὶς δαμάσαι δύναται ἀνθρώπων· ἀκα-

has been tamed; which would be manifestly untrue : but each of these four
great classes is considered as having a
special nature. An exact parallel is
I Cor. xv. 39, ἄλλη δὲ σὰρξ κτηνῶν
κ.τ.λ. What is there said of the outward flesh is here implied as to the
inward nature.

θηρίων τε καὶ πετεινῶν ἑρπετῶν τε καὶ
ἐναλίων, *of beasts and birds, of creep-
ing things and things in the sea*]
These classes are exactly and almost
verbally taken from Gen. ix. 2, which
is a modification of i. 28. Θηρία probably includes both θηρία and κτήνη of
i. 28, the fiercest and least tameable of
quadrupeds being taken as representatives of the whole class : πετεινά and
ἑρπετά are taken as they stand.

In the second pair ἑρπετῶν answers
to θηρίων in the first, and doubtless
was intended especially to include
serpents, with especial reference to
the tongue (see *v.* 8). The allusion
may be to the sacred tame serpents
which were kept in different temples,
for instance in those of Asclepius.
Tame fish, sacred and other, were
also known to the ancients (see Ael.
Nat. An. viii. 4; xii. 30). Ἐνάλια
answer to ἰχθύες. A poetic word,
used in prose in this general manner
in late writers only, as Ps.-Arist. *de
mundo* 5, οὗτος ἐναλίων ζῴων καὶ
πεζῶν καὶ ἀερίων φύσεις ἐχώρισεν;
Plut. ii. 911 D, τὸ τῶν ἐναλίων γένος
contrasted with τὰ χερσαῖα; also 729 E,
ἐφείδοντο μάλιστα τῶν ἐναλίων.

δαμάζεται καὶ δεδάμασται τῇ φύσει
ιῇ ἀνθρωπίνῃ, *is tamed and hath been
tamed into subjection to the nature
that is human*] First comes the
general statement that they are
tamed : then the thought occurs that
there are domestic races which have
been tamed long ago ; and so the
present acquires a more precise sense.

There is a long-established conquest
by the human race transmitted by
hereditary instinct, and it is being
perpetually renewed. Δαμάζω is sometimes applied to the mere crushing of
a foe : its proper sense is *taming*,
subduing not for destruction but for
orderly use, as with horses and oxen.
There is no clear indication that use
is contemplated here : but rather the
general notion of taming, involving
obedience and restraint. There is
probably a reminiscence of what has
been said above of the bridling of
horses.

The taming is part of the lordship
of the earth bestowed in Gen. i. 28,
and corresponds to the government
(ἄρχετε LXX.) over the lower animals
which there follows: cf. Ps. viii. 6 ff.
This is brought out by the emphatic
form τῇ φύσει τῇ ἀνθ.; lit. "the nature
that is human," i.e. the conquest is
connected with the characteristic pre-
rogative of the living soul which God
breathed into man. The dative is
probably not the simple dative of
agency with a passive verb, of which
(except with passive participles) there
is no clear case in the N.T. All the
instances seem to fall under one of
two heads, including the idea either
of *appearing to* (as εὑρεθῶ ὑμῖν 2 Cor.
xii. 20 ; αὐτῷ εὑρεθῆναι 2 Pet. iii. 14 ;
ἐγνώσθη Lk. xxiv. 35 ; Phil. iv. 5) or
of being subjected to (here, and ᾧ τις
ἥττηται 2 Pet. ii. 19). Thus the sense
is not simply tamed by the human
nature, but tamed into subjection to
it. See the chorus in the *Antigone*
332 ff., esp. 342—351.

8. τὴν δὲ γλῶσσαν οὐδεὶς δαμάσαι
δύναται ἀνθρώπων, *but the tongue can
no one, even of men, tame*] By a vivid
image the tongue is projected, as it
were, out of human nature and spoken
of as though it had a separate life of its

τάστατον κακόν, μεστὴ ἰοῦ θανατηφόρου. ⁹ἐν αὐτῇ
εὐλογοῦμεν τὸν κύριον καὶ πατέρα, καὶ ἐν αὐτῇ κατα-

own, over which no one can gain complete mastery. And though in strictness the tongue is nothing more than the organ by which what is in the heart and mind is expressed, yet experience shews that speech or utterance, as such, has what may well be called a magic power which acts reflexly on the mind within: so that St James' language does express a true fact, though it does not attempt to explain all the grounds of it. There may be, that is, a kind of conflict between a man and his own tongue, or his own impulse of utterance, in which his true self gets worsted.

The position of ἀνθρώπων is at once secondary and emphatic; it might be "the tongue no one can tame,—no one, that is, of men"; but is rather "no one, even of men," even of those beings so highly endowed, of whom he has been just speaking.

ἀκατάστατον κακόν, *a disorderly evil*] This is the true reading, not ἀκατάσχετον, which would be merely a feeble repetition of οὐδεὶς δαμάσαι δύναται. St James has used the word already in i. 8, and ἀκαταστασία in iii. 16, where it is coupled with πᾶν φαῦλον πρᾶγμα. To his mind it expressed the utmost evil, the disorder which is the entire opposite of God's perfect purpose and man's single-minded surrender to God's purpose. Cf. 1 Cor. xiv. 33.

Not ἀκατάστατον only, but ἀκ. κακόν. It is startling to hear the tongue called "an evil," rather than its misuse. But (1) the adjective explains how it becomes an evil; and (2) its evil arises from the very fact of its independence, i.e. from its isolation from the integrity of humanity. There is just the same abnormal and morbid independence as in the case of a desire which in like manner can be conceived of as something distinct from the man in whom it arises (i. 14 f.).

μεστή, *full of*] Not μεστόν: it cannot therefore agree with κακόν, but goes back to ἡ γλῶσσα. The tongue not merely contains deadly venom, it is charged with it: cf. Ps. lviii. 4; cxl. 3. There must be an indirect reference to a poisonous serpent, as in these Psalms; the image probably being derived in the first instance from the flexibility and mobility of the actual tongue.

9. ἐν αὐτῇ (bis), *therein*] The phrase is remarkable. The purely instrumental use of ἐν is Hebraistic, and found only in such writers of the N.T. as admit a certain (not very large) amount of Hebraism. It does not agree with the general colour of St James' language. Nor does this passage come well under the rather vague "causal" use of ἐν (Jelf 246 f.; Kühner ii. 403 f.). But St James' purpose is probably to identify ourselves with the tongue. If he had said δι' αὐτῆς, it would have expressed a pure instrumentality: *we* should have appeared solely as the speakers, the tongue as our organ merely. Now the whole passage implies a kind of independent power over us exerted by the faculty of utterance; so that St James intentionally makes the tongue an actual speaker as well as an organ of speech: *in* the tongue we bless God, almost in the sense "in the person of the tongue." The nearest parallel is in Rom. xv. 6, ἐν ἑνὶ στόματι δοξάζητε κ.τ.λ.: cf. also Mt. ix. 34, ἐν τῷ ἄρχοντι τῶν δαιμονίων; and Acts xvii. 31, κρίνειν τ. οἰκουμένην ...ἐν ἀνδρὶ ᾧ ὥρισεν.

εὐλογοῦμεν, *we bless*] This is the highest function of speech. As man's relation to God is the supreme fact of his nature which alone puts all others into their right place, so blessing God for His goodness and His benefits is

ρώμεθα τοὺς ἀνθρώπους τοὺς καθ' ὁμοίωσιν θεοῦ γεγονότας·

the supreme use of the powers of utterance. Thus (Lk. i. 64) this is the first use which Zacharias makes of the recovered power, ἀνεῴχθη δὲ τὸ στόμα ...καὶ ἡ γλῶσσα αὐτοῦ, καὶ ἐλάλει εὐλογῶν τὸν θεόν. Cf. Ps. li. 15.

τὸν κύριον (not θεόν) καὶ πατέρα, the Lord and Father] The less common phrase is the true reading. The κύριον expresses God's majesty and His rule over all His creatures, and especially over men who have the privilege of being able to render conscious obedience. Πατέρα expresses both rule and love, and also all the associations connected with the human word, in reference (i. 18) to the first origin of man as not merely owing his existence to God's fiat but a partaker of the Divine nature as being made in God's image.

καταρώμεθα, we curse] Καταρῶμαι originally took the accusative of the thing, the dative of the person : " imprecate this or that against a man," the thing imprecated being sometimes omitted. But in late writers (Plutarch, Lucian) it succumbs to the general tendency to pure transitiveness. The first person καταρώμεθα (as well as εὐλογοῦμεν) is singular, because St James does not seem to be speaking directly of a universal human shortcoming (πολλὰ πταίομεν ἅπαντες v. 2).

As far as this verse goes, the meaning might be only that blessing and cursing are both utterances of the tongue: but v. 10 shews that St James meant to say that they come from the very same tongue, and that he is in fact attacking not merely a vice of the tongue but a false kind of religion. He is dealing with a tendency, close akin to that which he combated at the end of chapter i., to a loveless religiosity, the combination of professed devotion to God with indifference and even hatred to men. He implies that the utterance of blessing must be spurious if it does not include men as its objects as well as God : cf. 1 Pet. iii. 9 ; Rom. xii. 14 ; 1 Cor. iv. 12 ; and their source, the use of the word in Lk. vi. 28, where it has a stronger force than appears at first sight.

It is to be observed that τὸν κύριον καὶ πατέρα here repeats the τῷ θεῷ καὶ πατρί of i. 27.

τοὺς ἀνθρώπους, men] Not simply individual men, but mankind : the curse uttered against the hated or despised individual persons was in effect a wrong done to mankind, and sprang from an evil spirit as towards mankind, a disregard of the second law, the law of love to neighbours. It was the temper of the Pharisees in Jn vii. 49, " This people which knoweth not the law are accursed."

τοὺς καθ' ὁμοίωσιν θεοῦ γεγονότας, which are made after the likeness of God] Here the latent doctrine of the Epistle breaks out into plain words. The connexion between the two supreme forms of love which together make up the sum of human duty is not accidental : the love of man is founded on the love of God. The tenderness and mercy shewn to the lower animals form but a small part in that true love of men which attaches itself to the Godlike in them, hidden as the image may often be; so that the cursing of them is a cursing of that which bears the stamp of the Creator's own nature.

St James chooses not the κατ' εἰκόνα, but the second phrase καθ' ὁμοίωσιν, not elsewhere found in the N.T. On these words it is worth while to refer to Delitzsch New Comm. on Genes. E.T. i. pp. 99 f., on the words צֶלֶם εἰκών, and דְּמוּת ὁμοίωσις. In image, he says, the representation of the primitive form or model predominates, in likeness the representation of the pattern or ideal. He accordingly treats the

¹⁰ἐκ τοῦ αὐτοῦ στόματος ἐξέρχεται εὐλογία καὶ κατάρα.
οὐ χρή, ἀδελφοί μου, ταῦτα οὕτως γίνεσθαι. ¹¹μήτι ἡ

difference as justifying the interpretation common in the Fathers, by which likeness is the gradual process of assimilation to the archetypal image; image belonging to fundamental nature, likeness to progressive character. The distinction is an important one, whether it was intended in Genesis or not; a point very hard to determine. There does not appear, however, to be any trace of it here, where the reference is rather to what God originally made men to be than to what they have grown to be under His fatherly nurture.

Γεγονότας with καθ' ὁμοίωσιν expresses at once the primitive origin and the present continuance of the state which it introduced: in St James' eyes mankind are still in the likeness of God for all their sin and evil. *Beresh. Rabb.* 24 fin. (on Gen. v. 1), "According to R. Akiba the words Lev. xix. 18, 'Thou shalt love thy neighbour as thyself,' are a comprehensive principle of the Law. Thou shouldest not say 'Because I have been despised, may my neighbour be despised with me; and because I have been cursed, may my neighbour be cursed with me.' If thou actest so, said R. Tanchuma, know that he whom thou despisest is made after the image of God." On the image cf. Ecclus. xvii. 3 (and context).

10. *ἐκ τοῦ αὐτοῦ στόματος, from the same mouth*] This merely states clearly and emphatically what was implied in *v.* 9. It excludes the notion of different tongues blessing and cursing: it is not "from the same source," but definitely "from the same *mouth.*"

Cf. *Testam. Benj.* 6, ἡ ἀγαθὴ διάνοια οὐκ ἔχει δύο γλώσσας εὐλογίας καὶ κατάρας.

οὐ χρή, ἀδελφοί μου, ταῦτα οὕτως γίνεσθαι, *It is not fitting, my brethren,*

that these things should so be] Here St James turns from his statement to direct expostulation, intermitted since *v.* 1; so that the division of verses is very awkward, though modern editions of the A.V. have partially mended it by putting a full stop in the middle.

Ἀδελφοί μου marks the sudden turn of language, kept up by the repetition in *v.* 12.

χρή occurs here alone in the N.T., not at all in the LXX. or Apocrypha. Though St James does not use δεῖ, χρή is not a synonym. It is a somewhat vague word, apparently starting from the sense "there is need." In ethical applications it comes nearer to πρέπει or καθήκει than to δεῖ, meaning rather "fitting," "congruous to a law or rather standard." Hence St James probably does not mean "this conduct of yours is wrong," but "this doubleness in the use of the tongue is an unnatural monstrous thing." Then ταῦτα has probably the definite sense, the blessing on the one hand and the cursing on the other: it is a monstrous state to be in that this blessing and this cursing should be constantly arising on this footing of identical origin, from the same tongue, the organ of the same mind. Thus there is no redundance in the two words ταῦτα οὕτως; and the present γίνεσθαι has also its force, for he is speaking not of casual sins but of a settled and deliberate habit.

11. *μήτι, Can it be that*] The τι added to μή strengthens it, suggesting impossibility. Two similar uses of it in the N.T. are Mk iv. 21 and Lk. vi. 39. In other places it is used where the possibility is recognised by the side of the unexpectedness.

ἡ πηγή, *the fountain*] The force of the article is not obvious: συκῆ has none, and a fountain, as such, has no

πηγὴ ἐκ τῆς αὐτῆς ὀπῆς βρύει τὸ γλυκὺ καὶ τὸ πικρόν ;
¹²μὴ δύναται, ἀδελφοί μου, συκῆ ἐλαίας ποιῆσαι ἢ ἄμ-
πελος σῦκα ; οὔτε ἁλυκὸν γλυκὺ ποιῆσαι ὕδωρ.   ¹³ Τίς

particular title to be spoken of gene-
rically. The true reason probably is
that St James is thinking of what the
fountain stands for, the heart. The
reference to ἡ πηγή in itself proves
that the tongue was to him merely
the organ of a power within. Doubtless he remembered (Mt. xii. 34) ἐκ
γὰρ τοῦ περισσεύματος τῆς καρδίας τὸ
στόμα λαλεῖ, the overflow. And so
ἡ πηγή = ἡ καρδία (cf. ὁ ὀφθαλμός, τὸ
σῶμα).

ὀπῆς, crevice] Ὀπή is properly a
chink in a wall for looking through.
It then comes to be applied to holes
and burrows in the ground, as those
of ants and of hibernating animals, or
somewhat larger clefts in the rock
(Heb. xi. 38, etc.). Here too it is
probably the crevice in a face of rock
through which a stream bursts forth.
The πηγή is not to be confounded with
the well. On the springs of Palestine
see Stanley Sinai and Palestine pp.
123, 146, and Grove's App. 500 ff.

βρύει, sends forth] Βρύω is chiefly
used of the fresh and vigorous putting
forth of herbage by the earth, or of
leaves, flowers, or fruits by plants and
trees ; but also sometimes of the
shooting forth of water by a source
(cf. Clem. Alex. Paed. i. 6. 45 ; iii. 7.
39). Usually also it occurs with a
dative, but occasionally in late writers,
as here, with an accusative.

τὸ γλυκὺ καὶ τὸ πικρόν, that which is
sweet and that which is bitter] The
articles are not easy. If we supply
nothing, and understand merely "that
which is sweet," etc., the articles are
quite justified, and on the whole this
is best, the most general abstract
opposites being used here in the first
instance, and then ἁλυκόν afterwards
substituted. The mere omission of
ὕδωρ would create no difficulty : but a
generalisation of water "the sweet

water," "the bitter water" does not
seem natural here.

St James would be familiar with
bitter springs from those of Tiberias
(see Reland Palest. 301 ff., 1039 f. ;
Robinson Bibl. Res. ii. 384).

12. Not only a new image comes
in here, but a new point of view, prepared for by part of v. 11. In 9—11
St James has dwelt on the inconsistency of the two kinds of speech as
coming forth from the same tongue,
as though bitter and sweet came alike
from the same spring. But ἡ πηγή
has carried us back from the springs
to the inner reservoirs, from the
mouth to the heart ; and so now a
comparison between the heart and
its utterance, rather than between
two utterances, comes into view. The
image is formed by examples of our
Lord's words, Lk. vi. 44, "Each tree
is known by its own fruit." Wishing
to treat them gently, he keeps within
the limits of that single sentence of
Christ, as though it were only one
kind of fruit tree as against another,
all three being good and useful. But
doubtless he intended them to apply
the associated words, which spoke of
"corrupt trees" and of "thorns" and
"thistles" (Lk. vi. 43 f. ‖ Mt. vii.
16—20). In so doing he was indirectly implying that the curses
uttered by their tongues expressed
the contents of their hearts more
truly than the blessings, which he
assumes to be unreal words. The
same comes out more clearly in the
next image.

οὔτε ἁλυκὸν γλυκὺ ποιῆσαι ὕδωρ,
neither can salt water yield sweet]
So we must read for οὔτως and
οὐδεμία πηγὴ ἁλ. καὶ γλυκύ, a vapid
repetition of v. 11. Οὔτε is hard and
some good mss. naturally substitute
οὐδέ, but by a manifest grammatical

σοφὸς καὶ ἐπιστήμων ἐν ὑμῖν; δειξάτω ἐκ τῆς καλῆς

correction. In late Greek the original difference of οὔτε and οὐδέ, μήτε and μηδέ, became to a great extent broken down. This may be seen in the N.T. (as Acts xxiii. 8), and still more in later MSS. of the N.T. See Win.-Moult. 614 ff. Probably the best way to explain this οὔτε, which Lachmann thought corrupt, and which seems to have no exact parallel, is to treat the previous questions as equivalent to negative assertions : "the fountain does not, the fig tree cannot, nor can," etc.

ἁλυκόν] Simply "salt" as an adjective : doubtless ὕδωρ, kept to the end, goes with both ἁλ. and γλυκύ. Ποιῆσαι is borrowed from above, being used of natural producing. As applied to ὕδωρ it means to rain, and this is a rare use. Doubtless St James purposely retained the same word as an image in the sense, out of a reservoir of salt water springs forth no fountain of sweet water. Thus he distinctly implies, though he still leaves the rebuke to implication, that not the verbal blessing of God but the cursing of men was a true index to what lay within. It is no longer merely a difference of kinds placed on a level, but one is evil, the other good. Thus this sentence is no mere repetition of v. 11, but goes far beyond it.

13. Here the long digression on the tongue ends, and St James returns with full recollection of what he has said in the interval, to the interrupted warning of v. 1 against being "many teachers." The excuse for this ambitious teachership was the possession of wisdom, and so he goes on now to consider the true and the false wisdom. Speech and wisdom, as good things liable to grievous abuse, appear in like manner in 1 Corinthians (i. 5, 17, and thence on through ii. ; also iii. 18 f., etc.).

Τίς is by no means equivalent to ὅς. The only passage in the N.T.

where this can be, and this at best is doubtful, is Acts xiii. 25. But it shews how the one sense can pass over into the other. St James rather calls upon anyone who makes this claim to come forward, and hear what the true demand upon him is. Cf. Ps. xxxiv. 12, LXX.

σοφὸς καὶ ἐπιστήμων, wise and understanding] As Deut. i. 13; iv. 6. Ἐπιστήμων especially expresses personal acquaintance with things, conversance with them : it thus includes experience.

δειξάτω, let him shew] Cf. ii. 18 bis; ἐκ also as there.

καλῆς, good] As directly beheld and contemplated, as distinguished from ἀγαθός good in fruit or result. Thus here it manifestly refers to a goodness which can be seen and recognised. This comes out strongly in the parallel but more limited passage 1 Pet. ii. 12, where conduct which even the heathen must honour and admire is expressed by καλός (also ἀναστροφή) : on this application of letting the light shine before men cf. Rom. xii. 17 ; 2 Cor. viii. 21.

ἀναστροφῆς, behaviour] Ἀναστροφή is "manner of life." Perhaps "behaviour" is the most exact rendering. Ἀναστρέφεσθαι (=versari) is first used of externals, to have your employment in a place, be going to and fro in it. Then in later Greek as Polybius it is used ethically : the verb, not the substantive, occurs once or twice in this sense in LXX., but the substantive in Apocr. In the N.T. in the Epistles generally (not Evv., Act., Apoc.), and doubtless widely used at that time. Chiefly, and perhaps wholly, it means in the N.T. acts performed towards others, social conduct, whether as towards fellow Christians or towards the world at large.

τὰ ἔργα αὐτοῦ, his works] This is no tautology : his works are not simply his acts, but the utterance and

ἀναστροφῆς τὰ ἔργα αὐτοῦ ἐν πραΰτητι σοφίας. ¹⁴εἰ
δὲ ζῆλον πικρὸν ἔχετε καὶ ἐριθίαν ἐν τῇ καρδίᾳ ὑμῶν,

outcome of his wisdom and understanding. It is assumed that the
use of wisdom and understanding is
practical (so i. 5 in connexion with
i. 4); so that τὰ ἔργα αὐτοῦ are
equivalent to "the works of the wise
man." Just as works in chap. ii. were
the manifestation of faith, so they are
here of wisdom. The works are to be
shewn forth in contrast to the words
to which vv. 1—12 refer.

ἐν πραΰτητι σοφίας, in meekness of
wisdom] Here comes in the con-
trolling spirit, the mention of which
indicates what it was that vitiated
the supposed wisdom. It was pride
and bitterness, exaltation of self and
not contempt only but hatred of
others. Both of these characteristics
are negatived together by "meekness,"
including at once humility towards
self, and gentleness and forbearance
towards others (contrast with v. 14).
The word itself stands twice in the
Gospels as spoken by Christ, Mt. v. 5,
"Blessed are the meek"; xi. 29, "for
I am meek"; and in Zech. ix. 9,
quoted by Mt. xxi. 5, it is a characteristic of King Messiah as He comes to
Jerusalem. It occurs a few times in
LXX. (chiefly for עָנָו), and is the word
applied to Moses (Numb. xii. 3). In
i. 21 St James had dwelt on meekness
as a condition of receptivity in hearing : here conversely he speaks of it
as a condition of the true shewing
forth to others for their instruction.
At first sight ἐν πραΰτητι σοφίας is
a paradox. The arrogant disputer is
ready to praise meekness as a fitting
virtue for the weak and foolish; but
thinks it out of place for himself.
St James lays down on the other
hand that it is a fruit and mark of
wisdom. He who is wise in a true
sense of the word, he means, cannot
but be meek. By meekness of behaviour wisdom will be displayed

rather than disguised. St James
leaves untouched the question whether
the possession of wisdom is a sufficient
ground for assuming the responsi-
bilities of teaching. He implies that
the καλὴ ἀναστροφή must come first,
and then much at least of the osten-
tatious teaching will disappear.

14. ζῆλον, jealousy] A word that
oscillates between a good and an evil
sense, both occurring in the N.T.
Arist. (Rhet. ii. 11. 1) distinguishes it
from φθόνος, as emulation from envy;
he says, καὶ ἐπιεικές ἐστιν ὁ ζῆλος καὶ
ἐπιεικῶν, τὸ δὲ φθονεῖν φαῦλον καὶ
φαύλων, etc.; and classical writers
generally incline to an at least not
distinctly evil sense, which they express rather by φθόνος or ζηλοτυπία.
But in the Acts ζῆλος is distinctly
evil, and so in at least St Paul and
St James. St James, however, though
in v. 16 he uses ζῆλος absolutely as
St Paul does, here precludes mistake
by adding πικρόν.

ἐριθίαν, ambition, rivalry] Combined with ζῆλος likewise in Gal. v. 20.
A curious word with an obscure
history : see Fritzsche Rom. 143—8,
the best account, but very imperfect. Ἔριθος (derivation doubtful) in
Homer's time is a hired labourer,
apparently an agricultural labourer
(Etym. Mag. κυρίως δὲ ὁ τὴν γῆν ἐργα-
ζόμενος ἐργάτης ἐπὶ μισθῷ): and a gloss
of Hesychius (ἐριθεύει εἰκῇ, ἐργάζῃ
μάτην) seems to shew that labour or
work was the main idea. The same
is always the force of the somewhat
commoner compound συνέριθος. The
fundamental passage is Odyss. vi. 32,
where Athene tells Nausicaa that she
will accompany her καί τοι ἐγὼ συνέριθος ἅμ᾽ ἕψομαι, when she goes with
the housemaidens to wash the linen.
This one passage apparently gave rise
to many others, one in Aristoph. Pax
785 and many in late poets; also

Plat. *Rep.* vii. 533 D; *Leg.* x. 889 D of the arts cooperative, coancillary with, philosophy, whence also Orig. *Ep. ad Greg.* i. Afterwards, probably from wrong etymology, it was used of women servants spinning wool. But in Arist. *Polit.* v. 2, 3 we find ἐριθεία, -εύομαι in a quite different sense. Speaking of changes of political constitution, some he says take place from arrogance, some from fear; some from preeminence, some from contempt and so on : and then some δι' ἐριθείαν. The term is explained by the next chapter : "Constitutions change without sedition also διὰ τὰς ἐριθείας, as at Heraea, ἐξ αἱρετῶν γὰρ διὰ τοῦτο ἐποίησαν κληρωτάς, ὅτι ᾑροῦντο τοὺς ἐριθευομένους," i.e. apparently they changed the mode of appointment to offices from election to lot, because they chose τοὺς ἐριθευομένους : this may mean either candidates who bribed, or who courted and gained a following in other ways. Suidas says, ἐριθία · ἡ διὰ λόγων φιλονεικία, λέγεται δὲ καὶ ἡ μισθαρνία. More definitely speaking of δεκάζεσθαι (bribery) he says, ὅμοιον καὶ τὸ ἐριθεύεσθαι τῷ δεκάζεσθαί ἐστιν, καὶ ἡ ἐριθεία εἴρηται ἀπὸ τῆς τοῦ μισθοῦ δόσεως (cf. *Etym. Mag.* 254). This points to the gaining of followers and adherents by gifts. It might, however, be by arts as well as gifts : see Ezek. xxiii. 5, 12, καὶ ᾑριθεύσατο (Sym.). But apparently the word came to be used not merely of the manner of winning followers, but of the seeking of followers itself. Thus Hesych., ᾑριθευμένων πεφιλοτιμημένων, ᾑριθεύετο ἐφιλόνεικει : hence to be ambitious, indulge in ambitious rivalry. The Schol. on Soph. *Ajax* 833, ὁ δὲ Σοφοκλῆς ἐριθεῦσαι μέν τι ὥς πρεσβυτέρῳ (sc. Aeschylus) μὴ βουληθείς, οὐ μὴν παραλιπεῖν αὐτὸ δοκιμάζων ψιλῶς φησι κ.τ.λ.; Polyb. x. 25. 9, οἱ δὲ τῆς στρατηγίας ὀρεγόμενοι διὰ ταύτης τῆς ἀρχῆς ἐξεριθεύονται τοὺς νέους, καὶ παρασκευάζουσιν εὔνους συναγωνιστὰς εἰς τὸ μέλλον. It is likewise implicitly coupled with φιλοτιμία in

Philo *Leg. ad Caium* 10 (ii. 555), ἡγεμονία δ' ἀφιλόνεικος καὶ ἀνερίθευτος ὀρθὴ μόνη. (The passages in Eust. *Opusc.* ap. Stephan. suit either "ambition" or "faction." Cf. *C.I.G.* 2671. 46, ἀνερίθευτοι.)

What sense the earlier Greek Fathers attached to it in St Paul does not appear. Chrys. on Rom. ii. 8 seems to identify it with φιλονεικίας τινὸς καὶ ῥαθυμίας as if he had ἔρις in mind : in the four other places we learn nothing, nor do we from Theodore : Didymus on 2 Cor. has ἔριδάς τε καὶ ἐριθείας. Theodoret on Rom. is strange and obscure. The Latin evidence is as follows :

Rom. ii. 8, contentione d g vg pp

2 Cor. xii. 20, dissensiones d g r vg Ambst

Gal. v. 20, provocationes simultates Cyp² (*om.* Nemesianus) simultates Ambst irritationes d g Iren rixae Luc Hier vg

Phil. i. 17, aemulatione Tert dissensione d contentione g Ambst vg contumaciam r Aug³ invidia(m) et contentione(m) Aug²

Phil. ii. 3, contentionem d g vg Aug Amb al aemulationem Hil irritationem Ambst

Jam. iii. 14, contentionem (es) f s vg Aug

Jam. iii. 16, contentio f s vg Aug

Most of these renderings suggest the erroneous association with ἔρις (also "contention" syr vg): but aemulatio (Tert Hil) may have another force. Some of the N.T. places are ambiguous : but wherever the context has a defining force, it is in favour of the sense found in Polyb. etc. The difficult Rom. ii. 8 must be taken with Phil. i. 17, which seems to point to the Judaizing leaders, who intrigued against St Paul. In 2 Cor. xii. 20 it is separated from ἔρις by ζῆλος and θυμοί and precedes καταλαλιαί, so also in Gal., though followed by διχοστασίαι. In Phil. ii. 3 it is coupled with κενοδοξία and contrasted with ταπεινοφροσύνη : so here with ζῆλος.

μὴ κατακαυχᾶσθε καὶ ψεύδεσθε κατὰ τῆς ἀληθείας.
¹⁵οὐκ ἔστιν αὕτη ἡ σοφία ἄνωθεν κατερχομένη, ἀλλὰ

Thus all points to the personal ambition of rival leaderships. There is no real evidence for "party spirit," "faction," etc., i.e. for the vice of the followers of a party: ἐριθία really means the vice of a leader of a party created for his own pride: it is partly ambition, partly rivalry.

ἐν τῇ καρδίᾳ ὑμῶν, *in your heart*] Here what answers to the πηγή is at last distinctly expressed.

μὴ κατακαυχᾶσθε, *boast not*] The imperative is not the most obvious mood: we should rather have expected some statement of the natural consequences of having bitter jealousy in the heart, viz. "how can ye do other than boast, etc.?" Μή with a question cannot mean "Do ye not?" so that the imperative is unquestionable. The meaning seems to be this, "Do not set up for teachers, for then your teaching will be a boasting, etc." It is thus in antithesis to δειξάτω in *v.* 13. He asks "Who is wise etc.?" The possession of wisdom was made a claim to teachership. He deals with it first positively. There is a right way to shew forth wisdom. But, he goes on, if when searching your hearts you find bitter jealousy and ambition there, do not speak and teach, for in shewing forth what you regard as your wisdom you will be boasting etc.

κατακαυχᾶσθε] As in ii. 13 (cf. 1. 9; iv. 16), but here followed by an additional κατά. This one word exactly expresses the true spirit and purpose of the ambitious teachership. It was boasting against other men, partly against the multitude, still more against rival teachers. But St James unexpectedly puts in another object. The boasting directed against other men would in effect be a boasting against the truth itself which was supposed to be spoken. Nay it would be more, it would turn to falsehood

uttered against the truth.

καὶ ψεύδεσθε κατά, *and lie not against*] If necessary the κατά might be repeated in sense from κατακαυχᾶσθε (Kühner ii. 1073 f.): but a better sense is given by the words as they stand: the adverse boast turns to simple falsehood, and the truth suffers from both.

τῆς ἀληθείας, *the truth*] For somewhat similar contexts of ἡ ἀληθεία see Rom. i. 18; ii. 8 (also ἐξ ἐριθίας), 20; 1 Jn i. 6, 8. The implied doctrine is a paradox, but amply attested by experience. The mere possession of truth is no security for true utterance of it: all utterance is so coloured by the moral and spiritual state of the speaker that truth issues as falsehood from his lips in proportion as he is himself not in a right state: the correct language which he utters may carry a message of falsehood and evil in virtue of the bitterness and self-seeking which accompanies his speaking. At bottom such speakers do not cherish the truth except as a possession of their own, or a missile of their own.

15. οὐκ ἔστιν αὕτη ἡ σοφία, *This wisdom is not*] These words are enough to confirm the interpretation of *v.* 14 just given. No evil wisdom has been directly spoken of. But it is implied in κατακαυχᾶσθε etc.: the speech there spoken of is the speech which claims to be the speech of wisdom: now therefore St James will say what the wisdom is. Wisdom as such is what he specially prized (i. 5; iii. 17), which made him all the more hostile to its counterfeit.

ἄνωθεν κατερχομένη, a wisdom *that cometh down from above*] ἔστιν... κατερχομένη is not equivalent to οὐ κατέρχεται. The participle is qualitative, i.e. in effect an adjective: "is not one that cometh down," "is not of

ἐπίγειος, ψυχική, δαιμονιώδης· ¹⁶ὅπου γὰρ ζῆλος καὶ

a kind that cometh down" : it is not such a wisdom as God gives (i. 5). Cf. Philo *Leg. All.* iii. 58 (i. 120), τούτοις (tried ascetes) συμβέβηκε μὴ τοῖς γηΐνοις ἀλλὰ ταῖς ἐπουρανίαις ἐπιστήμαις τρέφεσθαι.

ἀλλὰ ἐπίγειος, *but is earthly*] Opposed to ἐπουράνιος. It belongs to the earthly sphere. However it may discourse about heavenly things, it derives its aims and its measures from a mere transfer of things earthly to a higher sphere : it has none of the large vision which belongs to the spirit. Compare τὰ ἐπίγεια φρονοῦντες of Phil. iii. 19, likewise said, I believe, of Judaizers, and Col. iii. 2, which manifestly refers to them, and has the same context (ii. 23) λόγον μὲν ἔχοντα σοφίας. Speaking to Greeks St Paul analogously refers to ἡ σοφία τοῦ κόσμου τούτου (1 Cor. i. 20 ; iii. 19), τοῦ αἰῶνος τούτου (ii. 6). All these three words gain their proper sense only when understood in antithesis to characteristics of the true wisdom. The spurious wisdom, in relation to its source and sphere, is earthly not from heaven.

ψυχική, *of the mind*] A remarkable word, not known in this sense before the N.T. It occurs in four passages : 1 Cor. ii. 14, ψ. ἄνθρωπος contrasted with ὁ πνευματικός ; 1 Cor. xv. 44 (bis), 46, σῶμα ψ. contrasted with σῶμα πνευματικόν ; Jude 19, ψυχικοί, πνεῦμα μὴ ἔχοντες. These all contain express opposition to πνευματικός, and the same is doubtless implied here. It is not likely that St James and St Jude borrowed it, in such different connexions, from St Paul ; and St Paul's own manner of using it in both places does not suggest that he was giving it a new sense. Most probably all three writers took it from the Greek religious language of Palestine. In earlier usage the word means simply of or belonging to the ψυχή ; and this is fundamentally the biblical sense,

the only peculiar colouring coming from the way in which the ψυχή was regarded as not identical with the πνεῦμα but inferior to it. On this head there is very little Jewish evidence (Delitzsch seems to know of none : *Hor. Hebr.* on 1 Cor. ii. 14 in *Z. S. f. Luth. Th.* 1877 p. 209). But Joseph. *Ant.* i. 1. 2 describing the Creation says that God καὶ πνεῦμα ἐνῆκεν αὐτῷ (man) καὶ ψυχήν ; and in 4 Macc. i. 32 (perhaps from a Platonic basis) it is said that of desires some are ψυχικαί, some σωματικαί ; and reason (ὁ λογισμός) appears to rule over both ; which implies the inferiority of the ψυχή to reason. Cf. Iren. v. 6. 1 ; Orig. on Ezek. Schol. (iii. 727 Migne). What is implied then is that this wisdom does not rise above the lower parts of the mind. The rendering "sensual" is so far wrong that it suggests sensuality in the common sense : the Latin *animalis* is in like manner correct as taken from *anima*, but suggests "bestial," which is not the true sense, which is simply "of the mind" in contrast to "of the spirit."

δαιμονιώδης, *demon-like*] The word requires care. -ώδης properly denotes (1) fullness, (2) similarity. The word itself, a rare word, in all the known examples means "demon-like," except in two very late writers, where (like δαιμόνιος) it means "supernaturally sent." The interpretation "inspired by demons" is not unnaturally suggested by κάτωθεν ἐρχομένη and *v.* 6 φλογιζομένη ὑπὸ τῆς γεέννης ; cf. 1 Tim. iv. 1, διδασκαλίαις δαιμονίων. But that sense is stronger than really suits the context ; and the more correct sense "demon-like" or rather "such as demons have" makes the triad more natural and complete. The origin and sphere of the spurious wisdom is the earth not heaven ; its seat in man is his soul, not his spirit ; the beings with whom he shares it are the

ἐριθία, ἐκεῖ ἀκαταστασία καὶ πᾶν φαῦλον πρᾶγμα.
¹⁷ ἡ δὲ ἄνωθεν σοφία πρῶτον μὲν ἁγνή ἐστιν, ἔπειτα

demons, not the angels: thus the wisdom shared by demons answers to the faith shared by demons of ii. 19.

16. ὅπου γάρ, *For where*] A necessary justification of what has just been said: St James has just used strong language respecting the professed wisdom of these teachers, and the reasonableness of his language did not lie on the surface, but had to be explained. Ὅπου and ἐκεῖ express presence. Though wisdom is God's gift, it is also an energy of the human mind and heart, and therefore takes its colour from the condition of the human heart and mind. If jealousy and rivalry are present there, these other things inconsistent with a truly Divine wisdom must be present there likewise.

ἀκαταστασία, *disorder*] A Stoic word. Cf. ἀκατάστατος i. 8; iii. 8. In Lk. xxi. 9 (cf. 2 Cor. vi. 5) it is coupled with πολέμους, as outward commotions and disorders. In 1 Cor. xiv. 33 it is contrasted with εἰρήνη with reference to orderliness in assemblies of the Church. In 2 Cor. xii. 20 (μή πως ἔρις, ζῆλος, θυμοί, ἐριθίαι, καταλαλιαί, ψιθυρισμοί, φυσιώσεις, ἀκαταστασίαι) it follows ψιθυρισμοί, φυσιώσεις. The meaning here seems to be that the presence of jealousy and rivalry implies a disorderly state of mind leading to disorder of spiritual vision; so that everything is seen in a distorted and disarranged light, the true mark of wisdom being to discern the inward order of things.

καὶ πᾶν φαῦλον πρᾶγμα, *and every worthless matter*] Πρᾶγμα is a vague word, properly an act, a thing performed, but often used only as "a matter." Cf. Herm. *Vis.* i. 1. 8, ἢ οὐ δοκεῖ σοι ἀνδρὶ δικαίῳ πονηρὸν πρᾶγμα εἶναι ἐὰν ἀναβῇ αὐτοῦ ἐπὶ τὴν καρδίαν ἡ πονηρὰ ἐπιθυμία;

Φαῦλος expresses not so much

moral evil as worthlessness; it is applied to what is poor, paltry, worthless (four times in N.T. of acts and mostly contrasted with τὰ ἀγαθά: Jn iii. 20, contrasted with τ. ἀλήθειαν; v. 29; Rom. ix. 11; 2 Cor. v. 10. Tit. ii. 8 is different). Here apparently we have another antithesis to true wisdom: wisdom discerns not only the order of things, but their relative worth and dignity: and the presence of what is low and worthless in the heart and mind incapacitates it for this discernment. Both ἀκαταστασία and φαῦλον exactly agree with ἐπίγειος etc., implying not so much positive evil as the limitations and paltrinesses that belong to a low order of things.

17. ἡ δὲ ἄνωθεν σοφία, *But the wisdom that is from above*] That there is such a wisdom is not only implied in v. 15, but stated in i. 5.

πρῶτον μέν, ἔπειτα] Apparently express first the purely inward personal character, second the social character of the true wisdom, the conduct which it inspires towards others.

ἁγνή, *pure*] The word answers very nearly to "pure," καθαρός being rather "clean." It is an ancient word of Greek religion, denoting freedom from any kind of defilement, whether of sensuality or of things supposed to be of a defiling nature. Cf. Plut. *Qu. Rom.* i. (ii. 263 E), Διὰ τί τὴν γαμουμένην ἅπτεσθαι πυρὸς καὶ ὕδατος κελεύουσιν;...ἢ ὅτι τὸ πῦρ καθαίρει καὶ τὸ ὕδωρ ἁγνίζει, δεῖ δὲ καθαρὰν καὶ ἁγνὴν διημένειν τὴν γαμηθεῖσαν; It thus expresses religious purity, combining καθαρός and ἅγιος. But in due time it acquired an ethical sense. Theoph. (Bernays 68) and Clem. Alex. 652 quote an inscription from the temple at Epidaurus,

ἁγνὸν χρὴ ναοῖο θυώδεος ἐντὸς ἰόντα
ἔμμεναι· ἁγνείη δ᾽ ἐστὶ φρονεῖν ὅσια.

εἰρηνική, ἐπιεικής, εὐπειθής, μεστὴ ἐλέους καὶ καρπῶν ἀγαθῶν, ἀδιάκριτος, ἀνυπόκριτος· ¹⁸καρπὸς δὲ δικαιοσύνης ἐν εἰρήνῃ σπείρεται τοῖς ποιοῦσιν εἰρήνην.

Cf. Clem. 629 with reference to washings, εὖ γοῦν κἀκεῖνο εἴρηται Ἴσθι μὴ λουτρῷ ἀλλὰ νοῷ καθαρός. ἀγνεία γὰρ, οἶμαι, τελεία ἡ τοῦ νοῦ καὶ τῶν ἔργων καὶ τῶν διανοημάτων, πρὸς δὲ καὶ τῶν λόγων εἰλικρίνεια ("Let all thy converse be sincere"). 1 Jn iii. 3 applies it even to God Himself (=ἅγιος). Thus here it seems to mean purity from every kind of inward stain or blemish (the positive side of ἄσπιλον ἑαυτὸν τηρεῖν ἀπὸ τοῦ κόσμου), and that on the ground of consecration to God. A similar sense and sequence occur 1 Pet. i. 22, τὰς ψυχὰς ὑμῶν ἡγνικότες ἐν τῇ ὑπακοῇ τῆς ἀληθείας (leading on to) εἰς φιλαδελφίαν etc. [See note in loc.] Also Jam. iv. 8.

εἰρηνική, peaceable] The most general exhibition of wisdom inspired by love. The true purpose of wisdom is not to gain victories over others, which in an unchristian state of society is implicitly the purpose of speech, but to promote peace: Mt. v.9, "Blessed are the peacemakers"; cf. 1 Cor. xiv. 33 already cited (contrasted with ἀκαταστασία): also Eph. iv. 3; Phil. iv. 7 ff.; Col. iii. 15.

ἐπιεικής, forbearing] Originally "fitting," "appropriate": then "fair" or "reasonable," "justly just"; see Aristot. Rhet. i. 13. 13, τὸ γὰρ ἐπιεικὲς δοκεῖ δίκαιον εἶναι, ἔστι δὲ ἐπιεικὲς τὸ παρὰ τὸν γεγραμμένον νόμον δίκαιον... (17) καὶ τὸ τοῖς ἀνθρωπίνοις συγγινώσκειν ἐπιεικές (cf. Eth. Nic. v. 14). Cf. Plato passim. It may thus be sometimes rendered by gentleness; but expresses rather forbearance, unwillingness to exact strict claims.

εὐπειθής, compliant] This word is tolerably common in the sense "compliant," "obedient," especially as towards laws or morality. It is appa-

rently confined to action, not extended to belief in the sense "docile." The precise force here is probably to be gathered by antithesis. The false wisdom would be domineering and imperious : the true wisdom shews itself in willing deference within lawful limits.

μεστὴ ἐλέους, full of mercy] Perhaps in contrast to μεστὴ ἰοῦ θανατηφόρου (iii. 8); at all events the two passages illustrate each other. Filled with mercy and good fruits, so that they break forth in overflow. On ἔλεος see ii. 13 (cf. Mt. ix. 13; xii. 7 from Hos. vi. 6). The true wisdom takes account of the actual wants and sufferings of men, and never loses sight of practical aims. It is not self-contained, but of necessity issues forth in good fruits. "Good" in the sense of our Lord (Mt. vii. 17ff., etc.), though here ἀγαθούς, not καλούς, because the benefits to others are specially here in view.

ἀδιάκριτος, without dividings of mind] This word usually takes its sense from the active διακρίνω to "distinguish," and means (passive or neuter) "without distinction," "promiscuous," or (active) "without making distinctions"; in which sense it is usually employed as a term of blame, though rarely by some Fathers as a term of praise (implicit obedience). But no such senses are possible here; and we may fairly take it as negativing any sense of either διακρίνω or -ομαι. This being the case, the meaning is virtually fixed by i. 6 bis, ii. 4, founded on Mt. xxi. 21 || Mk xi. 23; Acts x. 20; Rom. iv. 20; xiv. 23. The prominent meaning there is doubting, but doubting as a result of division of mind. Ἀδιάκριτος is "without dividings of mind"; the negative form of single-

IV.   ¹ Πόθεν πόλεμοι καὶ πόθεν μάχαι ἐν ὑμῖν; οὐκ

ness or wholeness of heart; cf. i. 5—8.
These last two negative epithets seem
parallel to ἁγνή on the one side and
εἰρηνική etc. on the other; and ἀδιάκριτος to the inward character of the
wisdom in relation to God alone.

ἀνυπόκριτος, *without hypocrisy* or
feigning] This word expresses the
relation to men. The true wisdom
requires not only singleness before
God but truthfulness towards men,
and is incompatible with all playing
of parts. We may recognise here a
warning against the pharisaic leaven
still lingering among Jewish Christians.

18. καρπὸς δὲ δικαιοσύνης, *But the
fruit which is righteousness*] For
the whole verse cf. Heb. xii. 11 : for
this phrase cf. Prov. xi. 30; Amos vi.
12; (also Phil. i. 11); and Isa. xxxii.
17 (but with ἔργα not καρπός). It
might be either (as apparently in
Isaiah) the fruit which springs from
righteousness, or the fruit which is
righteousness, righteousness as fruit.
The latter alone suits this sentence.
It is as though St James feared that
the force of the one comprehensive
word εἰρηνική might be lost in the
additional cognate epithets; and so
returned to it with a fresh expansion
for the emphatic close of the paragraph. Καρπὸς δικαιοσύνης in like
manner catches up the μεστὴ καρπῶν
ἀγαθῶν : St James cannot too often
reiterate his warning, founded on our
Lord's, against anything that bears no
fruit, an unfruitful religion, an unfruitful faith, and now an unfruitful
wisdom. He had said before (i. 20)
"the wrath of man worketh no righteousness of God"; now he shews in
contrast how righteousness *is* produced, for the warning of those who
professed to be champions of righteousness. It is not the product of
angry vindications: but it grows
slowly up as the corn from the seed,
the seed which is inevitably and al-

ways sown by those who make peace.
ἐν εἰρήνῃ, *in peace*] It might be
doubted whether this goes with καρπὸς
δικ. or σπείρεται or both. It is difficult to see any clear force in connexion with σπείρεται, and the order
rather suggests at least a primary
connexion with δικαιοσύνης. The
righteousness which thus springs up
is a righteousness in peace. Righteousness and peace are connected Ps.
lxxxv. 10; lxxii. 7. Usually the relation would be reversed, as it were
εἰρήνη ἐν δικαιοσύνῃ, righteousness the
foundation of peace, as Ps. lxxii. 3 ;
Isa. xxxii. 17 (already cited). But the
other relation is true also : peace is
the condition required for the growth
of righteousness, though it may be
peace in the midst of turmoil and
trouble (cf. Lk. i. 74 f.). Compare the
use of the cognate ἐν ἀγάπῃ in Ephesians (i. 4 ; iii. 17; iv. 15 f.). As the
sowing is peaceful by the very fact
that the sowers are the peacemakers,
so the harvest of righteousness is in
peace too. The dative τοῖς as before
probably does not denote pure agency,
but also what redounds to them: they
have this fruit of their labour.

τοῖς ποιοῦσιν εἰρήνην, *for them that
make peace*] Only a resolved form of
οἱ εἰρηνοποιοί (Mt. v. 9). They who
make peace shew likeness to God the
great maker of peace. They do His
work.

IV. 1. The true reading has πόθεν
twice.

πόλεμοι] This of course is suggested
by the preceding εἰρήνην. A new
paragraph begins here, the last of
the middle or principal part of the
book, its subject being strife as proceeding from the inward strife of
desire. Till *v.* 11 the tongue is not
mentioned again : St James is now
about to deal more directly with the
inward nature, as he has already
spoken of action and of speech. The
word πόλεμοι is the simplest and

ἐντεῦθεν, ἐκ τῶν ἡδονῶν ὑμῶν τῶν στρατευομένων ἐν

broadest that could be used in opposition to "peace." He probably was not thinking of the wars of nations, though they too, on one side or on both, might usually be traced to the same origin; but of the factions which divided one set of Christians from another. What the factions of the Jews of Palestine were, almost every page of Josephus shews; and the temper may well have spread to the Jews of other lands, and have kept its hold even on those of them who became Christians.

καὶ πόθεν μάχαι] Battles bear the same relation to wars that single conflicts do to standing animosities and hostile states. Thus if πόλεμοι are here the factions and antagonisms among Christians, the μάχαι are their casual quarrels. μάχη in late Greek is often applied to philosophical disputes, and even to contradictions or inconsistencies in logic. But the context does not point to doctrinal disputes; rather to more ordinary quarrels and factiousnesses.

ἐν ὑμῖν] This might be either "among you" or "within you": but what follows fixes the sense to "among you."

οὐκ ἐντεῦθεν] Probably only preparatory to what follows: "from this source, viz."

ἐκ τῶν ἡδονῶν ὑμῶν] It is not easy to seize the precise force; it is not likely to mean simply "desires," which is expressed by ἐπιθυμία in i. 14 f. Nor can it be concrete pleasures, i.e. pleasant things, for they could hardly be said στρατεύεσθαι. Apparently it means "indulgence of desires," "indulged desires." There is no limitation to sensual "pleasures," which only supply as it were imagery for the rest. Possessions and places of dignity or fame (v. 2) may be as sweet (ἡδονή) to the soul as anything else; and in i. 14 f. there is a similar description of all kinds of desires in

terms specially applicable to desires belonging to the senses. So also St Paul (e.g. Gal. v. 19) includes among the works of the flesh such vices as enmities, strife, jealousy, anger etc.

τῶν στρατευομένων, that war] Στρατεύομαι like στρατεύω is used either of the general or of the soldiers who serve under him: chiefly the latter. But it is difficult here to see either command or service implied with ἐν following. Further against whom? The somewhat parallel passage, 1 Pet. ii. 11, has τῶν σαρκικῶν ἐπιθυμιῶν, αἵτινες στρατεύονται κατὰ τῆς ψυχῆς, but that does not of necessity rule the sense here. "Against each other" is difficult to explain, what follows having nothing to do with the occasional conflict of pleasure with pleasure; and we should then expect "against each other" to be expressed; indeed στρατεύομαι absolute probably could not mean this.

The answer to both questions is found by taking στρατευομένων ἐν τοῖς μέλεσιν strictly together. The pleasures are represented as making war in the members, i.e. as invading them as a territory. Though εἰς would be the preposition generally used of invading a territory, ἐν is quite suitable here where the invading power does not come from an extraneous region. It is not that the war is made against the members: properly war is not said to be made against the territory invaded, but against its owners. So here the war is against the true lord of the members, i.e. the human spirit acknowledging and obeying the will of God, since the true nature of man is formed to do God's will. Cf. Rom. vii. 23, ἕτερον νόμον ἐν τοῖς μέλεσίν μου ἀντιστρατευόμενον τῷ νόμῳ τοῦ νοός μου. Thus 1 Pet. ii. 11 agrees, if we give τῆς ψυχῆς its highest sense. [See note in loc.]

τοῖς μέλεσιν ὑμῶν; ²ἐπιθυμεῖτε, καὶ οὐκ ἔχετε· φονεύ-

2. φονεύετε.] φονεύετε

ἐν τοῖς μέλεσιν ὑμῶν, *in your members*] In contrast to ἐν ὑμῖν. The
outer strife is only a product of an
inner strife. The very reference to
"members" implies the compositeness
of human nature, and the need of
acting with reference to the relation
of the parts to each other and to the
whole. Reflexly it calls attention to
the fact that in the larger body, the
body corporate in which the πόλεμοι
and μάχαι arise, we are strictly
"members one of another."

2. ἐπιθυμεῖτε, *ye covet*]   "Desire"
in the widest sense. But in reference
to dealings with others it becomes
limited to "coveting," i.e. desiring
what is another's. Compare St Paul's
reference to Commandment X. in
Rom. vii. 7; xiii. 9.

καὶ οὐκ ἔχετε, *and have not*] The
order quite excludes that prior want
which leads to desire. The words
must mark the intermediate stage.
First comes the desire, next the
desire finds no satisfaction.

φονεύετε, *ye commit murder*] This
has long been recognised as a serious
difficulty, because it is a strange word
to couple with ζηλοῦτε, more especially
as preceding it. Jealousy or envy
would be the cause, not the result, of
murder. Moreover "murder" is a kind
of crime that we should hardly look
for among any early Christians. Accordingly Erasmus and many after
him have proposed to read φθονεῖτε.
There is absolutely no MS. authority
for this; and though it is possible
that slight errors occur here and
there in all MSS., and there are some
passages where this does appear to be
the case, it must not be accepted in
any single instance without clear
evidence. Now though φθονεῖτε is
certainly possible here, it would not
really be as natural a word as it
appears at first sight. St James has
already used ζηλοῦτε in a very strong

sense, strong enough for his purpose,
so that φθονέω is not *wanted*; and if
it were to be used, being the more
clearly disparaging word, it ought to
stand after ζηλοῦτε, not before it.
Cf. Plat. *Menex.* 242 A: "From prosperity," he says, "there came upon
the city πρῶτον μὲν ζῆλος, ἀπὸ ζήλου
δὲ φθόνος." Plut. ii. 796 A says of
φθόνος that "this passion, which befits
no time of life, yet among the young
is rich in specious names, being called
competition (ἅμιλλα) and ζῆλος and
ambition (φιλοτιμία)."

Thus φθονεῖτε followed by ζηλοῦτε
makes an anticlimax, though not so
startling an anticlimax as φονεύετε
ζηλοῦτε. The true solution seems to
lie in a change of punctuation. St
James' style is abrupt and condensed :
and apparently he intended φονεύετε
to be taken by itself as the single
consequent to ἐπιθυμεῖτε καὶ οὐκ ἔχετε,
and καὶ ζηλοῦτε to be the beginning
of a fresh series, not part of the conclusion of the first. This view is also
taken by Hofmann. It has, I think,
but two difficulties worth consideration. (1) The presence of καί before
ζηλοῦτε, where a sharper antithesis
would have seemed to be given by
the absence of a conjunction : but
ζηλοῦτε to say the least contains a
fresh element not in ἐπιθυμεῖτε, and
really expresses a different idea, and
Hebrew precedent is favourable to
either presence or absence of the
conjunction. (2) The reference to
murder remains. This difficulty must
remain if φονεύετε is genuine, whatever be the punctuation ; and it is
hardly greater than what μοιχαλίδες
in *v.* 4 presents, if taken literally, as
it doubtless must be. Murder and
adultery were both contemplated as
fast approaching those to whom the
Epistle was written, if not, as the
strictest interpretation of the words
would imply, actually among them.

ετε. καὶ ζηλοῦτε, καὶ οὐ δύνασθε ἐπιτυχεῖν· μάχεσθε
καὶ πολεμεῖτε. οὐκ ἔχετε διὰ τὸ μὴ αἰτεῖσθαι ὑμᾶς·

Of such murder Ahab and Naboth's vineyard would be a well remembered type. It is not unlikely that he first gives the extreme example of what leads to murder (in the spirit of the Sermon on the Mount; cf. 1 Jn iii. 15), and then (ζηλοῦτε) turns to what was clearly and widely present. Analogously the adulteresses of *v.* 4 seem to be an extreme example, leading to the widely spread and unquestionable friendship with the world.

As positive evidence for this punctuation independent of φονεύετε, may be noted its throwing καὶ οὐ δύνασθε ἐπιτυχεῖν into exact analogy with καὶ οὐκ ἔχετε, and its giving μάχεσθε καὶ πολεμεῖτε force by making them correspond to φονεύετε. The whole verse should, I believe, be read thus: "Ye covet, and have not: ye commit murder. And ye envy, and cannot attain : ye fight and war." The usual punctuation gives the whole verse a loose and apparently inconsequent structure.

καὶ ζηλοῦτε, *and ye envy*] The verb like the substantive has both a good and an evil sense. The evil is clearly meant here, as Acts vii. 9; 1 Cor. xiii. 4. As we have seen ζῆλος might be simply the first stage of φθόνος, and both might mean envy of possessions. But comparison with iii. 14 on the one hand, where ζῆλος is used and ambition not covetousness is in question, and with ἐπιθυμεῖτε...φονεύετε on the other, which clearly refers to covetousness, shews that ζηλοῦτε expresses not envy of possessions but envy of position or rank or fame. It is sordid and bitter personal ambition. In this sense much is said of ζῆλος in Clem. Rom., not only in the enumeration iii. 2, but iv. 7—13; v. 2 ff.; vi. 1 ff. etc. (On the word see Lightfoot on iii. 2 and Trench *Syn.* i.) The passage quoted above from Plutarch specially

illustrates the true sense here.

καὶ οὐ δύνασθε ἐπιτυχεῖν, *and cannot attain*] 'Επιτυγχάνω does not properly mean to "obtain," i.e. get possession, but to "attain," i.e. either fall in with or hit the mark, and is specially used absolutely of being successful. Here then it will be "succeed in attaining" the position of the rivals.

μάχεσθε καὶ πολεμεῖτε, *ye fight and war*] These words stand in exactly the same relation to καὶ ζηλοῦτε... ἐπιτυχεῖν as φονεύετε to ἐπιθυμεῖτε... ἔξετε. The words are repeated from *v.* 1, here naturally in inverse order, because the single and casual μάχαι are a step to the settled and continuous πόλεμοι.

οὐκ ἔχετε, *ye have not*] St James goes back to the former οὐκ ἔχετε. The desire, in so far as it included no coveting towards others, was not (or need not be) in itself evil. Men have various wants, and it is by Divine appointment that they have desires that these wants should be supplied. And so it is also of Divine appointment that these wants should be carried before God in prayer, and desires take the form of petitions. Except by prayer, men stand in this, as in all things, in a false relation to God and therefore to all things.

διὰ τὸ μὴ αἰτεῖσθαι ὑμᾶς, *because ye ask not*] It is remarkable that the middle is used here and in the next line, but the active between. αἰτέω is properly to ask a person, what is asked for being often added in a second accusative; it is as it were to "petition." αἰτοῦμαι is properly to ask *for* a thing: the person asked is sometimes also inserted, but rarely. Thus the two forms approach each other from different sides, and it is often difficult to distinguish them. Thus compare 1 Jn iii. 22 with v. 14 f. Here αἰτοῦμαι retains its proper force. δαπανήσητε requires an implied object, spending

³αἰτεῖτε καὶ οὐ λαμβάνετε, διότι κακῶς αἰτεῖσθε, ἵνα ἐν
ταῖς ἡδοναῖς ὑμῶν δαπανήσητε. ⁴μοιχαλίδες, οὐκ οἴδατε

must be a spending of something; and
the same object seems to be implied
throughout, viz. "what things ye desire." "Ye have not what things ye
desire because ye ask not [for them],"
and again, "ye ask [for them] amiss,
that ye may spend them" etc.

3.   Then the intermediate αἰτεῖτε is
probably due to an intentional reference
to our Lord's words in their Greek form
(Mt. vii. 7 f. ‖ Lk. xi. 9 f.; Jn xvi. 24);
he wishes the apparent contradiction
of them to be patent, that he may explain it. Thus αἰτεῖτε καὶ οὐ λαμβάνετε, "ye ask, and ye do not receive."
The apparent contradiction of v. 2
must also be noticed; but it is impossible to explain it by difference of
active and middle: St James could
never mean to say that they did αἰτεῖν
though they did not αἰτεῖσθαι. The
true solution is simpler. In a sense
they did ask, but it was an evil asking,
and therefore not a true asking. We
had a similar ambiguity in the language
about faith.

διότι κακῶς αἰτεῖσθε, because ye ask
in evil wise] Not all asking from God
is prayer. Asking is but the external
form of prayer, and no asking from
God which takes place in a wrong
frame of mind towards Him or towards
the object asked has anything to do
with prayer. It is an evil asking.

ἵνα ἐν ταῖς ἡδοναῖς ὑμῶν δαπανήσητε,
that ye may consume what ye desire
in your pleasures] The usual preposition with δαπανάω is εἰς, and no other
example of ἐν seems to be known: but
it is difficult to take δαπανήσητε alone
as the primary predicate, and doubtless
ἐν ταῖς ἡδοναῖς ὑμ. must be taken together, not precisely in the sense "consume upon your pleasures," but literally "consume in your pleasures," i.e.
by using for your pleasures. Throughout "what ye desire" is to be understood
as the object. There is force in δαπανήσητε; not simply spend, but consume,

expend, dissipate. This force is explained by ἐν ταῖς ἡδ. ὑμῶν, which as
before must be taken in the widest
sense, not limited to pleasures of the
senses. God's gifts, when rightly used,
are not dissipated in the using: they
are transmuted as it were to some fresh
form of energy, which lives on, and
turns to fresh use. But the use which
consists in nothing more than individual gratification, not tending in any
way to improve and enlarge the person
gratified, is pure waste, dissipation,
destruction. God bestows not gifts
only, but the enjoyment of them: but
the enjoyment which contributes to
nothing beyond itself is not what He
gives in answer to prayer; and petitions to Him which have no better
end in view are not prayers.

4.   μοιχαλίδες, ye adulteresses] Μοι-
χοὶ καί is spurious (Syrian). The
first question here is whether the
word is used literally or figuratively.
It is a common late word for "adul-
teress." It is usually taken figuratively
for these reasons, that adulterers are
omitted, that friendship with the world
seems too slight and too inappropriate
a charge to bring against adultery, and
that adultery was not a kind of offence
likely to be found in early Christian
societies. Hence it is assumed that
μοιχαλίδες is to be interpreted with
reference to the O.T. language, in
which all sin and apostasy are spoken
of as adultery, in reference to such
language as "thy Maker is thy husband." On that view the reference
may either be to whole communities
(backsliding Israel) or to individuals
(adulterous souls). The difficulty of μοιχαλίδες is undeniable. But it is hardly
credible that this figurative view
should have been brought in by a single
word, without any mark of its figurative intention; and moreover φονεύετε
and μοιχαλίδες in a literal sense confirm each other, and both stand on

ὅτι ἡ φιλία τοῦ κόσμου ἔχθρα τοῦ θεοῦ ἐστίν; ὃς ἐὰν

the same footing as the passage iv. 13 —v. 6, which likewise does not read as if addressed to Christians, least of all v. 6. It would seem as though in all this part of the Epistle St James extended his vision beyond the immediate state of things among those to whom he was writing and contemplated likewise that which would naturally spring from the roots which already were there, and what did indeed already exist among the unbelieving Jews. The other alternative would be to treat the Epistle as written to all Jews of the Dispersion, not Christian Jews only: and that is apparently excluded by ii. 1.

The mention of adulteresses alone may be founded on, and is at least illustrated by Mal. iii. 5, a passage which is probably referred to in v. 4: there in LXX. τὰς μοιχαλίδας represents a masculine in the Hebrew. But there is also a fitness in the word used. The whole passage is not exhaustive, it deals with representative evils. Peace has suggested war, war has suggested first wrong deeds of aggression (murder etc.) due to the action of indulged pleasures, which in this case are aptly represented as themselves making war. But St James wishes to point to another class of evils likewise due to pleasures but not of the aggressive type. Now a male adulterer as such is an aggressor, a maker of war, an invader of that which belongs to another man; so that he would not so well serve as an example for this second illustration. Unfaithfulness, disloyalty, breach of a sacred bond and covenant are the essence of this second type of evil; and of these the faithless wife serves as the clearest example, since the faithless husband, who as such is doubly an adulterer, does not exhibit *this* characteristic detached from the other.

οὐκ οἴδατε ὅτι ἡ φιλία] Here we reach the remaining difficulty, the

connexion between literal adultery and love of the world. The difficulty is greatly diminished when we remember that both in the Bible and in actual fact adultery includes much more than impurity. The broken bond and the price paid for the breach of the bond are doubtless here contemplated. The price might be gifts, or pride, or distinction, or other such things: they would at all events often belong to the world even more than to the flesh. (Cf. Ezek. xxiii. 5 f., 12, 14 ff.; also Hos. ii. 12; ix. 1 f.) Guinevere's disloyalty to Arthur for the sake of Lancelot has not a little in common with disloyalty to God for the sake of the world. It is the surrender to the glory and strength of visible things in forgetfulness of simple inward love and duty.

ἡ φιλία τοῦ κόσμου, *the friendship of the world*] To be compared with 1 John ii. 15, Μὴ ἀγαπᾶτε τὸν κόσμον κ.τ.λ.; both being closely connected with Mt. vi. 24 || Lk. xvi. 13. Yet the conceptions of the three passages, as represented by the three words δουλεύειν, ἀγαπᾶτε, φιλία, are different. φιλία, not occurring elsewhere in N.T. but several times in Prov. (LXX.), and in Apocr., is best rendered by "friendship," though it goes beyond it in Greek usage. It is used (see Rost and Palm) for any kind of family affection, but especially for friendship proper (see the singularly interesting and beautiful discussion in Aristotle's *Eth. Nicom.* viii.). As between God and men St James has already recognised it in the person of Abraham (ii. 23). The friendship of the world (i.e. standing on terms of friendship with it) in those days would mean or involve conformity to heathen standards of living (see on i. 27; iii. 6). At the time when St James wrote this, the eyes of all Jews must have been turned on one signal example illustrating this verse. The Empress Poppaea, the

οὖν βουληθῇ φίλος εἶναι τοῦ κόσμου, ἐχθρὸς τοῦ θεοῦ
καθίσταται. ⁵ἢ δοκεῖτε ὅτι κενῶς ἡ γραφὴ λέγει Πρὸς
φθόνον ἐπιποθεῖ τὸ πνεῦμα ὃ κατῴκισεν ἐν ἡμῖν; ⁶μείζονα

5. λέγει Πρὸς...ἡμῖν; μείζονα] λέγει; πρὸς...ἡμῖν; μείζονα v. λέγει;
πρὸς...ἡμῖν, μείζονα

wife of Nero, one of the vilest of women, was conspicuous at Rome; and there is reason to believe that she had embraced Judaism (Friedländer i. 413), for Josephus calls her θεοσεβής (*Ant.* xx. 8. 11), and she was the patroness and friend of the Jews at Rome.

Both φιλία and ἔχθρα doubtless denote here rather states than feelings. To be on terms of friendship with the world involves living on terms of enmity with God. It is neither simply hatred of God nor the being hated by God; but being on a footing of hostility. This explains the genitive.

ὃς ἐὰν οὖν βουληθῇ, *whosoever therefore chooses*] Here we pass from the footing to the state of mind. There might be much thoughtless and as it were casual love of the world of which St James might hesitate to use this language. But he wishes the contradiction to be recognised and faced. The relation between the two states as such being what he has described, any one who deliberately chooses the one makes himself to belong to the other. Βούλομαι implies purpose, intention, not mere will, but will with premeditation as i. 18. καθίσταται virtually "makes himself" as iii. 6.

5. δοκεῖτε ὅτι, *think ye that*] With a different subject, as Mt. xxvi. 53; Mk vi. 49; Lk. xii. 51; xiii. 2.

κενῶς, *in vain*] Cf. ὦ ἄνθρωπε κενέ ii. 20; and κενός is often used with λόγος and ῥῆμα, a word void of meaning.

ἡ γραφὴ λέγει] These words and those that follow stand almost on a level with iii. 6 for difficulty, and the number of solutions proposed is great (see Theile). It is impossible here to examine them in detail. As regards

the general construction, πρὸς φθόνον κ.τ.λ. may be joined to what precedes, as the quotation referred to, or it may be taken as a separate sentence affirmative or interrogative: and further τὸ πνεῦμα may be taken either as the subject to ἐπιποθεῖ or as governed by it, and πρὸς φθόνον may be variously understood.

At the outset κατῴκισεν, not -ησεν, is the reading: so that the verse contains a distinct reference to God, "which He caused to dwell in us." This of itself makes it highly probable that ἐπιποθεῖ has the same subject, making τὸ πνεῦμα accusative, "He longs for the spirit which He caused to dwell." The reference here is certainly, as in other parts of the Epistle, to God's breathing into man's nostrils the breath of life; probably also to Gen. vi. 3, where the LXX. and other versions [Jer. Onk. Syr. Sah.; but Sym. κρινεῖ] have οὐ μὴ καταμείνῃ τὸ πνεῦμά μου ἐν τοῖς ἀνθρώποις τούτοις εἰς τὸν αἰῶνα for the difficult יָדוֹן, for which they perhaps had another Hebrew word: also Job xxvii. 3 (cf. xxxiii. 4; xxxiv. 14). ἐπιποθεῖ is well illustrated by Alford, though he inverts the construction: it expresses God's yearning over the human spirit which He not only made but imbreathed as a breath from His own Spirit: for His yearning see Deut. xxxii. 11.

πρὸς φθόνον, *jealously*] This makes another step. Apparently it can only mean "jealously," in the same way that πρὸς ὀργήν means "angrily," πρὸς ἀλήθειαν "truly" etc. This is the only place in the N.T. where πρός is so used: but there can be no real doubt about it here.

Is then φθόνον used in a good or

δὲ δίδωσιν χάριν· διὸ λέγει Ὁ θεὸς ὑπερηφάνοις ἀντιτάσσεται

an evil sense? If we follow the usage of the word itself, it should have an evil sense. But in that case πρὸς φθόνον κ.τ.λ. must form a question expecting a negative answer "Is it jealously (or, for jealousy) that He yearns" etc., with the meaning "It is not from jealousy of others but for some other reason, as simply love to men, that He yearns" etc. But this does not suit the context: ἢ δοκεῖτε ὅτι clearly shews that St James is still pursuing the stern strain of v. 4, and maintaining the incompatibility of friendship with God and the world together. Now this is exactly what the Bible calls jealousy (see 2nd Commandment), and the difficulty here arises not from the *conception* of jealousy, but from the word used. This being the case it seems tolerably certain that St James *does* mean to attribute φθόνος to God (not of course in the sense in which Herodotus i. 32; iii. 40 said φθονερὸν τὸ θεῖον and Plato *Phaedr.* 247 A, φθόνος γὰρ ἔξω θείου χοροῦ ἵσταται, denied it, i.e. as grudging mankind happiness or prosperity), but in the sense that He does grudge the world or any other antagonistic power such friendship and loyalty as is due to Himself alone. We may therefore render the words "jealously (or, with jealousy) doth He yearn after the spirit which He caused to dwell in us."

Lastly, are these words independent or a quotation? No one probably would doubt that the form of language suggests a quotation. ὅτι κενῶς ἡ γραφὴ λέγει certainly does not sound as if it were meant to stand absolutely, and there are no words of the O.T. which could readily occur to any one as so clearly expressing the substance of v. 4 as not to need quotation. Also πρὸς φθόνον κ.τ.λ. comes in abruptly as St James' own words; though fitly enough if they belonged originally to another context.

The difficulty is that no such words can be found. The passages already cited contain however their substantial purport; so that our O.T. Scripture does in a manner furnish them. But it is likely enough that they come directly from some intermediate source now lost to us. There are other reasons for supposing the N.T. writers to have used Greek paraphrases of the O.T. resembling the Hebrew Targums, and the words may have come literally from one of these. In their vocabulary such paraphrases would certainly not always follow the same limitation as the LXX.; and though the LXX. sedulously uses ζῆλος etc. only (there is no trace of φθόνος as a rendering of קִנְאָה in Hexapla), and avoids φθόνος in speaking of God, it by no means follows that a Palestinian paraphrase would do the same.

6. Before examining the first six words of the verse, it will be well to consider the quotation which follows, from which the words δίδωσιν χάριν are derived. The form in which St James quotes Prov. iii. 34, διὸ λέγει Ὁ θεὸς ὑπερηφάνοις ἀντιτάσσεται ταπεινοῖς δὲ δίδωσιν χάριν, differs from the LXX. only by the substitution of ὁ θεός (so also 1 Pet. v. 5, doubtless from Jam.) for Κύριος. Both subjects of the verbs are absent from the Hebrew, but both come from the LXX. of 32 (Κυρίου), 33 (Θεοῦ), *Jehovah* in both places. The verse in the original is rather peculiarly worded, but probably means (contrast Delitzsch) "Though to the scorners He sheweth Himself a scorner, yet to the lowly He giveth grace." That is, unlike the scorners of the earth, who are specially scornful to the lowly, He is scornful only to scorners and to the lowly on the contrary a giver of grace.

ὑπερηφάνοις, *scorners*] ὑπερήφανος belongs to all periods of Greek in the sense "insolent," being especially used of such evil effects as follow from

ταπεινοῖϲ δὲ δίδωϲιν χάριν.   *7'Ὑποτάγητε οὖν τῷ θεῷ· ἀντί-*

wealth or position (Arist. *Rhet.* ii. 16. 1. Trench *Syn.* § 29 is worth reading, but he makes ὑπερήφανος too purely inward). In N.T. the substantive stands Mk vii. 22 between βλασφημία (not "blasphemy" but "reviling")and ἀφροσύνη(for this sequence cf. Arist. *Rhet.* ii. 17. 6 ὑπερηφανώτεροι καὶ ἀλογιστότεροι). The adjective (not to speak of Lk. i. 51, derived from Ps. lxxxix. 10) stands in 2 Tim. iii. 2 between ἀλαζόνες and βλάσφημοι, and in Rom. i. 30 between ὑβριστάς and ἀλαζόνας. This last collocation (adopted also by Trench, though in a peculiar way) best illustrates the force of ὑπερήφανος, as is seen in a passage of "Callicratidas"(Neo-Pythagorean) in Stob. *Fl.* 85. 16 (iii. 141 f. Mein.) ἀνάγκα γὰρ τὼς πολλὰ ἔχοντας τετυφῶσθαι πρᾶτον, τετυφωμένως δὲ ἀλαζόνας γίγνεσθαι, ἀλαζόνας δὲ γενομένως ὑπερηφάνως ἦμεν καὶ μήτε ὁμοίως μήτε ἴσως ὑπολαμβάνειν τὼς συγγενέας κ.τ.λ., ὑπερηφάνως δὲ γενομένως ὑβριστὰς ἦμεν (cf. Teles, ib. 93. 31 (p. 187. 6) ὑπερήφανος ἐξ ἀλαζονείας). The ἀλαζών is personally arrogant, and gives expression to his arrogance; in the ὑπερήφανος the personal arrogance has become insolence towards others, whether in thought, word or deed; in the ὑβριστής the impulse to assert self by actual contumely or violence to others has become the dominant characteristic. The whole range of the three words is exemplified in iv. 13—v. 6, which ends with ἀντιτάσσεται ὑμῖν, best explained as an echo of iv. 6.

The original of ὑπερήφανοι is לֵצִים, the scorners or scoffers, a word much used in Proverbs and occasionally elsewhere: see especially Hupfeld on Ps. i. 1. It is rendered in various ways by LXX., never very successfully; here alone by ὑπερήφανος, which fairly represents the temper expressed outwardly by לֵצִים.

ἀντιτάσσεται, *withstands*] Possibly

for יִתְיַצֵּב, "withstands,""stands in the way." But the words in Prov. are הוּא יָלִיץ לְ, "himself sheweth scorn," of which ἀντιτάσσεται cannot be a direct translation, but may perhaps be a paraphrase, in the sense "To the scorners God sets himself face to face," i.e. meets scorn with scorn (cf. the probable meaning of μὴ ἀντιστῆναι τῷ πονηρῷ in Mt. v. 39). However this may be ἀντιτάσσεται was probably taken by St James in its common and obvious sense of facing for resistance, as Esther iii. 4, and (by corruptions of the Hebrew text) 1 Kings xi. 34; Hos. i. 6. Ἀντιτάσσομαι is properly a military word, to set or be set in battle array, but often used figuratively, in the singular no less than the plural.

ταπεινοῖς δέ, *but to those of low estate*] The K'thibh here has עֲנָוִים, the Q'ri עֲנִיִּם. It is usually said (the case is well stated by Delitzsch on Ps. ix. 12) that the former word has a physical sense, outwardly lowly, afflicted, poor; the latter an ethical sense, inwardly lowly, humble, meek. Hupfeld *l.c.* has shewn the difficulty of carrying out the distinction consistently. Lowliness (downcastness, depression) is the fundamental idea in both cases. On the whole, whatever be the Hebrew reading, probably the physical sense was intended in Prov., if not always in O.T. The עֲנָוִים are the helpless or poor trampled on or insulted by the insolent rich or powerful. The same sense on the whole suits best in St James. The strictly ethical sense can never be clearly traced in the N.T. in the absence of some qualifying adjunct (ταπεινὸς τῇ καρδία Mt. xi. 29; ταπεινόφρων, ταπεινοφροσύνη Acts, 1 Peter, St Paul). Elsewhere ταπεινός, ταπεινόω, ταπείνωσις denote always some kind of external lowliness or abasement. Here we are especially reminded of ὁ ἀδελφὸς ὁ ταπεινός in i. 10, and the strong sympathy with the poor (אֶבְיוֹנִים) perceptible in the Epistle, as in early Jewish Christianity generally.

δίδωσιν χάριν, *giveth grace or acceptance*] Not to be interpreted as referring to "grace" in the traditional theological sense. Still less can the phrase δίδ. χάριν bear here the meaning found in classical writers (Eur. *Suppl.* 414; Plat. *Leg.* 702 c; 877 A; and later authors), to gratify, do a pleasure or favour to (*gratificor*). In the LXX. χάρις almost always represents חֵן, the primary force of which is seen in the phrase "find grace in the eyes of," common in the historical books. The same books four times have "give grace," but always with the same adjunct "in the eyes of," the giver of the grace or favourable estimation being thus distinct from the person whose favourable estimation is given. Of a phrase "give grace" in a sense directly correlative to that of "finding grace" i.e. "shew favour," there is no example with חֵן in the O.T., though it finds place in the solitary instance of the cognate חֲנִינָה (LXX. with a change of person δώσουσιν ἔλεος) Jer. xvi. 13: cf. Tob. vii. 17. On the other hand the Psalms and Proverbs three times speak of "giving grace" in a sense arising out of the absolute use of the word "grace" (almost always without any defining adjunct in these books and in Ecclesiastes. The fundamental sense "acceptance," which predominates a few times (Prov. iii. 4; xxii. 1; xxviii. 23; Eccl. ix. 11), is usually more or less merged in the sense of the quality or qualities which lead to acceptance and constitute acceptability, whether it be *graciousness* of speech and demeanour or the lesser "grace" of *gracefulness*, adornment, beauty. Acceptability and acceptance are blended in the two passages which most concern us here; Prov. xiii. 15 "Good understanding *giveth grace*" (cf. iii. 4 "So [by devotion to "mercy and truth"] shalt thou find *grace and*

good understanding in the sight of God and man"; also Ecclus. xxi. 16; xxxvii. 21); and Ps. lxxxiv. 11 "The Lord will *give grace* and glory" (cf. Prov. iv. 9 "a garland of *grace*" parallel to "a crown of *glory*"; also Ecclus. xxiv. 16 οἱ κλάδοι μου κλάδοι δόξης καὶ χάριτος). In like manner here, Prov. iii. 34, God is represented as granting to the lowly a "grace" or acceptance (before the more discerning of men as well as before Himself) doubtless founded on a disposition worthy of such acceptance, a lowliness of spirit (Prov. xvi. 19; xxix. 23; Mt. v. 3), which He denies to the scornful men of power, externally the monopolists of "grace" or acceptance.

This the original sense of Proverbs, illustrated by an almost immediately preceding verse, iii. 31, "Envy thou not the oppressor, and choose none of his ways," is also the sense of St James. He is giving a warning against the danger of courting the friendship of the world, the society ruled by powerful scorners. Refusal to seek that friendship meant acceptance of the lowly estate, held in no visible honour by God or men. But the ancient wisdom of Israel had pronounced the true judgement. Those who looked below the surface of things would find that the powerful scorners have God Himself set against them (cf. ἐχθρὸς τοῦ θεοῦ καθίσταται) while it is to the lowly ones that He gives "grace" or acceptance.

The introductory words μείζονα δὲ δίδωσιν χάριν can now hardly have any other meaning than this, "But He giveth a greater grace or acceptance than the world or its friendship can give": that is, their connexion is with *v*. 4, *v*. 5 being parenthetic. To connect them directly with *v*. 5, in the sense "He gives a (spiritual) grace to aid men to cleave to Him, proportionate to the jealousy with which He yearns after His spirit within them," renders the whole of the quotation irrelevant except the two words already cited, besides involving a

complete departure from the sense
of Proverbs. The subject of the verb
is naturally identical with the implied
subject of the preceding principal verb
ἐπιποθεῖ. By "greater" St James
doubtless means worthier, higher, as
1 Cor. xii. 31 (right text); Heb. ix. 11;
xi. 26.

διό, *wherefore*] The employment of
διό in the introductory formula of a
quotation is elsewhere found only in
Eph. iv. 8; v. 14 (διὸ λέγει both times,
as here); while the more obvious
διότι, "because," is confined to 1 Peter.
It seems to be derived from a Rab-
binic usage (Surenhuis Βιβλ. καταλ. 9),
but ultimately it may be traced to
Gen. x. 9; Num. xxi. 14 (עַל־כֵּן יֵאָמַר),
LXX. διὰ τοῦτο ἐροῦσιν, δ. τ. λέγεται).
The idea probably meant to be suggested is that the truth stated is *pre-
supposed* in the quotation appealed
to, forming as it were the basis, on
which it rests.

λέγει, the Scripture *saith*] Λέγει
may have as a subject ἡ γραφή from
v. 5, or the implied subject of δίδωσιν,
that is, God; or again it may be
virtually impersonal, as in Eph. v. 14,
and probably iv. 8. This use of λέγει
(or other such words) without an expressed or directly implied subject,
for introducing quotations from Scripture or quasi-Scriptural books, is not
identical with the common interpo-
sition of an impersonal ἔφη (*inquit*)
after the opening words of quotations
of all kinds: it doubtless implies an
appeal to an authoritative voice. The
Rabbinical illustrations cited by Surenhuis, p. 11, belong only to cases
(like Rom. xv. 10) where another quotation has immediately preceded. To
supply mentally either "God" or "the
Scripture" is in strictness to define
too much as there is no real ellipse,
but in translation into modern languages some supplement is needed,
and for this purpose "the Scripture"
gives the truest impression. Ἡ γραφή
is also the more probable of the two
possible subjects furnished by the

preceding context.

7. From vv. 7 to 10 we have a
hortatory digression, starting from the
suggestions of v. 6.

ὑποτάγητε οὖν τῷ θεῷ, *Submit
yourselves therefore to God*] It is
hardly credible that St James should
use this phrase without a conscious
reference to its associations in the
Psalm from which (LXX.) it virtually
comes, and that Psalm xxxvii. *Noli
aemulari*. See vv. 7, 9, ὑποτάγηθι
τῷ κυρίῳ καὶ ἱκέτευσον αὐτόν· μὴ
παραζήλου ἐν τῷ κατευοδουμένῳ ἐν τῇ
ζωῇ αὐτοῦ, κ.τ.λ. οἱ δὲ ὑπομένοντες τὸν
κύριον αὐτοὶ κληρονομήσουσιν τὴν γῆν:
so again Ps. lxii. 1, 5, Οὐχὶ τῷ θεῷ
ὑποταγήσεται ἡ ψυχή μου; παρ'
αὐτοῦ γὰρ τὸ σωτήριόν μου. ...πλὴν τῷ
θεῷ ὑποτάγηθι, ἡ ψυχή μου, ὅτι παρ'
αὐτοῦ ἡ ὑπομονή μου. This is but a
paraphrastic rendering of the original,
the Hebrew (דָּמַם, דּוּמִיָּה) meaning
"to be silent (or, still: σίγησον Aq.,
ἡσύχαζε Sym.) to the Lord," i.e. the
going forth of the soul to Him not
in speech (whether clamour to Him
or murmur against Him) but in reso-
lute suppression of speech. Similarly
Lam. iii. 26, "It is good that a man
wait and *be still to* the salvation
(saving help) of Jehovah" (LXX. ὑπο-
μενεῖ καὶ ἡσυχάσει εἰς τὸ σωτήριον
Κυρίου); and with another reference,
Job xxix. 21, "men...*kept silence to*
my counsel" (LXX. ἐσιώπησαν ἐπί).
Compare Ps. iv. 4; cxxxi. 2. This
deeply felt idea of a strenuous silence
to God, the expression of perfect trust,
loses somewhat by translation into the
common thought of submission, which
need imply no more than a sense of
inability to resist: but St James might
well assume that readers of the LXX.
Psalter would recognise the "submission" of which he spoke to be one
aspect of faithful endurance under
trials.

Yet doubtless St James' primary
meaning was the simple Greek meaning "submit yourselves." In 2 Mac.
ix. 12 the dying Antiochus Epiphanes

H. J.   7

στῆτε δὲ τῷ διαβόλῳ, καὶ φεύξεται ἀφ᾽ ὑμῶν· ⁸ἐγγίσατε

is made to say, Δίκαιον ὑποτάσσεσθαι τῷ θεῷ καὶ μὴ θνητὸν ὄντα ὑπερήφανα φρονεῖν. Epictetus uses the same word, applying it to both the fact of subjection to God (*Diss.* iii. 24. 65, ὡς τοῦ Διὸς διάκονον ἔδει, ἅμα μὲν κηδόμενος, ἅμα δ᾽ ὡς τῷ θεῷ ὑποτεταγμένος) and the duty of submission to Him (iv. 12. 11, ἐγὼ δ᾽ ἔχω τίνι με δεῖ ἀρέσκειν, τίνι ὑποτετάχθαι, τίνι πείθεσθαι, τῷ θεῷ καὶ τοῖς μετ᾽ ἐκεῖνον). In the N.T., which dwells much on submission as among men, human submission to God is spoken of only here and Heb. xii. 9 (ὑποταγησόμεθα τῷ πατρὶ τῶν πνευμάτων). Here as οὖν indicates, it is doubtless suggested by ὑπερηφάνοις (cf. 2 Mac. above). The insolence of the powerful implies a sense at once of having others in subjection and of being in subjection to none (cf. Ps. xii. 3—5). The lowly then are bidden to find refuge for their subjection to the tyrannous and too visible "world," not in wooing its friendship but in cherishing the submission or accepted subjection to the invisible God (compare Ign. *Eph.* 5, γέγραπται γάρ, Ὑπερηφάνοις ὁ θεὸς ἀντιτάσσεται· σπουδάσωμεν οὖν μὴ ἀντιτάσσεσθαι τῷ ἐπισκόπῳ, ἵνα ὦμεν θεῷ ὑποτασσόμενοι). The same word expresses both the external fact (subjection) and the voluntary acceptance of it (submission):—"be ye subject (in mind), as being already subject (in destiny); take up the attitude belonging to the position."

The aorist imperative (used in this verb by 1 Pet. ii. 13; v. 5; but not by St Paul) has here the force of a call out of a degenerate state, and it is repeated in nine succeeding verbs.

ἀντίστητε δὲ τῷ διαβόλῳ, *but resist the devil*] Δέ is omitted in the Rec. Text after the later Syrian text, doubtless because the following initial imperatives have no connecting particles.

The name ὁ διάβολος is used much in the N.T., somewhat more than the transliterated original ὁ Σατανᾶς. Both names occur in Mt., Lk., Jn, Acts, St Paul and Apoc. Apparently in most if not all cases the use of the Greek διάβολος involves a distinct reference to the etymology. The precise force of the Hebrew name is not free from doubt. Apparently the verb שָׂטַן (also שָׂטַם) meant originally to "lie in ambush for," and so to "bear a chronic grudge against" or "be a treacherous enemy to." The subst. שָׂטָן stands in Numbers for the angel waylaying Balaam, and in Samuel and Kings for (apparently secret) enemies, as it were thorns in the side. In the later books it becomes a proper name for the evil spirit, as an accuser (Ps. cix. 6; Zech. iii. 1, 2), as an insidious enemy (1 Chr. xxi. 1), and as both (Job i., ii.). The occurrence of the derivative שִׂטְנָה for "an accusation" in Ezra iv. 6 is sufficient proof that in the late language the original sense had become specialised to express in particular that form of insidious hostility which consists in malicious accusation; and there is ample evidence (see e.g. Levy-Fleischer, *N. Heb. W. B.* iii. 500 f.) that malicious accusation came to be regarded as a characteristic of Satan, as indeed appears by Apoc. xii. 10 (see Schöttgen, *Hor. Heb.* i. 1121 ff.). The Fathers usually interpret the name simply as ὁ ἀντικείμενος, *adversarius*, in accordance with a possible latitude of interpretation in several places where the verb or the substantive used appellatively occurs; and similarly [ὁ] ἀντικείμενος is the rendering of Theodotion in Job, and of both him and Symmachus in Zech. iii. 2, as they also (and Aquila likewise) use ἀντίκειμαι and its participle in passages of less direct bearing. But (except in the later revised text, once

τῷ θεῷ, καὶ ἐγγίσει ὑμῖν. καθαρίσατε χεῖρας, ἁμαρ-
τωλοί, καὶ ἁγνίσατε καρδίας, δίψυχοι. ⁹ταλαιπωρήσατε
καὶ πενθήσατε καὶ κλαύσατε· ὁ γέλως ὑμῶν εἰς πένθος
μετατραπήτω καὶ ἡ χαρὰ εἰς κατήφειαν· ¹⁰ταπεινώθητε
ἐνώπιον Κυρίου, καὶ ὑψώσει ὑμᾶς.   ¹¹ Μὴ κατα-
λαλεῖτε ἀλλήλων, ἀδελφοί· ὁ καταλαλῶν ἀδελφοῦ ἢ
κρίνων τὸν ἀδελφὸν αὐτοῦ καταλαλεῖ νόμου καὶ κρίνει
νόμον· εἰ δὲ νόμον κρίνεις, οὐκ εἶ ποιητὴς νόμου ἀλλὰ
κριτής. ¹²εἷς ἔστιν νομοθέτης καὶ κριτής, ὁ δυνάμενος
σῶσαι καὶ ἀπολέσαι· σὺ δὲ τίς εἶ, ὁ κρίνων τὸν
πλησίον;

¹³ Ἄγε νῦν οἱ λέγοντες Σήμερον ἢ αὔριον πορευσό-
μεθα εἰς τήνδε τὴν πόλιν καὶ ποιήσομεν ἐκεῖ ἐνιαυτὸν καὶ
ἐμπορευσόμεθα καὶ κερδήσομεν· ¹⁴οἵτινες οὐκ ἐπίστασθε
τῆς αὔριον ποία ἡ ζωὴ ὑμῶν· ἀτμὶς γάρ ἐστε πρὸς
ὀλίγον φαινομένη, ἔπειτα καὶ ἀφανιζομένη· ¹⁵ἀντὶ τοῦ
λέγειν ὑμᾶς Ἐὰν ὁ κύριος θέλῃ, καὶ ζήσομεν καὶ ποιή-

9. μετατραπήτω] μεταστραφήτω   12. ἔστιν] ἐστὶν ὁ   14. τῆς αὔριον...γάρ
ἐστε] τὰ τῆς αὔριον· ποία γὰρ ἡ ζωὴ ὑμῶν; ἀτμὶς ἐστε ἡ   15. θέλῃ] θελήσῃ

or twice) not so the LXX., which employs διαβάλλω, διαβολή, ἐνδιαβάλλω,
ἐπίβουλος, σατάν, and for the evil spirit
exclusively [ὁ] διάβολος.
There can be little doubt that the
writers of the N.T. adopted the term
διάβολος directly or indirectly from
the LXX.; and this consideration seems
to set aside the tempting interpretation suggested by abundant Greek
usage as regards the verb, the "severer,"
"putter at variance," in opposition to
a "reconciler." For the equally tempting interpretation "perverter," that is,
"one who turns good to evil," there
is no Greek evidence beyond the occasional sense of διά in composition (as
it were, one who casts awry). The
biblical origin of the name fixes upon
it the sense "malicious accuser," "of
God to men, and of us to God, and
again of ourselves to each other"

(Chrys. 2 Cor. p. 438 D). There is a
special fitness in the word, because
it is oftener applied in ordinary Greek
to suggested disparagement, whether
open or secret, to words or acts intended to produce an unfavourable
impression (see Aristotle's account of
διαβολή as a department of forensic
rhetoric, Rhet. iii. 15. 1, with Cope's
note), than to formal and definite
accusation.
This the proper biblical sense of
ὁ διάβολος, of which the sense in
which he is called ὁ πειράζων is only
another aspect, agrees well with the
context here. Trustful submission to
God involves resistance to him who
tempts men to faithlessness by in-
sinuating disparagement of God's
power or His goodness, backed up
with suggestion of the safer and
pleasanter friendship of "the world."

7—2

σομεν τοῦτο ἢ ἐκεῖνο. ¹⁶νῦν δὲ καυχᾶσθε ἐν ταῖς ἀλα-
ζονίαις ὑμῶν· πᾶσα καύχησις τοιαύτη πονηρά ἐστιν.
¹⁷εἰδότι οὖν καλὸν ποιεῖν καὶ μὴ ποιοῦντι, ἁμαρτία αὐτῷ
ἐστίν. V. ¹Ἄγε νῦν οἱ πλούσιοι, κλαύσατε ὀλολύ-
ζοντες ἐπὶ ταῖς ταλαιπωρίαις ὑμῶν ταῖς ἐπερχομέναις.
²ὁ πλοῦτος ὑμῶν σέσηπεν, καὶ τὰ ἱμάτια ὑμῶν σητό-
βρωτα γέγονεν, ³ὁ χρυσὸς ὑμῶν καὶ ὁ ἄργυρος κατίωται,
καὶ ὁ ἰὸς αὐτῶν εἰς μαρτύριον ὑμῖν ἔσται καὶ φάγεται
τὰς σάρκας ὑμῶν· ὡς πῦρ ἐθηϲαγρίϲατε ἐν ἐσχάταις ἡμέραις.
⁴ἰδοὺ ὁ μιϲθὸϲ τῶν ἐργατῶν τῶν ἀμησάντων τὰς χώρας
ὑμῶν ὁ ἀφυστερημένος ἀφ᾽ ὑμῶν κράζει, καὶ αἱ βοαὶ τῶν
θερισάντων εἰϲ τὰ ὦτα Κυρίου Σαβαὼθ εἰσελήλυθαν· ⁵ἐτρυ-
φήσατε ἐπὶ τῆς γῆς καὶ ἐσπαταλήσατε, ἐθρέψατε τὰς
καρδίας ὑμῶν ἐν ἡμέρᾳ ϲφαγῆϲ. ⁶κατεδικάσατε, ἐφονεύσατε
τὸν δίκαιον. οὐκ ἀντιτάϲϲεται ὑμῖν;

⁷Μακροθυμήσατε οὖν, ἀδελφοί, ἕως τῆς παρουσίας
τοῦ κυρίου. ἰδοὺ ὁ γεωργὸς ἐκδέχεται τὸν τίμιον καρπὸν τῆς γῆς, μακροθυμῶν ἐπ᾽ αὐτῷ ἕως λάβῃ πρόϊμον κὰι
ὄψιμον. ⁸μακροθυμήσατε καὶ ὑμεῖς, στηρίξατε τὰς καρδίας ὑμῶν, ὅτι ἡ παρουσία τοῦ κυρίου ἤγγικεν. ⁹μὴ
στενάζετε, ἀδελφοί, κατ᾽ ἀλλήλων, ἵνα μὴ κριθῆτε·
ἰδοὺ ὁ κριτὴς πρὸ τῶν θυρῶν ἔστηκεν. ¹⁰ὑπόδειγμα
λάβετε, ἀδελφοί, τῆς κακοπαθίας καὶ τῆς μακροθυμίας
τοὺς προφήτας, οἳ ἐλάλησαν ἐν τῷ ὀνόματι Κυρίου.
¹¹ἰδοὺ μακαρίζομεν τοὺϲ ὑπομείνανταϲ· τὴν ὑπομονὴν Ἰὼβ
ἠκούσατε, καὶ τὸ τέλος Κυρίου εἴδετε, ὅτι πολύϲπλαγχνόϲ
ἐϲτιν ὁ κύριοϲ καὶ οἰκτίρμων. ¹²Πρὸ πάντων δέ,
ἀδελφοί μου, μὴ ὀμνύετε, μήτε τὸν οὐρανὸν μήτε
τὴν γῆν μήτε ἄλλον τινὰ ὅρκον· ἤτω δὲ ὑμῶν τό
Ναί ναὶ καὶ τό Οὔ οὔ, ἵνα μὴ ὑπὸ κρίσιν πέσητε.
¹³Κακοπαθεῖ τις ἐν ὑμῖν; προσευχέσθω· εὐθυμεῖ τις;

3. ὑμῶν· ὡς πῦρ] ὑμῶν ὡς πῦρ·   6. ὑμῖν;] ὑμῶν.   11. ὁ κύριος] Κύριος

ψαλλέτω. ¹⁴ἀσθενεῖ τις ἐν ὑμῖν; προσκαλεσάσθω
τοὺς πρεσβυτέρους τῆς ἐκκλησίας, καὶ προσευξάσθωσαν
ἐπ᾽ αὐτὸν ἀλείψαντες ἐλαίῳ ἐν τῷ ὀνόματι [τοῦ κυρίου]·
¹⁵ καὶ ἡ εὐχὴ τῆς πίστεως σώσει τὸν κάμνοντα, καὶ
ἐγερεῖ αὐτὸν ὁ κύριος· κἂν ἁμαρτίας ᾖ πεποιηκώς, ἀφεθή-
σεται αὐτῷ. ¹⁶ἐξομολογεῖσθε οὖν ἀλλήλοις τὰς ἁμαρτίας
καὶ προσεύχεσθε ὑπὲρ ἀλλήλων, ὅπως ἰαθῆτε. πολὺ
ἰσχύει δέησις δικαίου ἐνεργουμένη. ¹⁷Ἠλείας ἄνθρωπος
ἦν ὁμοιοπαθὴς ἡμῖν, καὶ προσευχῇ προσηύξατο τοῦ μὴ
βρέξαι, καὶ οὐκ ἔβρεξεν ἐπὶ τῆς γῆς ἐνιαυτοὺς τρεῖς καὶ
μῆνας ἕξ· ¹⁸καὶ πάλιν προσηύξατο, καὶ ὁ οὐρανὸς ὑετὸν
ἔδωκεν καὶ ἡ γῆ ἐβλάστησεν τὸν καρπὸν αὐτῆς. ¹⁹Ἀδελ-
φοί μου, ἐάν τις ἐν ὑμῖν πλανηθῇ ἀπὸ τῆς ἀληθείας καὶ
ἐπιστρέψῃ τις αὐτόν, ²⁰γινώσκετε ὅτι ὁ ἐπιστρέψας
ἁμαρτωλὸν ἐκ πλάνης ὁδοῦ αὐτοῦ σώσει ψυχὴν αὐτοῦ
ἐκ θανάτου καὶ καλύψει πλῆθος ἁμαρτιῶν.

16. προσεύχεσθε] εὔχεσθε   18. ὑετὸν ἔδωκεν] ἔδωκεν ὑετὸν
20. γινώσκετε] γινωσκέτω   αὐτοῦ ἐκ θανάτου] ἐκ θανάτου αὐτοῦ

Note on "Brother" improperly used (see p. xx).

Gen. xiv. 14, 16, Abram and Lot (really nephew), LXX. ἀδελφὸς A etc., ἀνεψιὸς g n, υἱὸς τ. ἀδελφοῦ m, ἀδελφιδοῦς *codd.* Cf. xiii. 8, "for we be men, brethren," ἄνθρωποι ἀδελφοί; xiii. 11, ἕκαστος ἀπὸ τοῦ ἀδελφοῦ αὐτοῦ. *Contra,* xii. 5; xiv. 12; "brother's son," (τὸν) υἱὸν τοῦ ἀδελφοῦ (αὐτοῦ).

Gen. xxix. 12, Jacob Rachel's "father's *brother*" (i.e. father's *sister's son*), LXX. ἀδελφὸς τοῦ πατρὸς αὐτῆς; xxix. 15, Laban to Jacob, "thou art my *brother*" (i.e. *sister's son*), ἀδελφός μου. *Contra,* xxix. 10 ter, Laban Jacob's "mother's brother."

Gen. xxxi. 23, (32), 37, Laban's "brethren," and *vv.* (32), 37, 46, 54, Jacob's "brethren"; i.e. apparently all attached to their households.

2 Chron. xxxvi. 10, Zedekiah (Mattaniah) Jehoiachin's *brother* (i.e. *father's brother,* LXX. ἀδελφὸν τοῦ πατρὸς αὐτοῦ). *Contra,* 2 Kings xxix. 17, "father's brother" (LXX. unintelligibly υἱόν). 1 Chron. iii. 15 has the genealogy rightly.

Gen. ix. 25, Shem and Japheth Canaan's "brethren" (i.e. uncles), LXX. τοῖς ἀδελφοῖς αὐτοῦ.

Gen. xvi. 12, Ishmael is to dwell "in the presence of all his brethren," LXX. κατὰ πρόσωπον πάντων τῶν ἀδελφῶν αὐτοῦ. Cf. xxv. 18.

Numb. xx. 14, Israel (people) brother of (the king of ?) Edom.

Amos i. 9, Israel and Tyrus apparently brothers, perhaps from Hiram's friendship and brotherhood (1 Kings ix. 13, cf. xx. 32; both cases of brother-hood of kings).

Neh. v. 10, 14, Nehemiah's brethren (i.e. ? household).

Job vi. 15, "my brethren" (i.e. ? Job's friends), LXX. οἱ ἐγγύτατοί μου, Ἄλλος· ἀδελφοί μου.

Job xix. 13, ἀδελφοί μου; Ps. xxxv. 14; cxxii. 8; either friends or relatives.

Isa. lxvi. 20, "your brethren," apparently fellow-worshippers of Jehovah from other nations.

Persons or things in pairs, Gen. xiii. 11; xxvi. 31; (xliii. 33 LXX.); Exod. xxv. 20; xxxvii. 9; (1 Sam. xx. 41 Thdn): of the same nature, Job xxx. 29; Prov. xviii. 9.

Fellow-descendants of Israel, Exod. ii. 11; iv. 8; (xxii. 25 LXX.); Lev. xix. 17 (?); xxv. 35 etc.; and esp. Deut. xv. 2 (contrasted with ὁ ἀλλότριος); Jud. xiv. 3. Fellow-descendants of a tribal head, Judah 2 Sam. xix. 12; Levi Numb. viii. 26; xvi. 10; Nehem. iii. 1; (Gk Ezra *passim*); 2 Chron. xxxi. 15.

2 Sam. i. 26, David and Jonathan.
Cf. Tobit *passim*.

Similarly "sister."
(Gen. xxiv. 60, Laban and his mother *both* say to Rebecca "thou art our sister": but apparently only by a zeugma. The LXX. in consequence alters "thy brother" in *v.* 55 into οἱ ἀδελφοὶ αὐτῆς.) Job xlii. 11, Job's brethren and sisters (?). Nations of like nature and character, Ezek. xvi. 46; xxiii. 31. Metaphorically, of the same nature, Job xvii. 14; Prov. vii. 4. Term of endearment, Cant. *passim*. Things in pairs, Exod. xxvi. 3, 5, 6, 17; Ezek. i. 9; iii. 13. Member of the same nation (Midianite), Numb. xxv. 18.

Note on τῆς δόξης (*see* ii. 1).

[The following is a note by Dr Hort on Tit. ii. 13 (τῆς δόξης τοῦ μεγάλου θεοῦ καὶ σωτῆρος ἡμῶν, Χριστοῦ Ἰησοῦ).]

Χριστοῦ Ἰησοῦ is best taken as in apposition to τῆς δόξης, not to τοῦ μεγάλου θεοῦ καὶ σωτῆρος ἡμῶν. The obvious difficulties of the latter in reference to St Paul's usage are much increased by μεγάλου, partly by its sense, partly as an adjective merely.

By its sense: cf. 1 Tim. i. 11; vi. 15, 16 [see below].

As an adjective, because it compels θεοῦ to be a pure substantive, and thus individualises it. It to say the least suggests "division" of "substance," a *separate* Deity, the Deity of Tritheism, not the equally perfect Deity of a Person of the One Godhead[1]. This is very unlike St Paul and the N.T.

St Paul does not elsewhere categorically call our Lord the glory of the Father; but various phrases of his have the same effect. In 2 Cor. iv. 4 we have τὸν φωτισμὸν τοῦ εὐαγγελίου τῆς δόξης τοῦ χριστοῦ, ὅς ἐστιν εἰκὼν τοῦ θεοῦ, while in 1 Cor. xi. 7 εἰκών and δόξα are coupled (ἀνήρ,...εἰκὼν καὶ δόξα θεοῦ ὑπάρχων, ἡ γυνὴ δὲ δόξα ἀνδρός ἐστιν). In the same context in 2 Cor. (iv. 6) we have πρὸς φωτισμὸν τῆς γνώσεως τῆς δόξης τοῦ θεοῦ ἐν προσώπῳ Χριστοῦ, which must go along with 2 Cor. ii. 10, καὶ γὰρ ἐγὼ ὃ κεχάρισμαι, εἴ τι κεχάρισμαι, δι᾽ ὑμᾶς ἐν προσώπῳ Χριστοῦ, meaning in both cases *in the person of Christ*, so that St Paul describes God's glory as set forth (or as being) in the person of Christ. The sense is given without the word in 1 Tim. vi. 15, 16, where much stress is laid on the height and invisibility of the Father, φῶς οἰκῶν ἀπρόσιτον, who καιροῖς ἰδίοις will shew (δείξει) the ἐπιφάνεια of Ἰ. Χ.: unseen Himself, He manifests His Son as His glory. There is less certainty about 1 Tim. i. 11, τὸ εὐαγγέλιον τῆς δόξης τοῦ μακαρίου θεοῦ, though μακάριος probably denotes the supreme unapproachableness; and about Eph. i. 17, ὁ θεὸς τοῦ κυρίου ἡμῶν Ἰ. Χ., ὁ πατὴρ τῆς δόξης (a remarkable juxtaposition when compared with ὁ θεὸς καὶ πατὴρ τοῦ κυρίου ἡμῶν Ἰ. Χ. in Eph. i. 3 etc.). Still

[1] As if *Quicunque vult* had said "sicut unamquamque personam esse singillatim (or, per se) Deum et Do- minum confitemur," not "sicut singil- latim unamquamque personam Deum et Dominum confitemur."

more doubtful is I Cor. ii. 8, τὸν κύριον τῆς δόξης, and perhaps even Jam. ii. I, τὴν πίστιν τοῦ κυρίου ἡμῶν 'Ι. Χ. τῆς δόξης, where the order becomes quite easy if we may take τῆς δόξης, used quite absolutely, as in apposition to 'Ι. Χ. In Rom. ix. 4 ἡ δόξα is thus used absolutely, and seems to mean the Shechinah, and it is by no means unlikely that our Lord would be spoken of by the Apostles as the true Shechinah. In any case Apoc. xxi. 10, 11 is quite in point. Heb. i. 3 gives the same sense under the form ἀπαύγασμα τῆς δόξης.

Note on ὕλην (iii. 5).

[The following represents Dr Hort's notes from his letter to Dean Scott of January 28, 1878, written in answer to the Dean's list of passages intended to shew that ὕλη may mean "a forest."]

In St James "how great a forest" might be tolerated as a paraphrase of "how much woodland," but not as a literal rendering. Hence a reference to living wood seems rather unlikely, as often fire is connected with ὕλη meaning "cut wood."

Odyss. v. 63 f.,

ὕλη δὲ σπέος ἀμφιπεφύκει τηλεθόωσα,
κλήθρη τ', αἴγειρός τε, καὶ εὐώδης κυπάρισσος.

Rather "luxuriant tree-age" (like herbage) about the cave : so *Il.* vi. 147 f.,

φύλλα τὰ μέν τ' ἄνεμος χαμάδις χέει, ἄλλα δέ θ' ὕλη
τηλεθόωσα φύει.

Il. xi. 155 ff., *wood* and *a wood* equally pertinent :

ὡς δ' ὅτε πῦρ ἀΐδηλον ἐν ἀξύλῳ ἐμπέσῃ ὕλῃ,
πάντῃ τ' εἰλυφόων ἄνεμος φέρει, οἱ δέ τε θάμνοι
πρόρριζοι πίπτουσιν ἐπειγόμενοι πυρὸς ὁρμῇ.

Hes. *op.* 506 ff.,

μέμυκε δὲ γαῖα καὶ ὕλη·
πολλὰς δὲ δρῦς ὑψικόμους ἐλάτας τε παχείας
οὔρεος ἐν βήσσῃς πιλνᾷ χθονὶ πουλυβοτείρῃ
ἐμπίπτων, καὶ πᾶσα βοᾷ τότε νήριτος ὕλη.

"Woodland" (the forest region) is more coordinate with γαῖα than "a forest" would be : cf. also νήριτος, 509.

Thuc. ii. 77. If the sentence, ἤδη γὰρ ἐν ὄρεσιν ὕλη τριφθεῖσα ὑπ' ἀνέμων πρὸς αὐτὴν ἀπὸ ταὐτομάτου πῦρ καὶ φλόγα ἀπ' αὐτοῦ ἀνῆκεν, stood alone, it would be *Il.* xi. 155 over again. But just before ὕλη twice means "wood" indefinitely (cut wood): hence there is a presumption that here again ὕλη is "wood" indefinitely. The same thing is spoken of in two states, cut and living : a transition from cut wood to a forest would be much more violent.

Lucretius (i. 896 ff.) probably had the passage in view, but throws no light : the described phenomenon is the same on either view :

> At saepe in magnis fit montibus, inquis, ut altis
> Arboribus vicina cacumina summa terantur
> Inter se, validis facere id cogentibus austris,
> Donec flammai fulserunt flore coorto.

Aristot. *H. A.* ix. 11. 3 (615 a 15), ἔνιοι δὲ τῶν ὀρνίθων ἐν τοῖς ὄρεσι καὶ τῇ ὕλῃ κατοικοῦσιν, is distinctly in favour of the indefinite use. He coordinates τοῖς ὄρεσι with τῇ ὕλῃ (the forest region). So still more c. 32 (618 b 21), οὗτος (sc. the white-tailed eagle) κατὰ τὰ πεδία καὶ τὰ ἄλση καὶ περὶ τὰς πόλεις γίνεται ...πέτεται δὲ καὶ εἰς τὰ ὄρη καὶ εἰς τὴν ὕλην διὰ τὸ θάρσος, where τὰ ἄλση bears the same relation to τὰ πεδία that ἡ ὕλη does to τὰ ὄρη.

Theocr. xxii. 36,

> παντοίην δ᾽ ἐν ὄρει θηεύμενοι ἄγριον ὕλην.

Παντοίην favours the same use.

Soph. *O. T.* 476 ff.,

> φοιτᾷ γὰρ ὑπ᾽ ἀγρίαν
> ὕλαν ἀνά τ᾽ ἄντρα καὶ
> πέτρας ἅτε ταῦρος.

The sing. ὕλαν with plur. ἄντρα : ὑπό irrelevant, whether as "seeking the covert of," or simply "under the covert of."

Eur. *Hipp.* 215,

> πέμπετέ μ᾽ εἰς ὄρος· εἶμι πρὸς ὕλαν
> καὶ παρὰ πεύκας,

forest region, like "the (collective) mountain." Cf. Scott, *Lady of the Lake*, iii. 16,

> "He is gone on the mountain,
> He is lost to the forest."

On the other hand, Herodian's use, vii. 2. 4 (λίθων μὲν γὰρ παρ᾽ αὐτοῖς (sc. the Germans) ἢ πλίνθων ὀπτῶν σπάνις, ὕλαι δ᾽ εὔδενδροι), 5 (οἱ δὲ Γερμανοὶ ἀπὸ μὲν τῶν πεδίων καὶ εἴτινες ἦσαν χῶραι ἄδενδροι ἀνακεχωρήκεσαν· ἐν δὲ ταῖς ὕλαις ἐκρύπτοντο, περί τε τὰ ἕλη διέτριβον), also viii. 1. 2 (ἐν κοιλάσιν ὀρῶν ἢ λόχμαις ὕλαις τε), is at first sight individual, and may be so. But in the absence of other clear evidence, I suspect that it is collective. Thus Plutarch *Pyrrh.* 25, δασεῖαν ὕλαις ὁδόν; while also *Aratus* 32, τόπον ὕλης γέμοντα. Aristotle just after the above place has (618 b 28) οὗτος οἰκεῖ ὄρη καὶ ὕλας, though the evidence already given makes a strictly individual sense improbable.

Aristotle's collective sense of the singular with the article is well illustrated by Xenoph. *Cyn.* vi. 12 (δήσαντα δ᾽ ἐκ τῆς ὕλης τὰς κύνας); ix. 2 (τὰς μὲν κύνας δῆσαι ἄποθεν ἐκ τῆς ὕλης), 19 (εἰς δικρόας τῆς ὕλης); x. 7 (ἐπιβάλλοντας τοὺς βρόχους ἐπὶ ἀποσχαλιδώματα τῆς ὕλης δίκρα); Plato *Crit.* 107 c (γῆν μὲν καὶ ὄρη καὶ ποταμοὺς καὶ ὕλην οὐρανόν τε ξύμπαντα); *Polit.* 272 A (καρποὺς δὲ ἀφθόνους εἶχον ἀπό τε δένδρων καὶ πολλῆς ὕλης ἄλλης). No doubt forest trees were included, but the predominating and sometimes exclusive meaning is brushwood or even mere weeds of a shrubby or woody nature. Its leading idea, when it is used of living wood, seems to be nearly that of *loca silvestria*, the indeterminate wild rough country on the flanks of the hills, as distinguished from the cultivated land below.

Note on τὸν τροχὸν τῆς γενέσεως (iii. 6).

[The following references in further illustration of this phrase have been taken from the marginal notes in Dr Hort's Greek Testament and from his other MSS.]

On the wheel or circle of human affairs (their reverses) see a large collection of passages in Gataker on Marcus Aurelius ix. 28.

On the Orphic and Pythagorean wheel or circle of Genesis (metempsychosis) see Lobeck, *Aglaophamus*, 797—800.

On the *general* cycle of growth and decay see Simplicius *Comm. in Epict. Ench.* p. 94 B, ἀλλ' οὔτε τῇ ψυχῇ κακόν ἐστιν ἡ τοῦ σώματος νόσος, εἴπερ ἰατρεία οὖσα τῆς ψυχῆς δέδεικται καὶ φαίνεται πολλαχοῦ ἐναργῶς αὐτή. καὶ εἰ ἐπιβλαβὴς δὲ τῷ μερικῷ σώματι ἡ νόσος ἦν καὶ ἡ φθορὰ αὐτῆς, ὠφέλιμος δὲ οὖσα ἐφαίνετο τῇ τε τοῦ χρωμένου ψυχῇ, καὶ τῇ τοῦ παντὸς συστάσει τῶν ἐν αὐτῷ στοιχείων, καὶ τῷ ἀπεράντῳ τῆς γενέσεως κύκλῳ, διὰ τοῦτο ἐπ' ἄπειρον προϊόντι, διὰ τὸ τὴν ἄλλου φθορὰν ἄλλου γένεσιν εἶναι. So ὁ τῆς γενέσεως ποταμός, Plutarch, *de consolat.* (ii. 106 F).

Plato, *Leg.* x. p. 898 (Jowett's translation), "Of these two kinds of motion, that which moves in one place must move about a centre like globes (μίμημά τι κύκλων) made in a lathe, and is most entirely akin and similar to the circular movement of mind (τῇ τοῦ νοῦ περιόδῳ)....In saying that both mind and the motion which is in one place move in the same and like manner, in and about the same, and in relation to the same, and according to one proportion and order, and are like the motion of a globe (σφαίρας ἐντόρνου ἀπεικασμένα φοραῖς), we invented a fair image, which does no discredit to our ingenuity....Then, after what has been said, there is no difficulty in distinctly stating, that since soul carries all things round (ἐπειδὴ ψυχὴ μέν ἐστιν ἡ περιάγουσα ἡμῖν πάντα), either the best soul or the contrary must of necessity carry round and order and arrange the revolution of the heaven" (τὴν δὲ οὐρανοῦ περιφορὰν ἐξ ἀνάγκης περιάγειν φατέον ἐπιμελουμένην καὶ κοσμοῦσαν ἤτοι τὴν ἀρίστην ψυχὴν ἢ τὴν ἐναντίαν).

Iamblichus *de myster.* viii. 6, λέγεις τοίνυν ὡς Αἰγυπτίων οἱ πλείους, καὶ τὸ ἐφ' ἡμῖν ἐκ τῆς τῶν ἀστέρων ἀνῆψεν κινήσεως. τὸ δὲ πῶς ἔχει δεῖ δίχα πλειόνων ἀπὸ τῶν Ἑρμαϊκῶν σοι νοημάτων διερμηνεῦσαι. δύο γὰρ ἔχει ψυχάς, ὡς ταῦτά φησι τὰ γράμματα, ὁ ἄνθρωπος. καὶ ἡ μέν ἐστιν ἀπὸ τοῦ πρώτου νοητοῦ μετέχουσα καὶ τῆς τοῦ δημιουργοῦ δυνάμεως, ἡ δέ, ἐνδιδομένη ἐκ τῆς τῶν οὐρανίων περιφορᾶς, εἰς ἣν ἐπεισέρπει ἡ θεοπτικὴ ψυχή. τούτων δὴ οὕτως ἐχόντων, ἡ μὲν ἀπὸ τῶν κόσμων εἰς ἡμᾶς καθήκουσα ψυχή, ταῖς περιόδοις συνακολουθεῖ τῶν κόσμων· ἡ δὲ ἀπὸ τοῦ νοητοῦ νοητῶς παροῦσα, τῆς γενεσιουργοῦ κινήσεως ὑπερέχει, καὶ κατ' αὐτὴν ἥ τε λύσις γίνεται τῆς εἱμαρμένης, καὶ ἡ πρὸς τοὺς νοητοὺς θεοὺς ἄνοδος, θεουργία τε, ὅση πρὸς τὸ ἀγέννητον ἀνάγεται, κατὰ τὴν τοιαύτην ζωὴν ἀποτελεῖται.

Clement *Strom.* v. 8 (pp. 672 f.), ἀλλὰ καὶ Διονύσιος ὁ Θρᾷξ ὁ γραμματικὸς ἐν τῷ Περὶ τῆς ἐμφάσεως περὶ τοῦ τῶν τροχίσκων συμβόλου φησὶ κατὰ λέξιν· ἐσήμαινον γοῦν οὐ διὰ λέξεως μόνον, ἀλλὰ καὶ διὰ συμβόλων ἔνιοι τὰς πράξεις, διὰ λέξεως μὲν ὡς ἔχει τὰ λεγόμενα Δελφικὰ παραγγέλματα, τὸ μηδὲν ἄγαν καὶ τὸ γνῶθι σαυτὸν καὶ τὰ τούτοις ὅμοια, διὰ δὲ συμβόλων ὡς ὅ τε τροχὸς ὁ στρεφόμενος ἐν τοῖς τῶν θεῶν τεμένεσιν εἱλκυσμένος παρὰ Αἰγυπτίων καὶ τὸ τῶν θαλλῶν τῶν διδομένων τοῖς προσκυνοῦσι. φησὶ γὰρ 'Ορφεὺς ὁ Θρᾴκιος·

> θαλλῶν δ' ὅσσα βροτοῖσιν ἐπὶ χθονὸς ἔργα μέμηλεν,
> οὐδὲν ἔχει μίαν αἶσαν ἐπὶ φρεσίν, ἀλλὰ κυκλεῖται
> πάντα πέριξ, στῆναι δὲ καθ' ἐν μέρος οὐ θέμις ἐστίν,
> ἀλλ' ἔχει, ὡς ἤρξαντο, δρόμου μέρος ἴσον ἕκαστος.

Cf. Plutarch *Numa* 14 (i. 69 f.) τοῖς Αἰγυπτίοις τρόχος αἰνίττεταί τι.

Nilus *Sentent.* 193 (Orelli *Opusc. Sent.* i. 344) [1245 A, B, Migne], Γέλα μὲν τοῦ βίου τὸν τροχόν, ἀτάκτως κυλιόμενον· φυλάττου δὲ τὸν βόθρον [τροχὸν, Migne] εἰς ὃν κυλίει τοὺς ἐν αὐτῷ νυστάζοντας. Cf. 122, p. 334 [1260 D], Σκιᾷ καὶ τροχῷ τὰ λυπηρὰ τοῦ βίου καὶ τὰ φαιδρὰ παράβαλλε· ὡς γὰρ σκιὰ οὐ μένει, καὶ ὡς τροχὸς κυλίεται; and 140, p. 338 [1240 C], Εἰ τὴν ζωὴν τὴν ὄντως ποθεῖς, προσδέχου ἀεὶ τὸν ἀνθρώπινον θάνατον, καὶ μίσει τὸν παρόντα βίον· ὁρᾷς γὰρ τὸν τροχὸν ἀτάκτως κυλιόμενον.

On the whole passage cf. Andrewes, *Sermons* 603 f. [*Library Ang. Cath. Th.* iii. p. 122], "The tongue is the substantive and subject of all the rest. It is so; and God can send from Heaven no better thing, nor the devil from hell no worse thing than it. 'The best member we have,' saith the Prophet [Ps. cviii. 1 P. B. V.]; the worst member we have, saith the Apostle :—both, as it is employed.

"The best, if it be of God's cleaving; if it be of His lightening with the fire of Heaven; if it be one that will sit still, if cause be. The worst, if it come from the devil's hands. For he, as in many other, so in the sending of tongues, striveth to be like God; as knowing well they are every way as fit instruments to work mischief by, as to do good with."

Note on ἐσπαταλήσατε (v. 5).

Ezek. xvi. 49, ἐν πλησμονῇ ἄρτων καὶ ἐν εὐθηνίᾳ (οἴνου A) ἐσπατάλων αὕτη (Sodom) καὶ αἱ θυγατέρες αὐτῆς. הַשְׁקֵט, to be at rest, A.V. "idleness."

Ecclus. xxi. 15, λόγον σοφὸν...ἤκουσεν ὁ σπαταλῶν καὶ ἀπήρεσεν αὐτῷ (contrasted with ἐπιστήμων); xxvii. 13, ὁ γέλως αὐτῶν (μωρῶν) ἐν σπατάλῃ ἁμαρτίας.

Deut. xxviii. 54, "the man that is tender and very delicate (וְהֶעָנֹג) among you." Sym. ὁ σπάταλος, LXX. ὁ τρυφερός, Aq. τρυφητής.

Eccles. ii. 8 (Sym.) σπατάλας, תַעֲנוּגֹת, the *delights* of the sons of men. LXX. ἐντρυφήματα, Aq. τρυφάς.

Cant. vii. 7 (6): "Ἀλλος (? Sym.), ἀγαπητὴ, ἐν σπατάλαις, בַּתַּעֲנוּגִים. LXX., Aq. τρυφαῖς (ὦν), "O love, for *delights*." The same Hebrew word occurs elsewhere only Prov. xix. 10; Mic. i. 16; ii. 9, and is rendered τρυφή, τρυφερά, τρυφῆς by LXX.

Amos vi. 4, οἱ καθεύδοντες ἐπὶ κλινῶν ἐλεφαντίνων καὶ κατασπαταλῶντες ἐπὶ ταῖς στρωμναῖς αὐτῶν, סְרֻחִים, Jer. *lascivitis*. In vi. 7 the same Hebrew word is τρυφητῶν in Sym., *lascivientium* Jer., LXX. having another reading. The word seems to mean "hang" or "stretch languidly and effusely." Prov. xxix. 21, ὃς κατασπαταλᾷ ἐκ παιδὸς οἰκέτης ἔσται, מְפַנֵּק (cf. Arab. root "live softly").

Ps.-Theano *Ep.* I [p. 741] (Gale *Opusc. mythol.* 86), εἰδυῖα ὅτι τὰ σπαταλῶντα τῶν παιδίων, ὅταν ἀκμάσῃ πρὸς ἄνδρας, ἀνδράποδα γίνεται, τὰς τοιαύτας ἡδονὰς ἀφαίρει. The epistle is all about luxurious and indulgent education.

Nilus *Sentent.* 319 (Orelli i. 368) ὁ δὲ ἐμπλατύνων ἑαυτὸν ἐν τῷ παρόντι βίῳ διὰ σπατάλης καὶ μέθης καὶ δόξης ἀπανθούσης κ.τ.λ.

Anthologia Palatina xi. 402 σπατάλη bis, κατασπαταλᾷς, with reference to luxurious *eating*; ix. 642, σπατάλημα, of luxurious food.

Gloss ap. Steph., σπαταλάω *delicias ago*.

Polybius *excerpta Vaticana* p. 451 [xxxvii. 4, 6 ed. Didot] πλουσίους τούτους καταλιπεῖν (τ. παῖδας) καὶ σπαταλῶντας θρέψαι.

Clement *Strom.* iii. 7 (p. 538): We must practise ἐγκράτεια not only περὶ τὰ ἀφροδίσια, but also περὶ τὰ ἄλλα ὅσα σπαταλῶσα ἐπιθυμεῖ ἡ ψυχὴ ἡμῶν, οὐκ ἀρκουμένη τοῖς ἀναγκαίοις, περιεργαζομένη δὲ τὴν χλιδήν.

Eustathius bis ap. Steph., τῶν σπαταλώντων μνηστήρων.

Anth. Pal. v. 18: τοῖς σπατάλοις κλέμμασι,...ἐκ σπατάλης, of the ointments and other luxurious equipments of rich ladies (τῶν σοβαρῶν).

Ib. v. 27. 6,

καὶ σοβαρῶν ταρσῶν χρυσοφόρος σπατάλη
νῦν πενιχρὴ κ.τ.λ.
ταῦτα τὰ τῶν σπαταλῶν τέρματα παλλακίδων.

Ib. vii. 206. 6 (on a cat killed for eating a partridge),

οἱ δὲ μύες νῦν
ὀρχοῦνται τῆς σῆς δραξάμενοι σπατάλης.

Ib. vi. 74. 8,

παρρίψασα δὲ κισσὸν
χεῖρα περισφίγξω χρυσοδέτῳ σπατάλῃ.

Ib. v. 271. 2,

τὴν χρυσοκροτάλῳ σειομένην σπατάλῃ.

Epiphanius i. 812 A, εἰ ἑώρα τινὰ ἐν τρυφῇ καὶ σπατάλῃ.

"Bardesanes" ap. Euseb. *Prep. Ev.* vi. 10 (p. 276 A): From the conjunction of Ares and Paphia in Crius οἱ Χαλδαίζοντες say are born τοὺς ἀνδρείους καὶ σπατάλους. Cureton says the corresponding Syriac word is unknown to him: *dissolutos* is the Latin of Rufinus.

Philo *de sept. spect.* i. 5, σπάταλον καὶ βασιλικὸν τὸ φιλοτέχνημα (the Hanging Gardens).

Chrysostom (on 1 Tim. v. 6) evidently takes gluttony as the leading idea, but sometimes includes drunkenness, and apparently once over-sleep.

Barnabas x. 3, ὅταν σπαταλῶσιν men as swine.

Hermas *Sim.* vi. 1, τὰ πρόβατα ταῦτα ὡσεὶ τρυφῶντα ἦν καὶ λίαν σπαταλῶντα, καὶ ἱλαρὰ ἦν σκιρτῶντα ὧδε κἀκεῖσε. Ps.-Chrysost. *de poen.* (ix. 777 E), ὁ σπαταλιστὴς ἐκεῖνος, sc. Dives in the parable.

N.T. latt. (1) Jam. v. 5 : fruiti estis super terram et abusi estis, ff ; epulati estis super terram et in luxuriis (no verb), vg. (2) 1 Tim. v. 6 :

delicata est Cyp Tert 171
in deliciis agit d pp
„   „   est vg pp
„   „   vivit pp g¹
deliciosa   „   g²

All the biblical passages and some of the others suggest simply luxurious and self-indulgent living. The leading idea is probably luxurious feeding, as several times in *Anth. Pal.* and in Chrysostom.

Perhaps "ye lived delicately on the earth and were luxurious" (Jam. v. 5), and "she that is luxurious" (1 Tim. v. 6).

None of the passages bear out the supposed connexion with σπαθάω. to lavish. Rather (as Lobeck) from σπάω, to suck down.

Peculiarities of vocabulary in the Codex Corbeiensis of St James.

i. 3 (also 4 ; v. 11)¹	ὑπομονή	sufferentia²
4 bis (also 25 ; iii. 2)³	τέλειος	consummatus
7	οἰέσθω	speret
10 (also 11 ; ii. 5 ; v. 1)⁴	πλούσιος	locuples
11	εὐπρέπεια	dignitas
	πορείαις	actu
13	ἀπείραστός (ἐστιν)	temptator non (est)
14	δελεάζεται	elicitur (cod. eliditur)
15	ἀποκνεῖ⁵	(?) adquirit
17	δόσις	datio
	παραλλαγή	permutatio
	τροπή (? ῥοπή)	(?) momentum (cod. modicum)
	ἀποσκίασμα	obumbratio
18	κτισμάτων	conditionum
21	ἀποτίθεμαι	expono

¹ All the passages in Jam. in which ὑπομονή occurs.
² Occurs besides in vg. of v. 11 and twice in *d* (Lk. viii. 15; xxi. 19).
³ In i. 17 *perfectus*; ii. 22 ἐτελειώθη,
confirmatur. Cf. ii. 8 τελεῖτε, *consummamini.*
⁴ But in ii. 6 *divites.*
⁵ In i. 18 ἀπεκύησεν, *peperit.*

i. 21 (also iii. 13)	πραΰτης	*clementia*
22	παραλογιζόμενοι (ἑαυτούς)	(?) *aliter consiliantes*
23	γένεσις¹	*natale*
24	εὐθέως	*in continenti*
25	ἀκροατής²	*audiens*
26	θρησκός	*religiosus*
26, 27	θρησκεία	*religio*
27	θλίψις	*tribulatio*
ii. 1	προσωπολημψίαις	*acceptione personarum*
9	προσωπολημπτέω	*personas accipio*
1	τῆς δόξης	*honoris* (cod. *honeris*)
3	ὑποπόδιον	*scamellum*
4	διακρίνομαι³	*dijudicor*
5	ἐπαγγέλλομαι⁴	*expromitto*
6	ἠτιμάσατε	*frustrastis* (cod. *-atis*)
	καταδυναστεύουσιν ὑμῶν	*potentantur in vobis*
8	τελεῖτε	*consummamini*⁵
9	ἐλέγχω	*traduco*
12	ἐλευθερία⁶	*liberalitas*
13	κατακαυχῶμαι⁷	*superglorior*
14 (also i. 21: iv. 12; v. 15, 20)	σώζω	*salvo*
16	χορτάζεσθε	*estote satulli*
22	συνεργέω	*communico*
23	λογίζω	*aestimo*
25	πόρνη	*fornicaria*
	ἀγγέλους	*exploratores*
iii. 3	πείθομαι	*consentio*⁸
4	(ὅπου)	*ubicumque*⁹
6	γένεσις¹⁰	*nativitas*
7	ἐναλίων	*natantium*
11	βρύω	*bullio* (trans.)
12	πικρόν ⎱ ἀλυκόν ⎰	*salmacidum*
13	ἐπιστήμων	*disciplinosus*
14	(κατα)καυχᾶσθε¹¹	*alapamini*
15	ψυχικός	*animalis*
	δαιμονιώδης	*demonetica*
17	ἐπιεικής	*verecundie*
	εὐπειθής	*consentiens*¹²

¹ In iii. 6 *nativitas*.
² But in vv. 22, 23 *auditor*.
³ But in i. 6 bis *dubito*.
⁴ In i. 12 *promitto*.
⁵ Cf. i. 4.
⁶ But in i. 25 *libertas*.
⁷ Cf. i. 9 καυχάσθω, *glorietur*; iv. 16 καυχᾶσθε, *gloriamini*; καύχησις, *gloria*,

(?) *gloriatio*; but iii. 14 κατακαυχᾶσθε, *alapamini*.
⁸ Cf. iii. 17.
⁹ Apparently in the sense "anywhere."
¹⁰ In i. 23 *natale*.
¹¹ Cf. ii. 13.
¹² Cf. iii. 3.

iii.	17	ἀδιάκριτος	sine dijudicatione
		?	inreprehensibilis
		ἀνυπόκριτος	sine hypocrisi
iv.	2	ζηλοῦτε	zelatis
		μάχεσθε	rixatis
	3	ἡδοναί[1]	libidines
		δαπανάω	erogo
	4	μοιχαλίδες	fornicatores
	5	ἐπιποθέω	(?) convalesco
			(? concupisco as vg.)
	8	ἁγνίζω	sanctifico
	11 ter	καταλαλέω	retracto de
	12	νομοθέτης	legum positor
	13 (also v. 1)	ἄγε νῦν	jam nunc
	14	ἀτμίς	momentum[2]
		πρὸς ὀλίγον	per modica (? per modicū)
		ἀφανίζω	extermino
	16	καύχησις[3]	gloria (? gloriatio for
			talis follows)
v.	2	σητόβρωτα γέγονεν	tiniaverunt
	3	κατίωται	aeruginavit
		φάγεται	manducabit (of rust)
	4	τῶν θερισάντων	qui araverunt in
	5	σπαταλάω	abutor
		τρέφω	cibo
	7	τίμιον καρπόν	honoratum fructum
	8	στηρίζω	conforto
		ἐγγίζω	adpropio
	10	ὑπόδειγμα	experimentum
		τῆς κακοπαθίας[4]	de malis passionibus
	11	πολύσπλαγχνος (? -ως)	visceraliter
	12	ἄλλον τινά	alterutrum
	13	κακοπαθέω[5]	anxio
		ψαλλέτω	psalmum dicat
	16	ἐνεργουμένη	frequens
	17	ὁμοιοπαθής	similis
	18	βλαστάνω	germino (trans.)
	19, 20	ἐπιστρέφω	revoco

[1] But in iv. 1 voluptates.　　　　[3] Cf. ii. 13.
[2] [Dr Hort suggested flamentum. See　　[4] But see v. 13.
Studia Biblica (first series), p. 140.]　　[5] But see v. 10.

GREEK INDEX

(The references in brackets are to the occurrences in James of annotated words.)

ἀγαθός 29, 52, 86 (i. 17; iii. 17)
ἀγαπάω 21, 51 (i. 12; ii. 5, 8)
ἄγγελος 66 (ii. 25)
ἁγνός 85 f. (iii. 15)
ἀδελφή 58 (ii. 15)
ἀδελφός 14, 27, 45, 57, 58, 67, 78, 102
  (i. 2, 9, 16, 19; ii. 1, 5, 14, 15; iii. 1,
  10, 12; iv. 11 ter; v. 7, 9, 10, 12, 19)
ἀδιάκριτος 86 f. (iii. 17)
ἀδικία 71 f. (iii. 6)
αἰτέω 90 f. (i. 5, 6; iv. 2, 3 bis)
ἀκαταστασία 85 (iii. 16)
ἀκατάστατος 13, 76 (i. 8; iii. 8)
ἀκούω 50 (i. 19; ii. 5; v. 11)
ἀκροατής 38, 41 f. (i. 22, 23, 25)
ἀλαζών contrasted with ὑπερήφανος 95
ἀλήθεια 33 f., 83 (i. 18; iii. 14; v. 19)
ἀλυκόν 80 (iii. 12)
ἁμαρτία 26, 54 (i. 15 bis; ii. 9; iv. 17;
  v. 15, 16, 20)
ἀμίαντος 43 f. (i. 27)
Ἀναβαθμοὶ Ἰακώβου xxii
ἀναστροφή 80 (iii. 13)
ἀνατέλλω 16 (i. 11)
ἀναφέρω 63 (ii. 21)
ἀνέλεος 56 (ii. 13)
ἀνεμίζω 10 (i. 6)
ἀνήρ 12, 36, 68 (i. 8, 12, 20, 23; ii. 2;
  iii. 2)
ἄνθος 15 (i. 10, 11)
ἀνθρώπινος 75 (iii. 7)
ἄνθρωπος 35, 62, 77 (i. 7, 19; ii. 20,
  24; iii. 8, 9; v. 17)
ἀντιτάσσομαι 95 (iv. 6; v. 6)
ἀνυπόκριτος 87 (iii. 17)
ἄνωθεν 29 (i. 17; iii. 15, 17)
ἀπαρχή 35 (i. 18)
ἅπας 68 (iii. 2)
ἀπατάω 43 (i. 26)
ἀπείραστος 22 f. (i. 13)
ἀπέρχομαι 40 (i. 24)
ἁπλῶς 7 ff. (i. 5)
ἀπό c. gen. 21
ἀποκυέω 26 f., 33 (i. 15, 18)
ἀποσκίασμα 31 (i. 17)
ἀποτελέω 26 (i. 15)
ἀργός 62 f. (ii. 20)

ἀτιμάζω 51 (ii. 6)
αὐτός 23 (i. 13)
αὐχέω 70 (iii. 5)

βασιλικός xxvi f., 53 f. (ii. 8)
βλασφημέω 52 (ii. 7)
βλέπω 63 f. (ii. 22)
βούλομαι 32 f., 69 f., 93 (i. 18; iii. 4;
  iv. 4)
βραδύς 36 (i. 19 bis)
βρύω 79 (iii. 11)

γέεννα 74 (iii. 6)
γένεσις 39, 72 ff., 106 f. (i. 23; iii. 6)
γίνομαι 38, 41, 77 f. (i. 12, 22, 25;
  ii. 4, 10, 11; iii. 1, 9, 10; v. 2)
γινώσκω 5, 62 (i. 3; ii. 20; v. 20)
γλῶσσα 71, 75 f. (i. 26; iii. 5, 6 bis, 8)
γραφή, ἡ 54, 64, 93 f. (ii. 8, 23; iv. 5)
γυμνός 58 (ii. 15)

δαιμόνιον 61 f. (ii. 19)
δαιμονιώδης 84 f. (iii. 15)
δαμάζω 75 (iii. 7 bis, 8)
δαπανάω 91 (iv. 3)
δεῖ contrasted with χρή 78
δείκνυμι 80 (ii. 18 bis; iii. 13)
δελεάζω 25 (i. 14)
διά c. gen. 55 f.
διάβολος 98 f. (iv. 7)
διακρίνομαι 10, 49 (i. 6 bis; ii. 4)
dialogue in the Gospels 10
διαλογισμός 50 (ii. 4)
διασπορά xxii, f., 3, 67, 92 (i. 1)
διδάσκαλος 67 (iii. 1)
δίδωμι 9 f., 96 (i. 5 bis; ii. 16; iv. 6 bis;
  v. 18)
δικαιοσύνη 36, 87 (i. 20; ii. 23; iii. 18)
δικαιόω 63, 65 (ii. 21, 24, 25)
διό 36, 97 (i. 21; iv. 6)
δίψυχος 12 f. (i. 8; iv. 8)
δοκέω 93 (ii. 26; iv. 5)
δοκίμιον 5 (i. 3)
δόκιμος 19 (i. 12)
δόξα, ἡ 47 f., 103 f. (ii. 1)
δόσις 28 (i. 17)
δοῦλος 1 f. (i. 1)

ENGLISH INDEX

Heinsius 37
Heisen 37
Helvidian theory xix ff.
Herder 18
Hermas xxvi, 12, 48, 85, 109
Herodian (grammarian) 16
Herodian (historian) 5, 27, 105
Hesychius 10, 42, 81 f.
Hilary of Poictiers xxx
Hilgenfeld 72 f.
Himerius 8
Hofmann 89
Holder xiii
Hupfeld 46, 95

Iamblichus 5, 106
Ignatius and Pseudo-Ign. 5, 6, 13, 23, 37, 98
Irenaeus xxvi f., 41, 84
Isidore of Seville xiii

James (St) the son of Zebedee xiii f.
James (St) the son of Alphaeus xiv, xvi
James (St) the Just, the Lord's brother xiii ff, 1
James (St), The Epistle of, relation to O. and N.T. x f., xxxiii; to St Paul x f., xxiv f., 66 f.; to Synoptic Gospels xi, xxxiii, *et al.*; authorship xi ff.; readers xxii ff.; circumstances and date xxiv f.; reception xxv ff.; purpose and contents xxxi ff.; style xxxiii
Jerome xiii f., xix ff., xxix, 17, 49
John of Damascus 12
Josephus xv, xxi ff., 1, 2, 6, 8, 23, 48, 84, 93
Jude (St) xv
Junilius xxix
Justin and Pseudo-Just. 36, 58

Kern xii

Lactantius 62
Leontius xxviii
Libanius 7
Liber Jacobi 2
Liber Jubilaeorum 65
Lightfoot (Bp) xv, xix f., xxii, 12, 28, 30, 39, 49, 53, 64, 90
Lobeck 106, 109
Lucian 8, 18, 26, 40, 49, 69, 70
Lucifer of Calaris xxx
Luther xxix

Macarius Magnes 33
Marcion x
Marcus Aurelius 23, 106
Martianay xiv
Mary wife of Clopas xx

Megilla 65
Melito 43
Messiah 1
Midrash on Canticles 65
Muratorian Canon xxvii
mysteries, the Greek 61

Nilus 107, 108
Novatian xiii

Oecumenius 23, 37, 40, 42, 70
Origen xxi, xxvii, 22, 40, 82, 84
Orphic doctrine xii, 61, 72 f., 106 f.
Otto 3

Paul (St) and St James x f., xxiv f., 66 f.
Paul of Nisibis xxix
persecution xxxi
Philaster xiii
Philo Judaeus xxxiii, 6, 9 f., 14, 15, 19, 25, 29, 31, 48, 64, 66, 73, *et al.*
Philo *de sept. spect.* 108
Philostratus 25
Phlegon 27
Plumptre (Dean) xiv, xxii, xxv, 48
Plutarch 4, 6, 8, 25, 28, 30 f., 44, 62, 74 f., 85, 89 f., *et al.*
Pollux 13
Polybius 7, 8, 10, 13, 82, 108
Polycarp, *Martyrium* 20, 28
Poppaea 92 f.
Proclus 72 f.
Protevangelium Jacobi xxi
Psalmi Solomonis 5, 39, 71
Pythagorean doctrine 106

Reland 79
religio, religiosus 42
Robinson (Dr E.) 79
Rönsch 64 f.

Schiller-Szinessy 2
Schneckenburger 20, 57
Schöttgen 55, 98
Schulthess 37
Schürer 48
Sermon on the Mount xxxi f., 6, 38, 50 f., 54, 79, 90, *et al.*
Shabbath 55
Shechinah 47, 104
Sibylline Oracles 20, 57
simoom 17
simplex, simplicitas 8
Simplicius 72 f., 106
Stanley (Dean) 79
subjunctive mood 54
Suidas 16, 42, 82
Surenhuis 97
Syriac Canon and versions xiii, xxiv, xxviii, xxx